SUSTAINABLE TRANSPORTATION

SUSTAINABLE TRANSPORTATION

PROBLEMS AND SOLUTIONS

William R. Black

THE GUILFORD PRESS
New York   London

© 2010 The Guilford Press
A Division of Guilford Publications, Inc.
72 Spring Street, New York, NY 10012
www.guilford.com

Printed in the United States of America

This book is printed on acid-free paper.

Last digit is print number: 9   8   7   6   5   4   3   2   1

Library of Congress Cataloging-in-Publication Data

Black, William R. (William Richard), 1942–
    Sustainable transportation: problems and solutions / William R. Black.
        p. cm.
    ISBN 978-1-60623-485-3 (hard cover: alk. paper)
    1. Transportation—Environmental aspects.   2. Local transit—
Environmental aspects.   3. Sustainable engineering.   4. Green technology.
5. Environmental degradation.   6. Transportation and state.   I. Title.
    HE147.65.B57 2010
    388—dc22

                                              2009040112

For Tracy, Richard, and Eric,
who have made life worth living

Acknowledgments

This book grew out of a course that I began teaching at Indiana University in the late 1990s, and I wish to thank my students from that time to the present, whose input has been critical in developing many of the ideas expressed in these pages.

In the fall of 2006 I was invited by Dr. Pavlos Kanaroglou to spend part of a sabbatical leave at McMaster University's Centre for Spatial Analysis in Hamilton, Ontario. In addition to being an excellent research institute, the Centre and the Department of Geography have a very good program in sustainable transportation. Their research journal collection was also of tremendous value.

Prior to that sabbatical, I was involved in a 6-year National Science Foundation–European Commission project to increase research interaction between U.S., Canadian, and European sustainable transportation researchers. The benefit of interaction with scholars involved in that effort, including Tom Leinbach, Cristina Capineri, Don Janelle, Andy Gillespie, Martin Lee Gosselin, Veli Himanen, Roger Stough, Piet Rietveld, Kieran Donaghy, Georg Rudinger, and Peter Nijkamp, is also ingrained in the book in many subtle ways.

I am also grateful for the support of The Guilford Press staff. Kristal Hawkins, Acquisitions Editor, and her anonymous reviewers have helped in shaping the content of the book. Louise Farkas, Senior Production Editor, and her staff have done much to improve how the book reads.

In spite of all this assistance, I may have left out your favorite program, policy, or technology. This is one of the problems of working in a field as dynamic as sustainable transportation: Everything cannot be included. For any exclusions, oversights, or errors—which I hope are very few—I am solely responsible.

Preface

During the past two decades there has been a movement within the transportation planning, policy, and research communities toward a new paradigm—the paradigm of sustainable transportation. This paradigm seeks to develop and maintain a transport system that does more than simply enable people and goods to move from one place to another but rather to accomplish this end while causing far less damage to the local and global environments. This new paradigm strives to lessen the incredible toll of deaths and injuries resulting from our transport system. It tries to address the need to develop alternative sources of energy for our travel and transport, and it seeks to manage the high levels of congestion developing in our urban areas, on the interstate highway system, and on other byways and roads.

To be sure, the paradigm has not been adopted by all members of the transportation community. Some view it as antiautomobile or antihighway, but this is not what sustainable transport truly is. The automobile is very much an established presence in the United States, and sustainable transport recognizes this reality. But its most ardent admirers also recognize that this vehicle can pollute less, can be made much safer for its occupants as well as pedestrians, can be made to be much more efficient, and can require far fewer resources to produce and operate. Highways are an integral part of the system we have adopted, and they must be improved and rebuilt as needed. Expansion of the network may even be required in certain cases, but most of our transport problems today cannot be solved through more highways. Nearly all transport research, planning, and policymaking today ultimately seeks to address problems of sustainable transport, even though many working in these fields may not yet recognize this close connection.

During the past 10 years I have had the opportunity to direct the U.S. side of efforts by the National Science Foundation and the European Commission to foster transatlantic research in the area of sustainable transport. The experience has been heartening, and I came away impressed not only with the creativity of scholars on both sides of the Atlantic but also with the recognition that, while we may never have a fully sustainable transport system, it can clearly be made more sustainable than it currently is.

There have been questions during the past decade by many who did not understand what was meant by the term "sustainable transport." I would have fumbled in attempting to answer the question myself a couple of decades ago. Since then, sustainable transport has become clearer to me, and I have come to view nearly all transport research as sustainable transport research.

This book seeks to translate my understanding of sustainable transport in a formal way. It is not all-inclusive; that would be impossible in a single volume. I do not get into the transport planning process in any detail, but I do suggest how indicators can guide that process. Methodology is also missing from this volume. But the reader should understand that any attempt to better understand travel behavior from the four-step transport planning model (of generation, distribution, assignment, and mode choice) to microsimulation approaches will help us to plan for a more sustainable system.

Part I of this volume begins with a general introduction to sustainable transport by summarizing its various definitions (Chapter 1). Next there follows a history of some of the earlier transport modes and their sustainability (Chapter 2). Chapters 3 through 7 then examine in detail the five key problems—what might be called a pentad of problems—that keep the current transport system from being sustainable. These are, in order of treatment, climate change, urban air quality, the finite nature of petroleum reserves, the large number of motor vehicle accidents and related fatalities and injuries, and traffic congestion.

Part II examines possible solutions to the problem of creating a sustainable transport system (Chapter 8). Some proffered solutions deal with better costing of travel and transport, which incorporates the negative externalities generated by this activity, often referred to as full costing (Chapter 9). We also look at pricing and taxation (Chapter 10). Planning approaches, specifically those concerned with the geography of the urban environment, are summarized next (Chapter 11), and how we can best use indicators of sustainability in planning is then discussed in detail (Chapter 12).

The various policy initiatives for promoting sustainability are reviewed in Chapter 13, followed by specific policies related to speed (Chapter 14) and various national-level initiatives (Chapter 15). Travel-demand management techniques that could prove useful in moving toward sustainable transport are described in Chapter 16. There is a need for some very basic educational initiatives in persuading the public to recognize the current problems of sustainability in transport, and these are presented in Chapter 17. Of course, there is also a substantial role for technology in moving toward a more sustainable transport system. Included in this discussion is the use of information and communications technology, including telecommuting and e-commerce (Chapter 18); alternative fuels (Chapter 19); hybrid vehicles, fuel cells, and catalytic converters (Chapter 20); and intelligent transport systems

(Chapter 21). The final chapter (22) in Part III summarizes the whole volume and highlights recent developments and their implications for the future.

I once intended to make this volume one that would be useful to planners and policymakers on both sides of the Atlantic. That aim proved to be too great an undertaking, given that nearly every country in Europe is pursuing its own path to sustainable mobility. As a result, I have chosen instead to focus my labors and this volume on U.S. aspects of this phenomenon. Nevertheless, I will cite some interesting practices being undertaken in certain European Union countries, trusting that the definitive volume on sustainable transport in Europe will emerge from one of the many capable Europeans I have met over the past decade.

It is my fervent hope that this volume will prove useful to the planners and policymakers hard at work in the various public and private fields of transport planning and policymaking.

Contents

List of Tables

List of Figures

PART I

THE NATURE OF THE PROBLEM

CHAPTER 1

The Problem of Sustainability
in the Transport Sector

There can be no understanding of sustainability
at any level other than global.
—JOHN WHITELEGG (1993)

It is reasonable to begin a volume on sustainability with some of the definitions of sustainability and sustainable transport that have appeared in the literature over the past 15 years or so. Before we do that, let us see if we can find some common ground, or some consensus, as to the meaning of "sustainable." We would all agree that if something is sustainable it is something that can be maintained or is something that endures. When we begin to use the word to modify certain nouns, such as *development*, or *cities*, or *transport*, we do little to make them clearer concepts. While the discussion that follows will focus primarily on sustainable transport, the inherent ambiguity or impreciseness applies in all cases.

One of the first of these clarifying phrases was used in the so-called Brundtland Report of 1987 (United Nations World Commission on Environment and Development, 1987). That report discussed what was referred to as "sustainable development," which was defined as development that meets the needs of the present without compromising the ability of future generations to meet their own needs. Without major changes this definition can be extended to sustainable transport, which may be defined as transport that satisfies "the current transport and mobility needs without compromising the ability of future generations to meet these needs" (Black, 1996, p. 151). This is easy to understand on the surface, but soon we have to face the fact that the *needs* are not specified very well, and even if we resolve this matter, we must then stop and decide how many *future generations* we are talking about.

Another way of expressing these ideas would be to state that sustainable transport represents transport and mobility with nondeclining capital, where capital would include human capital, monetary capital, and natural capital (see Pearce et al., 1989; Daly, 1992). Followed to its logical end, this would imply that natural resources could not be used in the system (sometimes referred to as "strong sustainability") unless these were used to develop additional natural capital (sometimes referred to as "weak sustainability").

Daly (1992) does not define what he means by sustainability, but he specifies certain parameters for any sector to be considered sustainable. Within this context transport is sustainable if it satisfies three conditions:

1. The rate at which it uses renewable resources does not exceed the rate of regeneration.
2. The rate at which it uses nonrenewable resources does not exceed the rate at which sustainable renewable substitutes can be developed.
3. Its rate of pollution emission does not exceed the assimilative capacity of the environment.

If we apply Daly's conditions to the transport system of the 1700s and 1800s, which are often viewed as sustainable, we would find these systems were on the verge of becoming nonsustainable at the time. The major long-distance transport mode of the 1700s was sailing ships. Although they used renewable wind energy, they were becoming nonsustainable because they were depleting the lumber stocks used in their construction and repair. The typical transport mode of urban areas during the 1800s was the horse-drawn wagon, buggy, or carriage. This system resulted in tens of thousands of horses polluting the streams, wells, and streets of these urban areas, obviously exceeding the assimilative capacity of these environments.

Schipper (1996) states that sustainable transport is transportation where the beneficiaries pay their full social costs, including those that would be paid by future generations. He further notes that changes in travel are associated with a number of potential externalities, including accidents, air pollution, congestion, noise, damage to the species' habitat, increases in carbon dioxide production, and the importing of oil. "It is these externalities, not transportation or travel per se that threaten the sustainability of the system" (p. 1).

Gordon (1995) is less willing to be drawn into the debate over the definitions of "sustainable transport" and states instead that underlying these ideas of sustainable transport are three different visions. "The first of these visions centers on changing people and the way they live, the second on changing technology, and the third on changing prices" (p. 2). In effect, she is proposing, in rather broad terms, the actions that are necessary to make the transport system sustainable.

Probably in an attempt to be more comprehensive, the Centre for Sustainable Transportation in Canada states that a sustainable transportation system is one that (1) allows the basic access needs of individuals and societies to be met safely and in a manner consistent with human and ecosystem health, and with equity within and between generations; (2) is affordable, operates efficiently, offers a choice of transport mode, and supports a vibrant economy; and (3) limits emissions and waste within the planet's ability to absorb them, minimizes consumption of nonrenewable resources, reuses and recycles its components, and minimizes the use of land and production of noise (Centre for Sustainable Transportation, 1998).

Europeans generally refer to the notion of sustainable transport as "sustainable mobility." Some U.S. groups also prefer the use of this term. The Mobility 2001 report defines sustainable mobility as "the ability to meet the needs of society to move freely, gain access, communicate, trade and establish relationships without sacrificing other essential human or ecological values today or in the future" (MIT & CRA, 2001).

Transport Canada (that country's department of transportation) skirted the issue of directly defining the concept of a sustainable transport system and sought instead to define "a more sustainable transportation system" as "one which provides *affordable access* to freight and passenger service and does so in an *environmentally sound* and *equitable manner*" (Transport Canada, 2003, p. 10; emphasis in original).

It should be apparent from this discussion that the definitions have moved from the academic realm to more practical constructs that can be implemented. There is considerable interest in using the concept of sustainable transport to help guide future policies and to evaluate activities and programs in measurable ways. We have identified many of the elements of a sustainable transport system, but let us see if we can go further and conceptualize something that is substantive enough to be measured.

If one wants to measure anything, it is necessary to ask the fundamental question of what the phenomenon really is. Now, in some cases, we want to measure such vague notions as intelligence, safety, equity, faith, justice, freedom, and so on. Once again, we think we know what these terms mean, but do we really? It is more likely that, on closer examination, these words would yield precisely the same types of debates we hear about sustainability, but for the most part we are comfortable with the ambiguity that surrounds these terms and their use.

THE COMPONENTS OF NONSUSTAINABLE TRANSPORT

I once set out to measure sustainable transport. In order to do this, one has to ask the question "What is it that makes a transport system sustainable?" This is practically an impossible question to answer since everyone expects so much of such a transport system. Instead, let's turn this question around and ask "What is it that makes a transport system *nonsustainable*?" If we start from this vantage point, we can better come to some agreement on a definition. It will probably not be acceptable to everyone, but few definitions are. Now let us address this question.

Diminishing Petroleum Reserves

It is generally recognized that in the hundred or so years of motor vehicles using gasoline as a fuel, the world has used approximately 1 trillion barrels of petroleum for this and other purposes—all of this at a time when only a small proportion of the population of the world had access to such vehicles or other uses for petroleum energy. The major question at this point is "What is the future demand for this fuel, and will the planet be able to supply it?" Given that the developing countries, in particular, are expected to increase substantially their demand for energy resources for transport and other sectors—indeed, this trend is well established—global demand will surely increase significantly over the long term.

What can be said of supplies? The optimist would say that there are about 2 trillion barrels of recoverable conventional petroleum reserves out there. In general, current production roughly keeps pace with demand, but if demand increases significantly, as we now anticipate, additional production will be needed. Unfortunately, at the present time new consumption is exceeding new reserve discoveries by more than a 3:1 ratio. If we consider only the conventional sources, some experts believe that we have already discovered and largely exploited all of the major oil fields in the world. If more are found (one relatively new area of exploration is the South China Sea), the world's oil producers might be able to stage a delaying action (Deffeyes, 2001). Others would say that, while conventional sources may not last much beyond 2020, there is significantly more petroleum out there, but we will need to tap such "unconventional" sources as shale oil, oil sands, and tar sands (Greene et al., 2003). Estimates are that the first of these, shale oil, is substantially more expensive to produce and deliver, while the oil sands and tar sands oil entail costs that result in a price that is comparable to the price of gasoline from conventional sources, assuming the price is inflated by suppliers. If the price of gasoline drops, then production from these sands is not competitive. Depending on what the actual costs turn out to be, we will see the slower or faster development of alternative petroleum sources. In the final analysis our current transport systems are nonsustainable because at least at present they chiefly use a fuel that is finite, nonrenewable, and fast being depleted. This is true whether we are talking about oil from conventional or unconventional sources.

Global Atmospheric Impacts

Some scientists believe that humans are placing emissions into the atmosphere that will eventually have a catastrophic impact on the world's climate. Many of them believe the impact has already begun, with perceptibly higher global temperatures and a measurable rise in sea levels. The increased emissions of what are commonly called greenhouse gases may lead to the enhancement of the "greenhouse effect," which under normal conditions enables the planet to retain enough heat to make it conducive to life forms. More specifically, the increased burning of fossil fuels has released substantial amounts of carbon dioxide, a greenhouse gas, into the atmosphere, resulting in a higher global average temperature. As of 2001, carbon dioxide concentrations have increased 31% over their levels in the year 1750 and are now at levels not seen in the past 420,000 years (IPCC, 2001c). Since transportation's use of petroleum-based fuels is responsible for roughly one-third of these emissions, by this definition our current transport system is demonstrably nonsustainable.

One might reasonably ask whether global warming will create major problems or whether it will be only a minor inconvenience. We really don't know the answer conclusively, but the general consensus is that negative impacts could be substantial from only small changes in temperature. Although many sectors of the economy or society might remain relatively unaffected, for a while, transport is not one of these. Transit tunnels flooding due to a rise in sea level, airplanes not taking off due to high temperatures, highways and railroad tracks buckling due to excessive heat, coastal highway and railway flooding, and the submersion of dock facilities are not problems that can easily be dismissed. Even more important is the potential shift in agricultural production to new areas with moderate climates and away from areas that are too hot or too dry, which would result in having to relocate and redesign transport infrastructure in these areas (Black, 1990).

Local Air Quality Impacts

Motor vehicle emissions are a significant contributor to urban air quality problems, which is something that makes the current transport system nonsustainable. According to the U.S. Bureau of Transport Statistics (2009), mobile sources (as of 2007) accounted for 3.7% of sulfur dioxide, 57% of nitrogen oxide, 68.4% of carbon monoxide, 2.9% of PM10 particulates of and 11.8% of PM2.5 particulates, and 33.9% of volatile organic compounds emitted into the air. A substantial portion of the production of urban ozone also has its origins in mobile sources. These various pollutants must be viewed as contributors to nonsustainability, as they are by European countries and the Organisation for Economic Co-operation and Development (OECD), which encompasses the developed nations of the world. That these pollutants have not always been viewed as part of the sustainability problem in the United States may reflect the fact that these problems were and are being addressed, but this attitude seems to have changed in recent years.

The negative health impacts of these emissions, primarily on the human respiratory system, must be viewed as a significant problem that cannot be allowed to fester. While U.S. policymakers have made substantial progress in reducing the level of these emissions, some even asserting that they will cease to be a significant problem in the foreseeable future, nevertheless at this time these emissions are a major factor making the current transport system nonsustainable.

Crash Fatalities and Injuries

It should be an accepted premise that a transport system that kills off its users is not sustainable. However, many policymakers do not wish to include motor vehicle fatalities and injuries in the calculus underlying the sustainability debate. Indications are that the world's motor vehicle fleet is responsible for nearly a million fatalities each year and some 70 million injuries (WHO, 2001, as cited in Evans, 2003). Global forecasts of fatalities and injuries during the next 10 years are almost beyond comprehension, given the growth in demand for personal mobility in China and India, for example.

In the United States the number of fatalities per vehicle mile is dropping, but mostly as a function of increases in vehicle miles driven. Until recently, total fatalities were also dropping, but this improvement is now disappearing or at least leveling off. We are no longer sure what is happening with injuries. In March 2004 the U.S. Department of Transportation set a national target of a 33% reduction in fatalities during the next 4 years, largely through greater use of seat belts, stronger enforcement of drunk driving laws, and closer regulation of the hours worked by motor carrier drivers. This is an achievable target. Other countries have set even more ambitious targets (e.g., Sweden has a target of zero fatalities), but the actions taken by U.S. authorities represent a significant improvement over prior goals they have set. Most countries, however, have not set *any* goals in this area. In any event, motor vehicle accident fatalities and injuries matter enough to be included in any debate over sustainable transport systems.

Congestion

Policymakers generally do not regard congestion as a major barrier to transport sustainability, apparently because the resulting impacts are so diverse. Congestion decreases the speed of vehicles, resulting in both *lower* fuel efficiency and increased emissions detrimental to human health. While increasing motor vehicle incidents, congestion actually decreases fatalities. Perhaps congestion is viewed as a manifestation of all the other criteria leading to nonsustainability, making its inclusion as a negative factor seem redundant.

Several years ago at a Transportation Research Board (TRB) annual meeting the question was asked, "If we adopted a renewable transport fuel with zero harmful emissions, would we have a sustainable transport system?" The question was never properly answered, but it is one that should be posed again. Clearly, replacing gasoline with hydrogen as the universal fuel would eliminate concerns about depletion of fuel stocks as well as the problems of global atmospheric impacts and local air quality. It could also contribute to a reduction in fatalities, as motor vehicle accident fires would be reduced with the use of hydrogen fuel (hydrogen dissipates almost instantly, making hydrogen fires vertical and localized rather than lateral as with gasoline). However, we would still have the problem of congestion in urban corridors and increasingly on major interstate highways and this, along with eventual gridlock, must certainly be viewed as contributors to nonsustainability. So, the answer to the question is that even a "wonder" fuel would not necessarily make the transport system sustainable. We would still have congestion, which will only worsen in the future.

Noise

One major difference between sustainable transport in the United States versus Europe is the latter's greater concern with noise. Considerable research suggests that loud and continuous noise is harmful to human health. This harm may be psychological, resulting in nervousness and behavioral disorders, or it may be physiological, resulting in impacts as significant as heart disease (from an excess production of adrenaline). As a consequence, many European nations are attempting to lessen the level of noise, particularly in urban areas. Of course, the same psychological and physiological effects are inherent to the transport systems in North America, and researchers are at work trying to minimize these. However, the problem and reactions to it are rarely viewed as relevant to the debate over sustainable transport systems here. The greater density of urban areas in Europe undoubtedly makes this factor more significant there.

Level of Mobility

While it may be unnecessary to state this premise, a sustainable transport system should evidence a reasonably high level of mobility. Consider the lesser developed countries in the world. In most instances we find that transport systems there use lesser amounts of petroleum, contribute little carbon dioxide to the atmosphere, and the other pollutants that we associate with motor vehicles, while not absent are certainly present in significantly smaller amounts. Motor vehicle fatalities and injuries are also comparatively low. Congestion is largely absent. Is this a sustainable situation? No, because the level of mobility is so abysmal that the transport system actually prevents development from occurring. So, we must take as a given that the transport system must provide a reasonable level of mobility, and this factor must be added to our criteria.

Other Contributors to Transport Nonsustainability

Biological Impacts

Much attention has been directed at the need to protect our biological resources from the damage wrought by transport activities (TRB, 1997). Animals killed along U.S. highways (estimated to number 4–6 million annually; Black, 2003), rivers and streams polluted, plants destroyed by emissions, and marine animals killed by run-off from highways, runways, and the like are all representative of these diverse biological impacts.

Perhaps the most devastating and highly publicized transport incidents that affect biological resources are the oil spills occasioned by oil tankers breaking up and spewing countless barrels of oil into the ocean or waterway they are traversing. Marine animals and water fowl are the most visible victims of such incidents, as the evening television news makes clear, but long stretches of beach are often despoiled for months or even years at a time. While no species has been extinguished by such transport accidents, their consequences for the local marine environmental and habitat are nonetheless substantial. Richard Forman's *Road Ecology* (Forman, 2002) and the 1997 TRB report *Toward a Sustainable Future* (also known as the Dean Report; TRB, 1997), both attest to the seriousness of the adverse biological impacts of transport systems.

Equity

Some researchers who have examined what makes the transport system nonsustainable have focused on matters of equity (e.g., Bae & Mayeres, 2005; Feitelson, 2002; Litman, 1999a), that is, the notion that operations of the current transport system should not jeopardize the possibility of future generations also satisfying their transport needs adequately. This notion of equity is not meant to imply that future generations should necessarily have the same type of transport system that we have today, but simply that if we are going to continue with a system based on finite petroleum reserves, then we should have either adequate fuel or another fuel available for those future generations. In this way we would avoid profound shocks to the social and economic systems that we rely on.

Beckerman (2003), however, has attacked the equity notion as something that is not desirable, arguing that an "equitable" system does not really maximize social welfare and that the present generation moreover owes nothing to future generations. On logical grounds he argues that future generations have no inherent right to anything at this time and that, indeed, most of what the current generation relies on will probably be viewed as having very little value to future generations, and therefore it makes little sense to try to preserve resources for them.

Other commentators believe that if the transgenerational equity argument is legitimate, then the current transport system should be made to be equitable, that is, fair, impartial, and just. Contrary to popular belief, equity has nothing to do with transport facilities being equally accessible or available to all potential users—that confuses incomes policy with transport policy. These questions have not yet been adequately dealt with in the literature, but hopefully we will get better insight into these aspects of sustainable transport in the future.

To bring this discussion of definitions to a close, let us summarize it by reducing it to a single definition. *A sustainable transport system is one that provides transport and mobility with renewable fuels while minimizing emissions detrimental to the local and global environment, and preventing needless fatalities, injuries, and congestion.* The absence of equity considerations is not accidental but rather a reflection of the fact that if the conditions in the definition are met the system will be equitable.

Those who find this definition to be too narrow probably view sustainable transport as relating to all aspects of the transport system (facilities, services, and use as well as urban development patterns) that affect the ability to sustain a society or an economy without compromising the ability of future generations to do the same. If we expect a sustainable transport system to do all of this, we are dooming it to failure. Even if we expect it to meet the narrower criteria, this rigorous set of requirements for the transport system raises the question of whether transport can be truly sustainable.

CAN THE TRANSPORT SYSTEM BE MADE SUSTAINABLE?

The current transport system is nonsustainable. A colleague once asked me why anyone would work in an area such as sustainable transport since it is obviously something that is not attainable. I would reply that, first, it is not at all certain that a sustainable system is unattainable. Ed Jordan, the first chief executive officer of the Consolidated Rail Corporation, once said there isn't a single problem that—given enough time, money, and people—could not be solved. Is the same thing true of sustainable transport? One can possibly envision hydrogen fuel as ultimately eliminating our concerns about the problems of diminishing resources, global atmospheric pollution, and local air quality. Similarly, major safety programs in highway and vehicle technology (e.g., intelligent transport systems, or ITS) might one day virtually eliminate fatalities and injuries. There is even some possibility of eliminating congestion as a dimension of the problem, particularly so if some of the ideas of Garrison and Ward (2000) are ever implemented. However, the major stumbling block or obstacle to implementing these solutions is adequate funding. Thus, the major dilemma is not that we don't know how to solve the problems of sustainable transport but that we don't know how to do it in an affordable manner.

In addition, the types of changes endorsed here lie decades away or would require many years of transitions. It is unlikely that hydrogen as an alternative fuel will ever gain a competitive foothold so long as the price of gasoline remains as low as it is today (or gyrates so radically in price). Since hydrogen may be a key component in powering a sustainable transport system, the sustainability of that system must await the full development of hydrogen fuel technology.

What We Really Mean by "Sustainable"?

Given that we can't do it cheaply and it won't happen overnight, does this mean we should not try to solve the problems? The answer is, obviously, "No." If we move toward sustainability and in the process fall short of achieving it, this is still likely to be a major improvement over where things stand at present. To do nothing will result in a continuation of the buildup of carbon dioxide in the atmosphere and a more severe future warming than currently anticipated, deteriorating urban air quality, additional highway fatalities and injuries, and potentially severe socioeconomic adjustment problems as fuel supplies diminish or the price of these climb to unprecedented levels.

Should we expect to ever achieve a sustainable transport system? Some commentators believe this is an unattainable goal. In the case of "sustainable development," Glasby (2002) argues for a totally new paradigm since, in his view, the world is embarked on a course that is manifestly unsustainable. That may be so in the case of sustainable *development*, but that doesn't mean that we can't develop a transport system that is more sustainable than the one that currently exists.

IMPLEMENTING SUSTAINABILITY IN THE TRANSPORT PLANNING PROCESS

It is reasonable to ask to what extent the various perspectives on transport sustainability have an impact on the manner in which new initiatives are implemented by different agencies as part of the planning process. This is not an easy question to answer since the transport planning process differs from one place to another, whether we are talking about plans for the countries of North America, South America, Asia, Australia, or Europe, or even plans for particular cities.

In addition, the approach to transport problems varies significantly from one place to another. Note, for examples, the tendency in European nations to call for reduced transport use through regulatory and pricing mechanisms (e.g., confiscatory taxes on vehicle purchases as well as fuel). In the United States, by contrast, transport and vehicle taxes are a common revenue source, but their explicit use as a tool for implementing transport policy is rare and unusual. Mechanisms used to implement transport policy are more typically voluntary, containing no real punitive consequences if one fails to deliver. The United States prefers to champion technological solutions to most of its transport problems: air bags (front and side), seat belts, and front and rear vehicular radar to cut down on needless fatalities; catalytic converters to cut down on emissions; and GPS and GIS systems to eliminate "extra" driving. Even much of government's policy is technologically oriented. For example, the original California zero-emissions mandate for automobile manufacturers in 1990 required them to sell a specified percentage of electric cars in California by the year 2000. Despite setbacks on the timing, more recent proposals from that state will mandate zero carbon dioxide emissions from those vehicles during the next decade, a policy requirement with multifaceted technological implications.

CONCLUSIONS

This chapter initially explored several definitions of sustainable transport, finding some to be either too cursory or too complex. The question was then posed, What is it that makes a transport system *nonsustainable*? Several variables were identified: use of a finite and diminishing petroleum resource; emissions of carbon dioxide that are detrimental to the global environment; emissions harmful to urban areas; excessive crash fatalities and injuries; and congestion. The issue of biological impacts was discussed briefly, and the idea of devising an equitable system was reviewed and found to be implicit in one's properly providing for transport and mobility.

The definition derived from this review and analysis is: *A sustainable transport system is one that provides transport and mobility with renewable fuels while minimizing emissions detrimental to the local and global environment and preventing needless fatalities, injuries, and congestion.*

CHAPTER 2

The Historical Problem of Sustainability in the Transport Sector

> I have always considered that the substitution of the internal
> combustion engine for the horse marked a very gloomy
> milestone for the progress of mankind.
> —WINSTON CHURCHILL (1942, as cited in Enright, 2001)

On their face, nearly all transport modes are sustainable. This is true whether we are looking at a horse and rider or a Cadillac Eldorado, a sailboat or a 747 airliner. The problem is the coupling of these various transport modes with excessive demand. None of our most common transport modes can handle large numbers of users, and this is the problem. In this chapter we will slip back in time to what are often viewed in retrospect as sustainable transport modes—but we will demonstrate the myth of this perspective.

It is likely that primitive man could walk across the African savanna grass without doing much more environmental damage than modern man does by walking across his lawn. Over time it is possible that a path, absent plant or grass growth, could be formed by the repeated use of the same route. The failure of grass to grow is essentially a product of soil compaction, and it might represent the lower end of an array of impacts that begins with such compaction of soil and extends to the modification of global climate. At the lower end, however, we can often stop using the path, or dig up the soil, and allow the path to return to its former state as part of the grassland or part of the lawn.

Early man did create such paths in different parts of the world. In North America several of these were in evidence and use when Europeans first arrived. One of these in Pennsylvania was called Nemacolin Trace, named after a Delaware Indian chief who helped establish it, and it became the path that several later transport lines followed. The potential negative impact of these paths or trails was minor in terms of the natural environment, and it is likely that significant impacts rarely extended beyond the path.

Domestication of livestock may have resulted in some early travel by this mode in Europe, northern Africa, or Asia, but we have no evidence to suggest animals were used for transport. In North America horses of the size that could have been used for transport were not even present until the arrival of Europeans (Hernando Cortez in 1519). The mustang herds of the American West were said to be descended from those early European horses.

THE MEDITERRANEAN EMPIRES

The key civilizations dominating the Mediterranean basin over the years were notable for their military undertakings. Whether we are talking about the Phoenicians, the Carthaginians, the Greeks, or the Romans, each of these was a naval power with a relatively large fleet at the time of their preeminence. The construction of these fleets was in large part responsible for the gradual deforestation of the region. The vegetative cover that exists there today is still affected by that earlier use of timber.

There were other heavy uses of timber in the region. In the Roman era, wood was used for the smelting of metals for use in military equipment and armaments. It was also used for public baths, cooking, heating, the production of charcoal, and other activities. None of these uses would require the use of plank timber of the type that would go into a ship, and this is the very type of tree that is virtually absent from the area today.

Domestication of horses for transport had already taken place in Europe and Asia before that. Many of these horses were used to pull vehicles, and this led to severe congestion in many Roman cities. The problem became so acute in Rome in 45 B.C. that Julius Caesar declared the center of Rome off-limits between 6:00 A.M. and 4:00 P.M. to all vehicles except those of officials, priests, visitors, and high-ranking citizens (Lay, 1992, p. 176).

Transport-induced air pollution was also evident in cities of the Roman Empire, but it was quite different than today. Chemicals for the most part were absent, but suspended particulate matter was very common in that dust from the streets sometimes mixed with the dried excrement of horses and other livestock. Street sweepers were used to try to keep this dust under control, but the dust only increased over time.

THE EXPLORATION PHASE

Much of the exploration of the world has taken place during the past 600 years. While exploration was clearly a transport activity, its demands on resources were relatively minor. Europe's nations were involved in commercial transport among themselves, thus exerting pressures on timber resources, but sustainability was still possible. The circumnavigation of Africa, the discovery of America, and the circumnavigation of the world, which together represented the first wave of globalization, changed all that—not because of the immediate need for more timber but because these explorations significantly extended the area over which countries of the world could trade. In effect, these discoveries stimulated the growth of commercial navies, whose construction needs placed upward pressure on lumber resources to the breaking point in a relatively short time.

THE 18TH CENTURY

By the 18th century the sustainability problem became significant as most of the naval powers of Europe, specifically England, France, and Holland, were beginning to encounter problems securing sufficient lumber for their navies. England had earlier cut down most of its oak plank timber, and it began importing this timber as well as the timber for the main masts of its ships from the New England colonies in America. The Revolutionary War (known in England as the War with the American Colonies) brought this trade in ship lumber with the colonies to an immediate halt.

Construction of a typical naval vessel of the time consumed, on average, some 1,400 oak trees. Merchant ships were far more numerous but required only 97 trees, on average, for construction. In the aggregate, of the 15,300 vessels registered in Great Britain in 1790, 98% were merchant ships and 2% were naval vessels (Albion, 1965). The total weight of the vessels in this fleet was approximately 1.9 million tons of lumber; with the usable lumber of an average tree weighing about 0.9 tons, this meant that the fleet in 1790 had required the cutting down of approximately 2.1 million oak trees. Had this been all, the impact would have been significant, but ships sank, aged, or needed repairs, and this simply added to the demand for timber. It is easy to see how Britain could have become deforested during this period. These figures help elucidate the nonsustainability of the wind-driven ships of the 18th century. By the 19th century the long-term outlook for this transport mode had become clouded and uncertain. Further discussion of this problem is available in Bamford (1956), Phillips (1986), Knight (1993), and Hickman (1999).

THE INDUSTRIAL AGE

The Industrial Revolution overlapped with this period, which saw the invention of the steam engine and its introduction into boats and ships during the 19th century. This did little to change the overall problem of shortages in wood supply since the early vessels continued to be manufactured from wood and the new power source used wood as a fuel. Shortages of lumber led some in England and elsewhere to advocate the planting of major stands of timber for the first time. Major reforestation efforts were begun at this time. Although the logic was sound, the timing was off. Growing timber to the size needed for a major ship requires nearly 100 years. In the interim, technology moved on to iron-clad ships by the seventh decade of the century.

The smelting of iron and the fabrication of steel became major manufacturing activities during the second half of the 19th century. Although these materials were obviously used in many products, the construction of a merchant fleet represented a major market for the steel industry. In addition, this was the era of railroad expansion.

THE RAILROAD ERA

The beginning of the railroad era during the 1830s in Europe and North America represented some technological advancements, but railroads were not the solution to the problem of sustainable transport. Localities in the United States were eager to become part of the developing network of railroads that would eventually serve the country. Although a few states became involved in railroad construction, early activity was primarily reserved to the private sector. During the early years entrepreneurs secured a charter from a state legislature that granted them permission to lay out a right-of-way for their new railroad, and then they would order whatever lumber was needed for the railroad (see Black, 1987). Initially this involved lumber for use in railroad cross ties (sleepers), trestles, and bridges. Development of the rail network in the United States created significant impacts on timber stands throughout the eastern half of the country. As an illustration, typically some 2,640 cross ties were used per mile of track (Wellington, 1887); each tie would represent about 44.6 board feet of white oak, and over a mile this translated into 117,744 board feet, or about 140 average oak trees per mile of track. We have no good estimates of the amount of timber used for bridges and trestles, but it would simply add to these numbers. Since the ties were not treated with chemicals (that practice started much later, in the 1880s) they had shorter lifespans, depending on the amount of curvature in the rail. For straight sections the life might be 9 years, but on the tightest curves it might be only 5 years. In other words, most of the rail lines had their ties replaced three or four times prior to the introduction of such treatments as creosote. Creosote helped prolong the life of ties from roughly 9 years to 25–30 years, but it brought with its use one of the earliest forms of chemical pollution in the transport sector.

After the lines were built and the railroads began operating, a new pressure developed on the nation's timber stands in the form of the use of lumber as a fuel to generate steam for locomotives. The trains of the 1800s were appreciably shorter than they are today, with an average of 8.5 cars per train, requiring some 55.4 board feet of lumber to move these cars 1 mile. In other words, operating these short little trains required about one oak tree for every 15 miles of train movement. It is not surprising that the right-of-way land along many of the nation's rail lines was barren by the end of the 19th century.

By that time suppliers had begun treating crossties with creosote to extend their life, and coal replaced wood as the major fuel source. These events relieved pressures on the timber stands, but they also introduced phenols into the environment and a new type of atmospheric pollution from the burning of the fossil fuel coal. Creosote continues to be used in the United States, although plastic coatings may replace its use in the near future. The use of coal decreased during the post-World War II period and was replaced by diesel fuel shortly afterward.

The use of iron and steel by the railroad industry has been examined by Fogel (1964). His concern was with its impacts on American economic growth. No one has examined the indirect environmental impacts of manufacturing these metals, including water and atmospheric pollution, for the railroad industry. These had to be substantial since some steel mills were in the business of producing only railroad track until the 1980s.

Over the years of the 20th century the railroad industry has done its share of polluting through the use of various petroleum products as lubricants; by using polychorinated biphenyls (PCBs) in brake boxes to keep them from overheating; and, by using chemical defoliants along their rights-of-way. At the same time, considering the huge volume of freight that railways have moved, it is one of the cleanest transport modes. Our discussion here has focused primarily on the United States, but the situation has not been much different in Britain or the other nations of Europe. One notable exception in the British case is attributable to the fact that during the 19th century their cross ties were generally longer and heavier (Wellington, 1887) than those elsewhere, suggesting a greater impact on their limited timber stands; more recently, cross ties have been made of concrete, especially in Britain.

URBANIZATION BEGINS

The spread of urban areas in the United States during the colonial era of the late 1700s does not appear to have generated significant transport impacts. Walking was the primary transport mode, combined with various amounts of transport by horse, horse-drawn carriages, and stagecoaches, none of which generated significant impacts, with the exception of manure and horse urine. During dry periods of the year it would be common for communities to sweep their streets, while during the rainy seasons it was common to use a "stage" to disembark from coaches, as opposed to stepping into the quagmire of mud and manure that would cover the streets of many communities. So long as the use of these transport modes did not become excessive, they were manageable. We know of no case where urban residents became ill from the pollution due to runoff during this horse and coach era. Had this occurred, it would not be surprising. Perhaps everyone was lucky, or perhaps it occurred and was not recognized for what it was.

By the close of the 19th century the population had begun to soar in the United States and Europe, as had demand for transport buggies and horses. The outcome should have been predictable: excessive numbers of horses and carriages would errate unsustainable conditions in such cities as New York and London by the 1880s. It is said that in each day during the earliest years of the 20th century, horses in New York left an estimated 2.5 million pounds of manure on the streets along with an estimated 60,000 gallons of urine (Flink, 1990, p. 136). Lay (1992, p. 132) notes that about 20 horses died each day on the streets of that city, or more than 7,000 each year. Although much of this detritus would be removed, these cities would hardly be pleasant environments during the summer months, doubtless creating respiratory health problems for many residents.

Accidents involving horse riding were quite significant during the late 19th century. Estimates of human fatalities from horse riding suggest that these occurred at the rate of 29 per 100 million miles traveled. Similar estimates for automobile fatalities in the year 1900 were about 24 per 100 million vehicle miles traveled (VMT). Currently the rate for motor vehicle deaths in the United States is about 1.5 per 100 million vehicle miles traveled. In terms of fatalities and injuries it may be said that the horse and buggy era was also not sustainable.

THE 20TH CENTURY

Given the urban problems of the 19th century, it is not surprising that the introduction of motor vehicles was viewed with considerable favor during the early years of the 20th century. By the end of the second decade the manure and urine associated with the horse were significantly less on the streets of American cities. Horses had been replaced by motor vehicles powered by steam and internal combustion engines. Steam was unable to hold a significant share of the automobile market, and vehicles powered by it were quickly replaced by internal combustion engine vehicles. It is doubtful that anyone at the time anticipated the emissions problems that these vehicles would eventually generate. The new motor vehicle system seemed to be the answer to a host of problems.

At the same time, the switch to motor vehicles had to have created massive economic impacts for the workforce of the country. Blacksmiths, harness makers, carriage makers, horse ranchers, livery stable keepers, and others gradually found themselves out of work. While some carriage makers made the successful transition to automobile body manufacturing, far more did not. In spite of these economic impacts the new vehicles seemed to be sustainable, although it is doubtful that anyone thought of them in those terms.

Perhaps the first indication of sustainability problems came with the increase in transport fatalities. The new vehicles traveled at higher speeds than individuals were used to traveling for personal transport. In many cases the fatalities were pedestrians. The first motor vehicle fatality in the United States was recorded on January 14, 1899, in New York City, although earlier accidents occurred. These early incidents all involved pedestrians, but there was an increasing number of fatalities due to motor vehicle crashes as the years passed. The other indicators of nonsustainability such as air quality problems, global pollution concerns (global warming and acid rain), land use problems, and motor vehicle congestion were not perceived as major problems by writers or policymakers of the day. Apart from some concerns expressed about high speed limits and inadequate signage, little seems to have been done to reduce the loss of life attributable to the new transport mode.

It wasn't until the late 1940s that governments recognized that the accumulated exhaust from motor vehicles could create air quality conditions that were hazardous to human health. The region most chronically affected by these problems in the United States was the Los Angeles basin of California. The smog (smoke + fog) of that region was actually urban ozone created by the interaction of nitrogen oxides and hydrocarbons in the presence of sunlight. Human respiratory systems do not react well to urban ozone, nor do human eyes. By the 1960s the federal government recognized that the problem was not confined only to California but appeared to be present in several large cities elsewhere as well. In part, this awareness led to some of the first emissions legislation for automobiles during the 1960s and creation of the U.S. Environmental Protection Agency in 1970.

At about the same time, consumer advocate Ralph Nader leveled two attacks on the lack of vehicle safety. His book *Unsafe at Any Speed* (Nader, 1966) criticized the Chevrolet Corvair on the basis of safety concerns, and *Small on Safety* (Ralph Nader Study Group, 1972) similarly took on the Volkswagen. These books asserted that motor vehicles were not being designed with the safety of the driver and occupants foremost in mind. The books were significant in drawing widespread attention to the fact that vehicles could be much safer than they were.

A classic planning-related volume by the Council on Environmental Quality (1974) was published at about the same time, titled *The Costs of Sprawl*. It concluded that, in the words of a third party, "automobile-related pollution would be reduced significantly in planned developments and that the economic and environmental costs of high-density development were significantly lower than those of low-density development" (Burwell et al., 1991, p. 88). This research had its critics, and it was eventually redone in a TRB report *Costs of Sprawl—2000* (Burchell et al., 2002). This new report, also had its critics, as most studies of this type do. There are some who believe that urban/suburban sprawl has no value whatsoever and generates huge costs for urban areas that need not be incurred. On the other hand, there are those who see sprawl as having some benefits. This volume examines both viewpoints in a balanced way, though some critics would probably prefer to see one or the other argument favored unqualifiedly.

The recognition that the motor vehicle could create significant congestion was probably not evident until after World War II, and for good reason. Motor vehicles were on a growth track during the earliest decades of the century. However, the stock market collapse in 1929 followed by the Great Depression during the 1930s did little to stimulate the market for automobiles. World War II brought a halt to automobile production as the government diverted key resources to the war effort rather than producing cars. Additionally, gasoline was carefully rationed, further decreasing the use of vehicles. With the end of the war, and the discharge of thousands of servicemen and -women who suddenly had disposable income to spend, automobile ownership began to skyrocket. By 1950, significant levels of congestion began developing as a result of increases in the level of automobile ownership. Passage of the Interstate Highway Act in 1956 was in part a response to this congestion, but an unintended consequence was to move congestion from the intercity portion of most trips to the central city since the new interstate links literally dumped traffic into city thorough fares that were ill equipped to handle it.

Perhaps the last component of motor vehicle nonsustainability to be recognized was its contribution to global warming. Many still would dispute that causality has been conclusively demonstrated, but given that motor vehicles emit carbon dioxide into the atmosphere at the rate of approximately 20 pounds per gallon of gasoline (Gordon, 1991; Miles-McLean et al., 1993) and given that carbon dioxide accounts for much of the greenhouse effect (see Chapter 1), there is no sound basis for refusing to accept this fact.

Aviation Transport

The aviation sector has significant impacts on both consumers and employees as well as communities. Most of the consumer/employee impacts are manageable, but the impacts on communities are more serious and have received less attention. Table 2.1 lists the primary impacts discussed in the literature (e.g., Upham et al., 2003). The two most common problems are noise and emissions, both of which have significant impacts on communities. The exact nature of the emissions is not well understood. In other words, the specific measurement of aircraft as the source of emissions is uncommon, and the relevant figures are normally just combined with those for other sources of the known pollutants.

Current aviation is not a sustainable transport mode. A clean alternative fuel could help solve many of the problems, but such a fuel has not yet been developed. For example, several possible alternatives do not work well at the low temperatures prevailing in the upper atmosphere, tending to result in too frequent engine stall (Hadaller & Momenthy, 1993). Until this problem is solved, the aircraft sector will not likely move toward long-term sustainability in any meaningful way.

Marine Transport

Marine transport is a reasonably sustainable sector (see Black, 2007). It certainly moves massive freight tonnage with relatively little impact on the natural environment. Container vessels developed over the past several years can now each move as many as 7,000 20-foot equivalent units (TEUs), and the newest designs call for this capacity to rise to 10,000 TEUs shortly.

TABLE 2.1. Environmental Impacts of Aviation

Nature of the impact	Impacted party or area
Deep vein thrombosis	Passengers
Airborne disease spread (e.g., tuberculosis)	Passengers
Cosmic radiation exposure	Crew
Aircraft noise pollution	Communities and airport personnel
Emissions—nitrogen oxides	Communities
Emissions—carbon monoxide	Communities
Emissions—nonmethane volatile organic compounds	Communities

TABLE 2.2. Major Oil Tanker Spills, 1967–2008

Ship	Year	Location	Spill (in ton)
Torrey Canyon	1967	Scilly Isles, U.K.	119,000
Sea Star	1972	Gulf of Oman	115,000
Jakob Maersk	1975	Oporto, Portugal	88,000
Urquiola	1976	La Coruna, Spain	100,000
Hawaiian Patriot	1977	Pacific near Hawaii	95,000
Amoco Cadiz	1978	Off Brittany, France	223,000
Atlantic Express	1979	Off Tobago, West Indies	287,000
Independenta	1979	Bosphorus, Turkey	95,000
Irenes Serenade	1980	Navarino Bay, Greece	100,000
Castillo de Beliver	1983	Off South Africa	252,000
Nova	1985	Gulf of Iran	70,000
Odyssey	1988	Off Nova Scotia, Canada	132,000
Exxon Valdez	1989	Prince William Sound, Alaska	37,000
Khark 5	1989	Off Morocco	80,000
Haven	1991	Genoa, Italy	144,000
ABT Summer	1991	Off Angola	260,000
Katina P.	1992	Off Maputo, Mozambique	66,700
Aegean Sea	1992	Off Spanish Coast	74,000
Braer	1993	Shetland Islands, U.K.	85,000
Sea Empress	1996	Milford Haven, U.K.	72,000
Prestige	2002	Off the Spanish Coast	63,000

Source. Copyright 2009 by the International Tanker Owners Pollution Federation (ITOPF). Reprinted by permission.

The most prominent area of marine transport that can be improved involves the oil tanker. There have been numerous incidents since 1967 involving the release of crude oil into the oceans (see Table 2.2). Some of these could have been prevented by utilizing double-hull tankers, but these also cost more to the shippers, and as a result they do not receive all the available cargo. Two related problems with tankers involve the release of methane into the atmosphere when the oil is removed and using oil as ballast on trips from source areas. The former problem can be solved by technology, while the latter problem requires the shipper to forgo some of its "cargo" and to use water instead for ballast (see Black, 2007). The long-term solution will probably require formalized international agreements.

CONCLUSIONS

We have examined the historical development of transport systems, focusing variously on wind-powered wooden ships during the 17th and 18th centuries, railroads and horse and carriage transport in the 19th century (verging into the 20th century), and motor vehicle transport in the 20th century. In every case these modes start off at a scale that is manageable and environmentally benign. However, as the use of the mode increases, it becomes more and more threatening to the society that uses it. The merchant and naval ships of Europe eventually resulted in the deforestation of large sections of England, France, and Holland. The railroad industry ultimately deforested huge swaths of land though North America because of its demand for large quantities of wood for construction and operating fuel. Horse and carriage transport grew to the point where it was beginning to pollute urban areas seriously with animal wastes. Motor vehicles now threaten to alter the climate of the planet as they consume huge quantities of petroleum. Nevertheless, each of these transport systems could have been sustainable if the numbers involved could have been kept well under control. This observation suggests that part of the answer to attaining long-term transport sustainability may lie in diversity, that is, not relying unduly on a single transport mode or fuel source.

CHAPTER 3

Climate Change

> Most of the observed increase in global average temperature
> since the mid-20th century is very likely due to the observed
> increase in anthropogenic greenhouse gas concentrations.
> —INTERGOVERNMENTAL PANEL ON CLIMATE CHANGE (2007)

This planet is surrounded by an atmosphere made up of numerous gases. Some of the incoming short-wave ultraviolet solar radiation passes through this atmosphere and heats the surface of the planet. The heat from the surface is then transformed into long-wave infrared heat radiation. Although our atmosphere acts as somewhat of a barrier to some of the heat passing through it to outer space, some does get through. The analogy of a greenhouse has been used to describe this retention of heat by the planet, and the process of retaining the heat has been referred to as "the greenhouse effect."

The greenhouse effect is basically a good thing because it makes the planet Earth warm enough to sustain life. If we did not have the effect, the average global temperature would be –18°C (–0.4°F) instead of the 15°C (59°F) that we enjoy.

Although there is nothing particularly new about this greenhouse effect, it was suggested in the 1960s that rapid increases in carbon dioxide could increase global temperatures, or "force" the greenhouse effect (Menabe & Wetherald, 1967). What this means is that it might be possible to increase the gases that contribute to the greenhouse effect—sometimes called greenhouse gases (GHGs)—and in doing this we might create a situation in which more of the heat is retained by the planet. Were this to happen, a warming of the planet would result—what we generally refer to as global warming.

The Intergovernmental Panel on Climate Change has noted that "it is likely that the rate and duration of the warming of the 20th century is larger than any other time during the last 1,000 years. The 1990s are likely to have been the warmest decade of the last millennium in the Northern Hemisphere, and 1998 is likely

23

to have been the warmest year" (IPCC, 2001a). While the idea of a warmer planet may have some natural appeal in the northern temperate zone during a particularly harsh January winter, the reality with its attendant consequences may be quite different. We will examine these potential impacts later in this chapter, but let us first look at the current thinking about greenhouse gases.

GREENHOUSE GASES

There are several specific greenhouse gases. In this section we examine the major ones and in particular note whether transportation is involved in any way in their production. Our focus is on gases resulting from human activities rather than those produced by natural sources. This is important to differentiate because certain gases that contribute to the effect are derived almost entirely from natural sources. One of the major natural gaseous forms is water vapor. Certainly swimming pools, reservoirs, and man-made lakes contribute to the formation of water vapor, but in comparison to the world's oceans that contribution is negligible.

We examine three sets of gases here: carbon dioxide, methane, and nitrogen oxides. In addition, we discuss several engineered or man-made gases.

Carbon Dioxide

The major greenhouse gas is carbon dioxide (CO_2). It is an extremely common gas that is found, for example, in every bottle or can of carbonated soft drink. It is also released whenever we burn fossil fuels (coal, natural gas, petroleum), when plants die, and whenever humans or animals exhale. Transportation is a significant source of this gas since gasoline is derived from petroleum. For each gallon of gas that is burned in a motor vehicle, as we earlier noted, some 20 pounds of carbon dioxide are emitted into the atmosphere. Transportation accounts for about 25% of the world's greenhouse gas emissions attributable to human activity, but there are several other important sources.

In the United States, transportation accounts for 32% of the carbon dioxide energy-related emissions (GAO, 2009). Of this amount, 60% comes from the burning of gasoline, 22% from the use of diesel fuels, 12% from the use of jet fuel, and 2.8% from various maritime fuels. Carbon dioxide emissions from transport have grown an average of 1.5% annually since 1990. Other energy sources of carbon dioxide emissions are the residential sector, with 21% of total emissions; the commercial sector, with 17% of emissions; and the industrial sector, with 29%. The annual growth rates for emissions attributable to these three sectors since 1990 have been 1.7%, 2%, and 0.2%, respectively.

Electricity production is a major source of carbon dioxide emissions, but we generally do not look at it independently. Instead, it is allocated to the end use sectors above, that is, transportation, commercial, residential, and so on. Of course, there are other non-energy-related anthropogenic sources of carbon dioxide. These include trash burning, cement production, removing carbon dioxide from natural gas, and natural gas flaring, but these are minor sources, accounting for less than 2% of annual emissions.

Although we have fairly good data on total carbon dioxide levels in the atmosphere, we have very reliable data only for the last 150 years or so. Prior to that, the levels sometimes have to be inferred from gases trapped in polar ice, statues, and various sealed containers that have survived. At the present time the level of carbon dioxide in the atmosphere is approximately 380 parts per million by volume (ppmv). This is approximately 30% higher than it was in 1800, or prior to the beginning of the Industrial Revolution, that is, prior to the time when we began burning coal on a large scale to produce steam power.

Figure 3.1 depicts the level of carbon dioxide in the global atmosphere since 1959, with Figure 3.2 representing the last several years of these levels. These data are from the Mauna Loa Observatory in Hawaii. The zigzag nature of the unadjusted monthly trend is due to the dying off of plant life in the northern temperate areas of the planet in the fall and the absorption of carbon dioxide by new plant growth in the

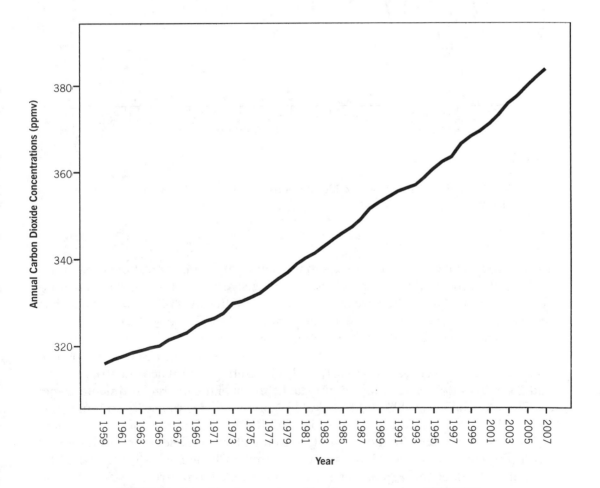

FIGURE 3.1. Monthly mean carbon dioxide concentration, 1959–2007.

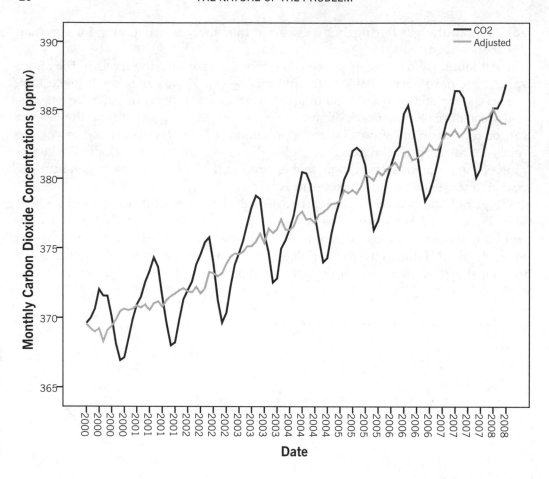

FIGURE 3.2. Monthly mean carbon dioxide concentration at Mauna Loa with seasonal variation and adjusted values.

spring. The same process also occurs in the Southern Hemisphere, but land masses in that half of the world are appreciably less extensive and therefore have little influence on the overall monthly trend. As can be seen, the level of carbon dioxide has increased from 315 to 380 ppmv over the period 1959–2007, or about 20.6%.

Recognition of the potential problems of carbon dioxide and its effect on global warming led scientists from a number of countries to begin discussing possible ways to curb these emissions as early as 1985. Meetings in Villach, Austria, in 1985 and Toronto in 1988 were followed by establishment of the Intergovernmental Panel on Climate Change in 1988 by the United Nations Environment Programme and the World Meteorological Organization. The Rio Earth Summit (officially known as the United Nations Conference on Environment and Development) in June 1992 led to the UN Framework Convention on Climate Change, which was signed by 155 nations; under this agreement, signatories pledged to return emissions to 1990 levels by the year 2000, but the agreement was not binding on the parties.

The next major relevant event was the signing of the Kyoto Protocol in December 1997. Under this agreement, the ratifying parties were to decrease carbon dioxide emissions an average of 5.2% below 1990 levels by the period 2008–2012. Specific individual targets for the developed nations were set at the time. The less developed nations were not given specific carbon dioxide reduction targets, and this difference in treatment became one of the stumbling blocks for U.S. participation in the treaty. The Clinton administration believed (probably correctly) that Senate ratification of the bill was a foredoomed exercise, the Republican leadership declaring it "dead on arrival." Concerns over exclusion of the developing nations, and potential negative impacts on economic growth kept the United States from ratifying the agreement.

The Bush administration did not even give any thought to sending the treaty forward for ratification. President George W. Bush made it clear that he thought the entire question of climate change needed more study, so the Kyoto Protocol has never been officially ratified or implemented by the United States to date.

Nevertheless, enough countries to activate it did ratify the agreement, and so it took effect in 2003. Few if any countries will be able to achieve the targeted reductions set for them by 2008–2012, but even if they manage to reduce their emissions only slightly—or, failing that, slow the growth in their emissions—that will be an improvement over the situation that existed.

Inaction by the U.S. federal government domestically led the state of California to enact a rule requiring significant reductions in carbon dioxide emissions, beginning in late 2008, and 11 other states subsequently adopted similar rules. California also insisted that it is the responsibility of the U.S. Environmental Protection Agency (EPA) to regulate carbon dioxide emissions. While EPA officials in the Bush administration disagreed, the U.S. Supreme Court ruled in April 2009 in California's favor. The full implications of this ruling are not yet clear at this writing.

On August 31, 2006, the legislature of the state of California passed and Governor Arnold Schwarzenegger signed into law a statute to limit the carbon dioxide produced by the state's industries. This legislation, known as the Global Warming Solutions Act of 2006, sought to reduce greenhouse gas emissions to 1990 levels by 2020. The California Air Resources Board (CARB) has developed a plan for implementing the 2006 act. Legislation enacted in 2008, the Sustainable Communities and Climate Protection Act, seeks to help reduce emissions from automobiles by providing financial incentives to cities to develop compact neighborhoods that encourage residents to walk, bike, and use mass transit more. The act also requires CARB to set vehicle emission reduction targets regionally within the state.

Methane

Methane emissions, while substantially less significant than carbon dioxide emissions in their overall ill effects, are nonetheless about 25 times stronger at forcing the greenhouse effect; in other words, they cause more heat to be retained per unit of volume. The primary sources of methane pollution are energy production (40%), agriculture (29%), and waste management (31%), with industrial processes accounting for very small amounts of the remainder (EIA, 2005). Key energy sources are coal mining, natural gas systems, petroleum systems, stationary combustion, and mobile source combustion. Agricultural sources include livestock management, rice cultivation, and crop residue burning. Waste management sources of methane pollution are predominantly landfills (92% of the emissions) and waste water treatment facilities. Overall, transport sources are a relatively minor contributor to methane pollution, chiefly emanating from getting the fuel from the oil wells to the vehicle itself.

Nitrogen Oxide

Nitrogen oxide emissions chiefly emanate from agricultural processes (75%) that encompass nitrogen fertilization of soils, the solid waste of domesticated animals, and crop residue burning; energy use (both mobile and stationary combustion); industrial processes; and waste management. Of these amounts, transportation accounts for 79% of the energy use sector, with the majority of this coming from vehicles with catalytic converters.

Engineered Gases

Other gases that also contribute to emissions problems—ones that are not naturally occurring but rather result primarily from human engineering—include hydrofluorocarbons, perfluorocarbons, and sulfur hexafluoride. The first of these, hydrofluorocarbons (HFCs), is primarily used as a replacement for chlorofluorocarbons (CFCs) in automotive air conditioning systems. CFC production was halted by the Montreal Protocol on Substances That Deplete the Ozone Layer (promulgated in 1987). CFCs had other uses, but this was the major transport use. HFCs can be detrimental to the atmosphere, but they have a relatively short atmospheric life.

Perfluorocarbons (PFCs) are emitted as by-products of aluminum smelting. They are not produced in abundance, but they can remain in the atmosphere for up to 10,000 years. Sulfur hexafluoride (SF_6) is a by-product of magnesium smelting, but it is also used as an insulator in large-scale electrical equipment. It, too, has a long atmospheric lifetime—up to 3,200 years. While the latter two engineered gases are not produced in great quantities, their prolonged atmospheric lifetimes potentially make them significant emissions pollutants. These have little relevance to transport and are noted here only for completeness.

Global Warming Potential

Some gases are detrimental primarily because of the quantities produced, while others create problems because they persist in the atmosphere for long periods of time. The global warming potential (GWP) measure seeks to convert all emissions into a common gauge. This value, when weighted by carbon dioxide equivalents, suggests that of the three gases and the engineered gases, the annual GWP in 2001 for these was 5,973 for carbon dioxide, 639 for methane, 354 for nitrogen oxide, and 156 for the engineered gases.

THE IMPACTS OF GLOBAL WARMING

As suggested above, the addition of greenhouse gases to the atmosphere will inevitably warm the planet over time. In this section we discuss the general impacts that will result. We examine the full range of impacts first and then focus on the impacts within the transportation sector.

While the exact amount of the expected rise in temperature is not known, current estimates range from 1.8°C to 4.0°C by 2100 (IPCC, 2007). The expected increase will not be uniform but rather will vary across the planet, with the least increase occurring near the equator and the largest in the polar regions. This will result in several sets of temperature-related impacts, including the melting of the polar ice caps and glaciers, increasing drought in semiarid regions, increases in evaporation and therefore more precipitation events, changes in ocean temperatures and possibly ocean currents, the mass migration of plants and animals, massive crop losses attributable to changing temperatures, an increase in the area over which insects range, and an increase in the likely geographic range of diseases. These are the major impacts that have been highlighted in the literature, with others likely to join them as our knowledge increases.

Some of these impacts may appear to be minor, but they are not. A glacier can sometimes be the major source of water for a locality during the summer, as is the case with Mount Kilimanjaro in Africa, for example. Loss of the glacier atop that mountain could make living on its slopes or in the grasslands at its base untenable. None of the impacts noted is at all minor.

A second set of impacts results from the anticipated sea-level rise, currently estimated to be 0.18–0.59 meters (IPCC, 2007), depending on one's assumptions. As the polar ice caps and glaciers melt, there will be an increase in the levels of oceans. In some cases this will simply result in the inundation of low-lying areas around the world's oceans. This will not occur overnight, and there will be more than enough time for individuals in these areas to move to higher ground. On the other hand, complacency could create a disaster in the wake of sea-level surge events. These are, for example, the large waves created by storms that usually come crashing ashore as part of a hurricane or typhoon. There is a tendency to point at the impact of Hurricane Katrina on New Orleans to illustrate this point, but that disaster had numerous levels of causation, ranging from failure to vacate the area, a compromised dike and levee system, and the abject failure of governments to respond to the crisis. So, this may not be the best example of the destruction that may result from a rise in sea levels.

There will be other tropical storms that generate disasters even when areas are comparatively "ready." We know this because we also know that there will be an increase in such storm events. These storms generate their strength from the warm water they pass over, and ocean water is only likely to grow warmer overtime, based on research of late (Emanuel, 2005; Webster et al., 2005).

There is a growing belief that current temperatures are accelerating the melting of the Greenland Ice Sheet, possibly nearly doubling the expected amount of sea level rise (Dowdeswell, 2006). Similar ideas also exist regarding certain middle latitude glaciers in New Zealand, China, the Alps of Europe, and Russia.

THE IMPACTS OF GLOBAL WARMING ON TRANSPORTATION

The general impacts of global warming on transportation derive from (1) temperature and precipitation changes, (2) water- and sea-level change, and (3) possible abatement activities. Several of these possibilities were suggested as early as 1990 (see Black, 1990); let us now look at the expected impacts. Some of these have also been suggested in the impact reports issued by the IPCC (e.g., IPCC, 1995, 2001a, 2001b, 2007).

In North America global warming could result in a significant disruption in the flow of goods and people as agricultural production shifts northward due to increased temperatures. "Many U.S. producers have been using aquifers to irrigate, but increases in temperatures will make this impractical in the short term and impossible in the long term" (Black, 1990, p. 3). Widespread irrigation may become increasingly impractical in the drier areas of the country, which could lead to substantial outmigration from the areas most affected by greater heat.

At one time it was believed that regions specializing in fossil fuel production could see significant decreases in demand for these fuels as a result of their high carbon dioxide emissions and resultant global pollution and warming. This trend has not yet been set in motion and may be delayed or averted due to technological improvements in carbon dioxide sequestration. At the same time, there appears to be a general reluctance to move away from fossil fuels completely such that the burning of coal will likely be with us for quite some time.

Streets and Highways

The major impact of global warming on streets and highways will be the constant flooding of these roads during storm events. This phenomenon, for example, appears to have occurred during the surges and subsequent levee collapses associated with Hurricane Katrina in 2005.

During the early 1990s one might have expected some positive impacts from snow removal costs decreasing as various areas of North America warmed up, but these would be offset by increasing snow-removal costs in the northern part of Canadian provinces as more and more people move into that area (for example). Nowadays we are less certain of this type of tradeoff in that, since a warmer planet will increase the amount of evaporation, there may be an overall increase in snowfall during the winter months.

One might reasonably expect that warmer temperatures would exacerbate air quality problems in most places since driving tends to increase during the warmer seasons of the year, but it is not in any way evident yet. Other roadway problems would include increased "heat buckling" of highways in warmer areas, damage to highways from the melting of permafrost in areas of northern Canada and Alaska, and increased fatalities associated with increases in population in Canada as residents of the United States seek cooler environments during the summer. These possible outcomes are not yet evident but still likely to evolve.

If extreme weather events increase—and science suggests they should—then we can expect significant flooding of streets and highways and damage to transport infrastructure in the affected areas. Hurricane Katrina demonstrated that high winds and flooding waters are capable of destroying highway bridges, covering streets and roads with debris that makes them impassable, and destroying signal systems or making them inoperable. That colossal storm actually managed to uproot the massive concrete roadbed underlying the U.S. route 90 bridge over St. Louis Bay (*Business Week*, 2005). Even in the absence of a hurricane, a gradual sea-level rise will exacerbate the damage caused by storm surges, that is, the surges will be higher and increasingly result in chronic coastal flooding.

The extent to which global warming is a problem for the highway system depends on where the highways are located. A northward shift in warmer temperatures not only would lower snow removal costs in the once cooler areas but also could result in decreased damages attributable to freeze–thaw activity. In northern areas of Canada it is not uncommon for travelers to rely on ice roads, frozen areas that have been specifically cleared for vehicle use (Lemmen & Warren, 2004). Premature thawing could necessitate making other arrangements for transport byways or the use of infrastructure less impacted by thawing.

Water Transport

Eventually the accelerated melting of polar ice and icebergs could make whole areas of North America's northernmost coasts much more navigable, resulting in the proliferation of ice breakers, coast guard operations, lighthouses, and the like. This eventuality remains a distinct possibility.

Inland transport on the Great Lakes, rivers, and seaways, similarly could also encounter numerous unfamiliar problems of a different sort. Were rainfall to diminish significantly, navigation would be more difficult between the Great Lakes unless remedial measures were undertaken. Similar problems might develop in the Mississippi River system if precipitation levels in that region drop. Droughts in that area are much more serious, and forced diversion of water from the Great Lakes to allow navigation on that waterway has occasionally been resorted to in the past (Changnon & Glantz, 1996). Forced channelization has existed on the Mississippi River since the late 1800s, and further human-engineered channelization may be necessary if increased global warming results in less water flowing into that river system. This development would potentially reduce the amount of navigation that could occur on that waterway.

A possible positive impact of global warming on this sector could be an increase in the number of ice-free days for the St. Lawrence Seaway. This improvement could lead to an increase in traffic, but the major barrier to increased traffic on that waterway continues to be limitations on the size of vessels that can use the canal.

Finally, a significant rise in sea level could result in the need to raise port termi-
nal facilities. This problem has not arisen to this point, but drastic measures might
be necessary if some of the higher sea-level rise projections occur. Of course, port
facilities on the Great Lakes could experience a similar problem as well as the problems that would result from a precipitous drop in lake levels.

In general, global warming impacts on water transport have changed little
during the past couple of decades. Increases in precipitation in coastal areas could
increase runoff and lead to greater erosion. This erosion, in turn, could increase
sedimentation of silt in harbors and result in the need to dredge more. In certain
areas this same runoff could result in landslides, which could block rail or highway connections. Once again, scientists are still unable to pinpoint precisely where
increased precipitation will appear, but some progress in predicting this phenomenon has in fact occurred (Barnett et al., 2005; Milly et al., 2005).

Railroads

The gradual sea level rise and occasional storm surges have long been seen as potential problems for rail lines that run alongside U.S. coasts in storm-prone coastal
areas. Some discussion arose during the 1980s about relocating certain rail lines
further inland, and some of this relocation work occurred.

Permafrost thawing has lately been seen as a problem for the railroads of Alaska
and parts of northern Canada, and this climatic trend remains on the rise and much
in evidence today.

The flooding of at-grade and subway rail transit systems in metropolitan areas
of the eastern United States is also seen as a potential problem if the observable sea
level rise and damaging storm surges increase significantly.

Additional impacts on the rail sector accrue from the occasional extreme event.
Hurricane Katrina demonstrated dramatically that such storms could tear out rail
lines and rail bridges with impunity. The CSX, a railroad company that serves the
eastern United States, suffered the worst damage, losing 39 miles of track that runs
along the Gulf Coast between New Orleans and Pascagoula, Mississippi (*Railway
Age*, 2005). The storm displaced track 10–50 feet at a time, often leaving it in a con-
torted upside-down position. Six railway bridges were also destroyed or heavily
damaged. Estimates of the total storm damage to the railroads was in excess of $60
million, excluding loss of revenue traffic during repairs. Additional impacts from
the storms included flooding and debris on the tracks, as was true of the highways
in the area.

Air Transport

Global warming impacts on air transport were initially seen as primarily associated
with storm surges and flooding for airports located in coastal areas. The flooding of
airports and the possible construction of sea walls to mitigate rising sea levels has
also received attention (see duVair et al., 2002; Titus, 2002). Titus (2002) has observed
that a 1-foot rise in sea level will normally result in a reduction in runway length of

20 feet (based on an assumed 3-degree descent angle and a runway that stretches all the way to the dike). This amount of reduction would not be a major problem for long runways (e.g., 10,000 feet) such as those at Boston's Logan Airport or Reagan National Airport in Washington, DC, but the problem bears watching.

There always remains the possibility of some potential impacts resulting from regulations intended to decrease emissions of greenhouse gases from jet aircraft. Switching to an alternative fuel has never been mandated on any large scale, but there have been initiatives aimed at moving toward blends or mixtures in the 15–85% range.

Our knowledge about the potential impacts of climate change, particularly atmospheric conditions, on the safe and efficient operation of aircraft has improved over time (Kulesa, 2002). The positioning of runways is determined by wind direction in order for aircraft to gain maximum lift (Thornes, 1992), and changes in wind direction and strength related to atmospheric conditions could be of concern in the future. Air temperature can impact flights if, when the temperature exceeds a certain threshold level, air density becomes too low to allow the aircraft to gain lift (*AWST*, 1990).

There are potentially several other impacts of climate change on the transportation sector (USDOT, 2002). An excellent volume on the science of climate change as well as its impacts has been published by the National Research Council's Transportation Research Board, and the reader is referred to that source (TRB, 2008).

ABATEMENT

The possibility of stopping the "forcing" of the greenhouse effect that has been leading to further global warming has been viewed as relatively unfeasible for more than 20 years. Instead, the talk even back then was about abatement, decreasing emissions through various policies and technological approaches.

Among the abatement strategies considered during the 1980s was a shift to methanol, which was not viewed as much of a solution, whether natural gas or coal was used as the feedstock. Compressed natural gas was viewed as a more likely fuel, but its use has not grown much beyond those early efforts. Ethanol was also suggested, and its use has only recently begun to increase significantly. Electric power was viewed as feasible, but only if produced from nuclear sources. Purely electric vehicles were viewed at the time as being of only marginal value in reducing emissions, and the intervening years have seen little demand for these vehicles in the United States.

Hydrogen-powered transport was seen as holding some promise. Although electricity for hydrogen production was thought to be best derived from solar energy sources, it was not viewed as an immediate solution to the alternative fuel problem.

Another set of possible solutions suggested during the 1980s involved shifting to other modes of transport by implementing various policies: exclusive bus lanes, tolls on low-occupancy vehicles, high taxes on parking and gasoline, and providing for high-quality mass transit. A major technological innovation in the passenger sector was creation of a high-speed rail system to absorb some of the short-haul air travel volume. Although these policies and technologies have not seen large-scale adoption, that possibility continues to be discussed.

Increasing vehicle efficiency through decreasing fuel use was not seen as a panacea for this problem during the 1980s. Many of the fuel-efficiency improvements that could be made had already been made in response to the CAFE (Corporate Average Fuel Economy) standards. In air transport, improvements had occurred in response to deregulation, which led to the use of fewer planes, the abandonment of unprofitable routes, and improvements in engine performance. An ongoing switch to smaller regional jets has also contributed positively to lesser emissions in the atmosphere. Improved communications have also increasingly served as a substitute for travel during this time, particularly through telecommuting and, more recently, teleconferencing, thereby helping to decrease the level of demand for transport.

Conservation of energy sources has long been seen as a way of decreasing travel demand and therefore as a way of diminishing fuel consumption and the production of greenhouse gases. While the conservationist impulse grows strongest during such crises as the oil embargo of 1975–1976, however, global warming still has not been viewed by government policymakers as a serious enough problem to gain the public's support. A paper I wrote in 1990 concluded pessimistically that probably "little, if anything, will be done to control the emission of greenhouse gases during the next 50 years" (Black, 1990, p. 7). In the paper I argued that

> global warming, with its rising temperatures and sea levels, dropping lake levels, droughts and disturbance of existing commodity flow patterns for grains and fossil fuels, could have a serious effect on the transport sector. Avenues for abatement of these impacts do not seem to offer much hope for control of the total problem, but research must continue in this area. To mitigate the likely impacts on all sectors, something must be done to lessen the trends in greenhouse gas emissions. (Black, 1990, p. 8)

CHANGES IN OUR KNOWLEDGE AND POLICIES RELATED TO GLOBAL WARMING

The cited passage above is most disturbing not because it misperceived the nature of possible transport-related problems and potential solutions associated with global warming but because it foresaw them so clearly and yet no action intervened to prevent the full-blown crisis we now encounter. Nevertheless, the problems and some solutions are better understood now, as we will show in the remainder of this chapter.

One might well expect significant initiatives aimed at emissions abatement at the federal level as public officials moved to limit the potential damage from global warming. Unfortunately, the administration of George H. W. Bush fought tooth and nail against the Global Warming Treaty during the Rio Earth Summit in

1992. The Clinton administration, though cognizant the problem, seemed unable to do very much about it, and the subsequent George W. Bush administration did not even perceive a problem—or so it said. President Bill Clinton did in 1993 create the Partnership for a New Generation of Vehicles (PNGV), which was intended to accelerate the development of electric propulsion, ultra-efficient technologies, light-weight materials, and advanced manufacturing processes. It brought together the Big Three automakers (General Motors, Ford, and Chrysler) and the U.S. national laboratories to accomplish these goals, but with only minimal funding (Sperling, 1995). It is questionable whether the Big Three automakers were the appropriate players to seek a change in the status quo, and it is not clear that anything worth noting emerged from these efforts.

The election of Barack Obama as President of the United States in 2008 promises to bring with it more U.S. government activity on climate change than has occurred in quite some time. At this writing (May 2009), of course it is too early to judge what will happen, but there is reason for some optimism, given the new president's statements and the strong control that Democrats currently wield in the House of Representatives and the Senate.

CONCLUSIONS

This chapter addresses one of the basic causes of nonsustainability in the trans-port sector: climate change. Carbon dioxide and other emissions from transport and other sectors have led to a forcing of the greenhouse effect, or global warming. While most sectors have seen some success at limiting these emissions, this has not been the case with transport.

We also examined the major impacts of global warming, noting that these broadly fall into two areas: impacts from increasing temperatures and impacts from sea level rise. The impacts that may befall the transport sector and its various modes if emissions continue unabated were also discussed. In this discussion Hurricane Katrina was used as an illustration of some of these impacts simply because the storm surges associated with sea level rise would be similar.

Abatement was briefly mentioned, but dismissed as something that does not now seem like a possible strategy for limiting the impacts of climate change. Never-theless, it does make some sense to try and limit the emissions of greenhouse gases to prevent the impacts from being worse than currently anticipated.

CHAPTER 4

Urban Air Quality

The contribution of the transport sector to total emissions
of air pollutants is higher than in the past and high
compared with the contribution from other sectors.
—JOHN WHITELEGG (1993)

It seems reasonable to assume that substandard urban air quality could keep
the transport system from being considered sustainable, although initially most
researchers in the United States did not consider it a critical factor. This relative
lack of concern may reflect the fact that air quality was already being given substantial attention by most transportation agencies. In any event, it is now generally
conceded to be a chief obstacle that prevents an area's transport system from being
considered sustainable.

EMISSIONS AND EMISSIONS STANDARDS

Air quality problems have been evident in the United States for well over 100 years,
beginning with the rapid industrialization of the late 19th century. Industrial plants,
steel mills, coke ovens in the coal regions, chemical plants, and later utility companies contributed to a less than optimal air quality situation. Little was done about
this air pollution until the middle of the 20th century, when some of the first legislation was passed to clean up the urban atmosphere.

The National Environmental Policy Act of 1969 and the Clean Air Act (CAA) of
1970 were major steps forward in this area. In particular, the Clean Air Act established the National Ambient Air Quality Standards (NAAQS), which set area-wide

standards for carbon monoxide (CO), sulfur dioxide (SO$_2$), lead (Pb), nitrogen dioxide (NO$_2$), ozone (O$_3$), and particulate matter of less than 10 microns in size (PM$_{10}$). These six pollutants are often referred to as the "criteria pollutants."

Carbon Monoxide

Carbon monoxide is produced when organic materials, such as gasoline, are not completely combusted. Motor vehicles are the largest source of emissions of this particular pollutant. Such on-road sources are responsible for 47% of the emissions, while off-road sources account for another 21% of these emissions. Concentrations are high in urban areas, particularly at intersections, and motor vehicles may account for as much as 95% of the carbon monoxide found there.

Emissions from this source have decreased on a per vehicle basis because of increases in fuel efficiency largely attributable to catalytic converters. Nevertheless, carbon monoxide continues to be a problem, owing to increases in the number of automobiles, the total vehicle miles driven, and the failure of catalytic converters to last as long as the vehicles.

Exposure to carbon monoxide levels as low as 0.001% for a prolonged period can result in death. This pollutant attaches to hemoglobin, inhibiting the ability of blood to carry oxygen. The amount of carbon monoxide that a driver often is typically exposed to may be sufficient to cause headaches, blurred vision and drowsiness. This is not a persistent pollutant, that is, it does not stay in the atmosphere. It rapidly converts to other compounds, such as carbon dioxide, and normally dissipates relatively quickly.

Sulfur Dioxide

Sulfur dioxide is produced when sulfur-containing fossil fuels are burned. It has a strong odor and can be harmful to the respiratory system. One of the primary problems created by this pollutant is "acid rain," which can be harmful to both humans and structures. We will not focus long on it here because transportation is not a major source of this pollutant. The overwhelming source is the burning of coal by electric power plants.

Lead

In the past, lead in urban areas traditionally came primarily from the lead in gasoline. Tailpipe emissions would deposit substantial amounts of lead in the environment. It was originally put into gasoline during the early 1930s to prevent engine knock. Among its most harmful side effects were blood disorders in children as well as problems with children's mental development. It has now been completely eliminated from gasoline in the United States, owing to its phaseout during the 1980s, and most of Europe. Some assert that lead was removed from gasoline because of its harm to children, but another factor was its tendency to clog catalytic converters. One might prefer to think that health effects were the key to its elimination, but these were known decades earlier. Lead is still found in gasoline in less developed parts of the world.

Nitrogen Oxides and Nitrogen Dioxide

Nitrogen dioxide forms when fuel is burned at very high temperatures, such as in motor vehicle engines. In fact, mobile sources are responsible for about 57% of such emissions in the United States. This class of pollutants includes nitrogen oxides and nitrogen dioxide. The former is controlled in part by catalytic converters, but again increases in vehicles and total vehicle miles driven have resulted in high concentrations of this pollutant in urban areas. Nitrogen dioxide is involved in the production of photochemical smog.

Ozone

Ozone is created in the atmosphere from nitrogen oxides and hydrocarbons in the presence of sunlight. It usually covers very large areas once it is produced. It may be harmful to human lung tissue, causing difficulties in breathing. It may also be injurious or irritating to eyes. Photochemical smog is usually composed of ozone and peroxyacetyl nitrates. Therefore, photochemical smog can be controlled if these two compounds are controlled.

Particulate Matter

Particulate matter less than 10 microns in size (PM_{10}) are actually pieces of solid matter. They have numerous sources, and mobile sources may be responsible for about 2.9% of these particles. Other sources include fires, industrial plants, and wind-blown dust. The negative health effects, again, primarily affect the respiratory system. These effects can range from asthma to lung cancer, since some particulate matter can be carcinogenic.

These six criteria pollutants were the original pollutants of interest. Over time we have had some success in reducing the emission of PM_{10} particles, and have moved on to focus on $PM_{2.5}$ particles, those less than 2.5 microns in size. The harmful effects remain the same. Lead is also of much less concern today since its removal from gasoline in the United States has virtually eliminated its presence in most cities. The current (2009) National Ambient Air Quality Standards appear in Table 4.1.

Emission Standards

When the original NAAQS were put into place, one way that urban areas could meet the standards was to control emissions from transportation (mobile) sources. Legislation initiating emission controls was enacted earlier, with the Motor Vehicle Air Pollution and Control Act of 1965. That federal law was based on legislation enacted

TABLE 4.1. National Ambient Air Quality Standards (February 2009)

Pollutant	Primary standard	Averaging times	Secondary standards
Carbon monoxide	9 ppm (10 mg/m^3)	8-hour	None
	35 ppm (40 mg/m^3)	1-hour	None
Lead	1.5 µg/m^3	Quarterly average	Same as primary
Nitrogen dioxide	0.053 ppm (100 µg/m^3)	Annual (arithmetic mean)	Same as primary
Particulate matter (PM$_{10}$)	Revoked 150 µg/m^3	24-hour	
Particulate matter (PM$_{2.5}$)	15.0 µg/m^3 35.0 µg/m^3	Annual arithmetic mean 24-hour	Same as primary
Ozone	0.075 ppm	8-hour	Same as primary
	0.12 ppm	1-hour (applies in limited areas)	Same as primary
Sulfur oxides	0.03 ppm	Annual arithmetic mean	
	0.14 ppm	24-hour	
		3-hour	0.5 ppm (1,300 µg/m^3)

Source: U.S. Environmental Protection Agency, *www.epa.gov/air/criteria.html*.

in 1963 in California that set emission standards for hydrocarbons and carbon monoxide for that West Coast state. It was the 1965 act that gave the federal government the authority to set emission standards for new motor vehicles and engines. These standards were to be set for pollutants that "cause, or contribute to, air pollution which may reasonably be anticipated to endanger public health and welfare."

The 1970 Clean Air Act went further, actually setting numerical standards for automobile emissions and specifying the reductions that were to occur. There were to be 90% reductions in hydrocarbons and carbon monoxide from 1970 levels by 1975, and a 90% reduction in nitrogen oxides from levels of the 1971 model year by the 1976 model year. These targets were not met, and the U.S. Environmental Protection Agency, which was created in 1970 by presidential order, then set interim standards that were also reasonably stringent.

The emission standards have been revised numerous times since then. These standards are usually targeted to be accomplished by a particular future date. If the current standards for light-duty vehicles (i.e., most automobiles) are all met by 2009, the level of carbon monoxide emitted will be 96% lower than at precontrol rates, total hydrocarbons will be 99% lower, and nitrogen oxides will be 98% lower. Standards covering nitrogen oxides and particulate matter have also been promulgated for heavy-duty diesel engines that, if met by 2010, will result in a 98% reduction in these emissions from precontrol levels. The standards have doubtless been effective on an individual vehicle basis.

The picture is not quite as bright when viewed from the perspective of total emissions from transportation sources since 1970. From that perspective, we see that the annual tonnage of carbon monoxide has dropped by about 40%, while nitrogen oxides have actually increased 22%, volatile organic compounds have declined by 53%, and PM_{10} particulates have dropped by 16%. These less-than-stellar changes in annual tonnage emitted primarily reflect substantial increases in total vehicle miles traveled.

EFFECTS OF EMISSIONS ON HUMAN HEALTH

The chief reason for concern regarding emissions is the detrimental impact these have on human health. Although we have noted them, they are worth underscoring here because they are the primary reason for attempting to control these emissions. For the most part, these emissions all have potential impacts on the human respiratory system, ranging from difficulty in breathing to death. The adverse health effects of carbon monoxide have been known for some time. Carbon monoxide entering the bloodstream links to hemoglobin sites normally reserved for the oxygen transported to all the organs of the body. This competitive binding (CO having a special affinity for hemoglobin) results in severe problems for those with cardiovascular diseases while it can also interfere with cognitive functioning, work capacity, and vision. Urban ozone concentrations formed by the interaction of nitrogen oxides and volatile organic compounds in the presence of sunlight can also create major health problems, ranging from chest pain and decreased lung functions to premature lung aging and chronic respiratory illnesses (EPA, 2001). Particulates can be very detrimental to human health as well, with problems ranging from making existing ailments (e.g., asthma) much worse to causing cancer and premature death. Although the precise effects of the various pollutants are not always well understood, clearly what we know is sufficient to want to take action to limit them. Researchers have variously estimated the health-related costs of air pollution; suffice it to say they are substantial (see McCubbin & Delucchi, 1999).

Air Toxics

Another set of emissions not yet been discussed here is generally referred to as "air toxics." These emissions in certain instances are known carcinogens, but they can also lead to cardiovascular and respiratory diseases as well as birth defects. These air toxics may emanate from various sources, but we will focus only on those significantly derived from mobile sources. These toxics and the percentage of their emissions that arise from mobile sources include benzene (76%), 1,3-butadiene (60%), acetaldehyde (70%), diesel PM (100%), formaldehyde (49%), and acrolein (39%). Relatively little is known about these air toxics beyond the fact that they represent a significant public health hazard (U.S. Government, 2001).

PLANNING AND THE CMAQ PROGRAM

Under the NAAQS rubric, there are two types of areas, those that meet the standards and those that do not; the latter are designated nonattainment areas. To bring an area into compliance (conformity) and to keep areas in compliance (maintenance), we have the Congestion Mitigation and Air Quality Program (the CMAQ program), created under the Clean Air Act of 1970.

It may not be readily apparent why this is a congestion mitigation program. Most of the criteria pollutants discussed in this chapter are released in comparatively greater quantities when the motor vehicle's engine is cold or when the vehicle is moving at slow speeds. Concerning the latter, motor vehicles operate most efficiently (vis-à-vis minimizing emissions) when at about 50–55 miles per hour (see Figures 4.1–4.4). At speeds significantly less than this, the combustion process results in the release of relatively more air pollutants in the emissions. When a highway is congested and traffic moves at a slow speed, less efficient operation of vehicles results. Therefore, reducing congestion is completely consistent with the goal of improving air quality. The question is how best to attain this goal.

The CMAQ program funds numerous actions that can be taken toward increasing conformity with maintenance of the standards while reducing congestion. These include programs that are explicitly spelled out in the Clean Air Act Amendments of 1990 (TRB, 2002a), such as:

1. Programs for improving public transit.
2. Restriction of certain lanes or roads, or construction of lanes or roads, for use of buses or high-occupancy vehicles (HOVs).
3. Employer-based transportation management plans, including incentives.
4. Trip-reduction ordinances.
5. Traffic-flow improvement programs that achieve emissions reductions.

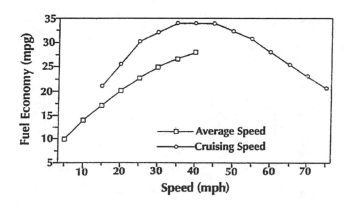

FIGURE 4.1. The relationship between speed and fuel economy. *Sources:* After Ross (1994), Davis (1995), and Greene (1996).

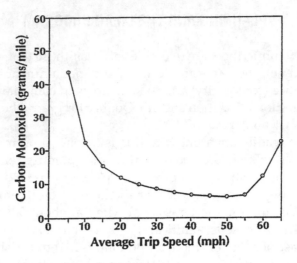

FIGURE 4.2. Generalized carbon monoxide emissions as a function of speed. *Source:* TRB (1995).

6. Fringe and corridor parking facilities serving multiple-occupant vehicle programs or transit operations.
7. Programs to limit or restrict access to areas of high emissions during periods of peak use.
8. Programs for providing high-occupancy or shared-ride services.
9. Programs to restrict a portion of the road surface to nonmotorized vehicles or pedestrians.

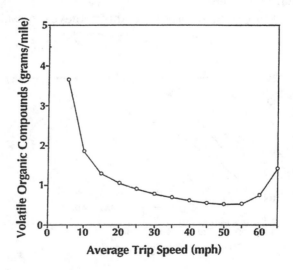

FIGURE 4.3. Generalized volatile organic compounds emissions as a function of speed. *Source:* After TRB (1995).

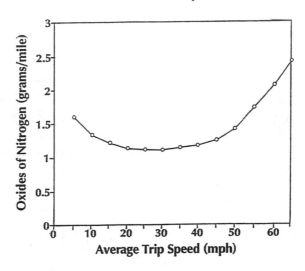

FIGURE 4.4. Generalized nitrogen oxide emissions as a function of speed. *Source:* After TRB (1995).

10. Programs for bicycle storage facilities and bicycle lanes in public and private areas.
11. Programs to control excessive idling of vehicles.
12. Programs to reduce emissions from cold starts (new under the Transportation Equity Act of the 21st Century, or TEA-21).
13. Employer-sponsored programs to permit flexible work schedules.
14. Programs and ordinances to facilitate nonautomobile travel.
15. Programs for new construction or reconstruction of paths, tracks, or areas for pedestrian and nonmotorized vehicles.
16. Programs to encourage removal of pre-1980 vehicles (excluded under the Intermodal Surface Transportation Efficiency Act and TEA-21).

These provisions are discussed in detail and evaluated later in this volume.

CONCLUSIONS

In this chapter we have identified the major air pollutants that make transport systems nonsustainable and have explored the legislative background of motor vehicle emission standards. Although per-vehicle emissions have been decreasing rapidly in the United States, and indeed throughout the developed world over the past three to four decades, the level of total emissions annually has not fallen as rapidly for all of the air pollutants (in the case of nitrogen oxides, even rising). This trend mostly reflects substantial increases in the total vehicle miles traveled in the United States over the same period.

We also reviewed the negative health consequences of these pollutants as well as those six air toxics emitted by transport sources. The air toxics have only recently drawn the attention of policymakers and researchers, and relatively little is known about them. The costs to society of both the criteria pollutants and the air toxics is an active topic of research and public discussion.

Finally, we reviewed the provisions of the Congestion Mitigation and Air Quality Improvement Program, noting in particular the importance of congestion relief in helping to curb emissions. Localities can use these programs to get into conformity with or to maintain adequate air-quality standards.

CHAPTER 5

The Finite Nature of Petroleum Reserves

It is by no means too early to begin preparing for the inevitable day,
which may come even before the end of the present century, when
world production of oil will be inadequate for world needs.

—KIRTLEY F. MATHER (1947)

INTRODUCTION TO THE RESOURCE

The future of petroleum is that it has no future. Whether we are talking about diesel fuel, propane, jet fuel, gasoline, or reformulated gasoline, we must not lose sight
of the fact that the source of these fuels is petroleum. Crude petroleum is a *finite*
resource and the *finite* source of these fuels. We began using significant amounts of
this transport fuel during the early years of the 20th century, and it is questionable
whether there will be enough of this energy source to power the world's vehicle
fleet in another half-century. Depending on whom you believe regarding reserves,
we may be able to stretch this fuel so that it goes into the 22nd century, but this is as
doubtful as it would be undesirable.

Based on 2005 data, the world is using about 83.8 million (83.8×10^6) barrels of
petroleum each day, or 30.6 billion (30.6×10^9) barrels a year (EIA, 2006a). We don't
know the total reserves, but estimates are that these are in the vicinity of 1.293 trillion (1.293×10^{12}) barrels. Assuming there is no growth in the rate of consumption
and the reserves don't increase, the world will deplete its oil reserves in slightly
more than 42 years from 2005, or in the year 2047. If we assume that consumption grows at the current growth rate for energy consumption, there will be a 1.4%
annual growth in petroleum consumption, which would result in the depletion of
global reserves by the year 2038. This is not a bright picture in either case. While
total discoverable reserves are obviously greater than the current estimated reserves
of 1.3 trillion barrels, we think it unlikely that these would yield more than another
decade of petroleum production. The continued use of petroleum-based fuels for

our transport system is therefore not sustainable since demand will far outstrip supply within a human lifetime, leading to its elimination or stringent rationing.

This projected scenario is based on the current set of players. If China and India were to consume substantially more than is reflected in the anticipated growth rate, the target year of 2038 for depletion would appear to be overly optimistic.

Of course, many people don't accept the notion that petroleum reserves are this limited. If you assume that substantial new reserves will be found and that the technological efficiency for recovering fuel from existing fields will also increase, some scientists estimate that discoverable reserves may range from 1.8 trillion to 2.6 trillion barrels. Working with these numbers, MacKenzie (1995) projected that global production will peak in 2018–2025 and then begin its inevitable decline. Assuming that all 2.6 trillion barrels are ultimately recovered, and the annual rate of growth ranges as high as 2.3%, then we will run out of petroleum by the year 2050. Campbell (1997) and Hatfield (1997) have raised similar concerns regarding petroleum reserves and petroleum use, but they are not as optimistic in their projections as MacKenzie (1995).

Economists argue that we will never run out of petroleum, noting that, as the resource becomes scarce, the price system will tend to ration the stocks that remain. Put another way, were the price of gasoline to rise to $20 a gallon, demand would decrease significantly. From a practical point of view, petroleum will cease to be a viable fuel when its price is no longer competitive with the available alternatives.

Many developments could slow the depletion of petroleum. The use of ethanol from biomass could delay the inevitable, but as the world's population doubles during the next 100 years it is quite possible that corn, sugar cane, and other suitable stock for biofuels will be used as foodstuffs instead and that arable land not already dedicated to food production will be transferred to that purpose.

Alternatively, if the price of corn and other ethanol stocks increase sufficiently, we could see land currently dedicated to food production shifted over to ethanol stocks, which in turn could potentially increase the price of food crops and cause significant "food panics" in the less developed parts of the world. To some extent, a significant price run-up occurred in the spring and summer of 2008, but speculators also played a role in driving up commodity prices at that time. We do not mean to suggest that ethanol has no role to play in meeting future fuel requirements. It will be one of the several fuels that will replace our nearly complete reliance on gasoline today.

Recycling may also play a role in the future of petroleum-based fuels. The production of petroleum-based fuels from recycled plastic and other materials could also boost supplies, but only marginally. The recycling of used automotive oil will also add to supply stocks marginally. One could also raise gasoline taxes to the point where consumption was radically affected. However, all of these are measures that will not solve the problem of the long-term sustainability globally of petroleum-based transport fuels. The reality is that petroleum is not sustainable as a fuel. Later, in Chapter 19, we will look at the potential alternative energy sources to petroleum, not as fuels to slow the depletion of petroleum-based fuels but as replacements for that fuel.

Taking another tack, Garrison (1999) gently reminds us that we may be entirely wrong about the likely depletion of petroleum reserves. He cites W.S. Jevon's 1865 book on *The Coal Question*, in which the author, observing English coal production increasing at 3.5% annually, confidently predicted the exhaustion of this resource within several decades. Jevon proved to be incorrect, suggesting that there are good reasons to be cautious when speculating about the potential depletion of any natural resource whose total reserves are still unknown.

THE RESOURCE BASE: SUPPLY

We actually know surprisingly little about the total supply of crude petroleum in the world. There are two kinds of oil reserves. The first, generally referred to as "proven reserves," is the oil that has been discovered and is known to exist in fields but has not yet been pumped out of the ground. These proven reserves are estimated to be in the neighborhood of 1.7 trillion barrels. This total is the sum of all the annual estimates supplied by the various companies and countries that have significant reserves (see Table 5.1). However, these numbers can fluctuate quite a bit from one year to the next, and it is difficult to place a lot of confidence in the total obtained.

The second type of reserves is referred to as "unproven reserves." These reserves have never been confirmed but are viewed as very likely to exist by petroleum geologists and other experts in the field. The U.S. Geological Survey places these undiscovered reserves at about 900 billion barrels, and this estimate, when combined with the proven reserves, gives us the total estimate of 2.6 trillion barrels of petroleum in the world.

It is also known that we have used approximately 850–900 billion barrels of petroleum over the past 120 years. Considering that we are talking about all of the 20th century, this total may suggest that the picture is fairly bright, but the reality is that many of the world's countries were not consuming significant amounts of oil in the past, and these countries are now stepping up their consumption, suggesting that demand in the current century will be much higher than in the past.

In recent decades a number of geologists and petroleum experts have suggested that world oil production is peaking. Much of this speculation is based on initial work by M. K. Hubbert (1956), who developed a method of estimating when oil production in a region would peak. Once such a peak is reached, the subsequent decline tends to be fairly predictable, describing a normal curve of production for the region. Hubbert, for example, estimated that U.S. production would peak in 1971 and decline substantially therefore closely approximating what, in fact, occurred (see Figure 5.1).

Hubbert also used his approach to estimate when world oil production would peak, based on an assumed total oil recovery of 2.1 trillion barrels (Hubbert, 1981), and concluded that it would peak in 2003 or 2004. During the 1990s Campbell (1997) examined several regions of the world with essentially the same procedure and concluded that many of these areas were then peaking in their production rates as

TABLE 5.1. Location of Production and Proven Reserves of Conventional Oil (Millions of Barrels)

Continent and country	Annual production (2002)	Proven reserves (2004)
North America		
Canada	808	4,500
Mexico	1,160	15,674
United States	2,097	22,677
South America		
Argentina	269	2,820
Brazil	546	8,500
Colombia	211	1842
Ecuador	143	4,630
Venezuela	834	77,800
Europe		
Denmark	135	1,277
Norway	1,149	10,447
United Kingdom	842	4,665
Africa		
Algeria	310	11,314
Angola	326	5,412
Chad		1,000
Congo	93	1,506
Egypt	274	3,700
Gabon	91	2,499
Libya	480	36,000
Nigeria	710	25,000
Asia		
Australia	227	3,500
Azerbaijan	110	7,000
Brunei	69	1,350
India	242	5,371
Indonesia	407	4,700
Iran	1,252	125,800
Iraq	735	115,000
Kazakhstan	299	9,000
Kuwait	584	99,000
Malaysia	281	3,000
Qatar	235	15,207
Russia	2,703	60,000
Saudi Arabia	2,500	261,000
Syria	186	2,500
United Arab Emirates	684	97,800

Source: EIA, 2006b.

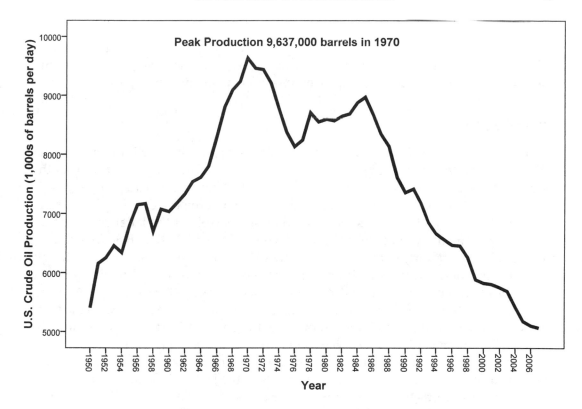

FIGURE 5.1. U.S. crude oil production (1950–2007). *Source*: EIA, 2000; EIA, 2008.

well. Once again, a peak represents not the end of production but rather the beginning of a trend of declining annual oil production.

Many researchers, objecting to Hubbert's approach, prefer to base their approaches on trends in consumption and increases in demand. Both approaches make assumptions about the total recoverable oil, and these assumptions are not that different.

With regard to the United States, the Energy Information Administration (EIA, 2006) notes that crude oil production is in decline from onshore wells in the lower 48 states, from the wells in Alaska, and from shallow-water offshore wells. Although EIA sees an increase in production from deep-water offshore wells over the next decade, it expects this source to begin declining around 2016, although this assessment was given prior to discoveries in the Gulf of Mexico during the summer of 2006 that are discussed below.

The Role of Technology in Recovery

It was not at all uncommon for petroleum recovery methods of the last century to leave as much as 30% or more of the oil in the ground. This was often in pockets that could not be reached. Today it is common to pump large amounts of water into the well, extract the water, and then separate the oil that is mixed in with it. This is just one of many technological changes that have developed over time. It is now also possible to map the approximate size of underwater fields using sonar, and this development has significantly improved prospects when deciding where to drill.

New Discoveries

During the summer of 2006 Chevron, Devon Energy, and StatOil announced the discovery of a major oil field in the Gulf of Mexico, approximately 270 miles southwest of New Orleans. Yield from the well was 6,000 barrels of crude oil per day. It is estimated that the Jack field, as it is called, may contain between 3 billion barrels of extractable oil and gas to as much as 15 billion barrels. If the latter proves to be the case, this would exceed the 13 billion barrels found at Prudhoe Bay, Alaska, and would add significantly to the nation's nearly 23 billion barrels of reserves. Although 6,000 barrels of crude per day is an impressive output, one should realize that the 1901 Spindletop discovery near Beaumont, Texas, yielded 5,000 barrels *per hour*. As for the size of the Jack field (3–15 billion barrels), this hardly compares with the largest known field in the world, the Ghawar field in Saudi Arabia, which has already yielded 55 billion barrels (its reserves being undetermined; Simmons, 2005).

Of course, the Gulf of Mexico is already the site of considerable drilling and numerous oil and gas concessions. Nevertheless, the Jack field is believed to be the largest oil find in the area. Of course, large parts of the Gulf are still not open to drilling. The U.S. Congress may reconsider a moratorium that currently prevents offshore drilling of the Atlantic and Pacific coasts of the continental United States. Legislative bills under consideration in 2007 and 2008 would have allowed drilling in areas at least 50–100 miles from the shore, the distance to be determined by the state affected. It is likely that similar ideas will emerge for the Gulf Coast region as well, given the recent promising finds in that area.

Other sizable fields may be discovered over the coming years, particularly in Siberia, western Africa, eastern South America, and the Caspian Sea region (Roberts, 2004). However, we will not likely see a repeat of the "monster" finds made during the 19th century in North America or during the 20th century in the Middle East.

THE DEMAND FOR PETROLEUM

As we noted at the beginning of this chapter, worldwide demand for oil is running at about 30.6 billion barrels a year (as of 2005). First we assumed that this total demand might remain constant into the future, and, second, we postulated that demand might continue to increase at a 1.4% annual growth rate, as in the recent past. How realistic are these alternative assumptions?

Obviously, the second is the more realistic scenario. However, one should be aware that the rate of growth may fluctuate widely. It was 2.3% during the mid-

1990s but now has moderated to 1.4% annually. In reality, we are not very good at forecasting changes in such rates.

The Growth of New Markets

Nevertheless, unusually high rates of growth are anticipated over the next decade for China and India in particular, and China is expected to become the largest consumer of world energy by the next decade. Demand for automobiles in China is growing at a very high rate, roughly 15–20% annually, but their absolute number is currently at a reasonably low level (Schipper & Ng, 2006). However, even if we assume that only a small fraction of the Chinese population manages to be able to purchase an automobile during the next decade, the resulting demand for petroleum will soar. China's population is currently about 1.6 billion, and even if only one-fifth of these people are eventually able to purchase an automobile, the 320 million vehicles will vastly exceed the number of automobiles in the United States. Thus, the estimated annual change in oil consumption postulated in our initial model may be too conservative to be realistic. Sperling and Gordon (2009, p. 209) see significant growth occurring in China, with the number of motor vehicles surpassing those in the United States by 2030 and ultimately reaching 500–600 million by 2050—even excluding motorcycles and rural vehicles, three- and four-wheel vehicles that have developed outside of government control.

Of course, economic events during 2007–2009 have had a significant impact on fuel consumption and motor vehicle sales, both in the United States and worldwide. The first event was a significant rise in the price of gasoline, which led to a reduction in the total amount of travel taking place in the United States and a change in the types of vehicles being purchased there and elsewhere. Suddenly smaller vehicles were much preferred, and the sale of larger vehicles plummeted. The second event was the general global economic recession (or depression), which resulted in a significant decrease in the sale of all types of motor vehicles in all parts of the world. The widespread collapse of bank credit availability following the collapse of the housing market has made it very difficult for individuals to purchase motor vehicles. Gasoline prices have fallen significantly in response to a major drop in demand for the fuel. The long-term impact of these events is difficult to forecast. If the global economy recovers in a few years, then the increase in motor vehicles and fuel consumption in new markets will continue and the decreases in vehicle sales and oil consumed will appear only as a slight dip in the long-term trend line. Alternatively, if the global economy fails to recover as fast as expected, future vehicle growth and oil consumed will be significantly less than currently anticipated.

NONCONVENTIONAL SOURCES OF PETROLEUM

The discussion up to this point has been entirely about conventional sources of petroleum; the petroleum that is found in a liquid state that we simply pump out of the ground. There are other sources of petroleum. These are the so-called oil sands and tars and the oil found in some shale deposits. These nonconventional sources of petroleum are found in great amounts in North America. Specifically, the oil sands are found in the province of Alberta, Canada, and very extensive deposits of oil shale are found in the Green River formation that encompasses portions of Colorado, Wyoming, and Utah. Estimates are that the oil sand deposits of Alberta represent potentially 174 billion barrels of oil (Greene et al., 2003). Of course, we cannot put tars and sands into the gas tank; on the other hand, we can remove the petroleum from these—but not without considerable effort and expense, mostly for heating the substrates to extract the petroleum.

Oil shale refers to sedimentary rocks that contain solid bituminous materials. These materials can be released as a petroleum type of liquid through a heating process called retorting. The oil shale deposits in the United States are the largest in the world, with estimates placing them at roughly the equivalent of 1.5–1.8 trillion barrels of oil. Of course, *recoverable* petroleum might be considerably less, the range of 500 billion to 1.1 trillion barrels (Bartis et al. 2005).

The retorting can take place after the shale is mined or while it is still in the ground. The former process generates a significant number of problems, ranging from emissions to the disposal of the rock after retorting. The process also requires large amounts of water, which is relatively scarce in the region of the oil shale deposits. Retorting in the ground is environmentally less harmful and would be accomplished by thermal heating of the rock.

There are numerous technological barriers that must be overcome before oil shale would be a reliable source of petroleum. Time estimates range from 10 to 30 years, depending on the quantity of petroleum to be produced, before the mining and environmental problems could be solved. Although the oil shale deposits of the western United States were considered a potential source of petroleum during the 1970s, the environmental standards of the day made development of them nonviable. These standards have only been strengthened over the intervening decades, making the processing of oil shale nonsustainable as a petroleum source in the present context.

CONCLUSIONS

In this chapter we have briefed the reader on the petroleum problem, emphasizing that petroleum is a *finite* resource with obvious limits to its long-term use. We reviewed the supply situation for this fossil fuel and discussed the possibility of large-scale new finds of major fields, which appear unlikely to materialize. On the demand side, we noted the growth of new markets for petroleum, mostly in Asia. The thus far unpredictable impact of the global recession in 2008 and 2009 was also addressed.

While nonconventional sources of petroleum admittedly exist in the tar sands of Canada and the extensive shale deposits of the United States, the recovery of oil from these sources would entail significant outlays of energy and require overcoming significant environmental problems. Nevertheless, increasing interest in these sectors may persist in the years to come.

The overall picture would appear to be one of growing demand for petroleum as the less developed nations of the world pursue the traditional path of industrial development—and, paradoxically, a decrease in reserves of petroleum to meet these new demands. The world's citizens appear little inclined to abandon petroleum as a fuel until the very last minute of its economic life, at which point we will more than likely begin to see the void filled by a mix of alternative fuels and improvised solutions.

CHAPTER 6

Motor Vehicle Crashes and Safety

> Clearly, we tacitly agree to accept a certain level of carnage in order to use the highways in ways we value. At the present time in the U.S., this tacit agreement says that it is acceptable to sacrifice between 40,000 and 42,000 lives annually.
>
> —PATRICIA WALLER (2001)

In the United States in 2007 there were 41,059 motor vehicle fatalities. If someone were to suggest that no one is listening to Dr. Waller, it would be difficult to summon a persuasive counterargument. It is lamentable that having 41,000 men, women, and children killed annually on the nation's byways is not a sufficient impetus for the U.S. government officials (federal, state, or local) to get serious about minimizing road fatalities. Apparently such carnage is, as Dr. Waller suggests, an acceptable sacrifice, in the view of most people.

Transport modes have never been particularly safe. Even the wind-powered ships of centuries ago sank, steam-powered vehicles (ships and locomotives) blew up, horses threw their riders, and planes crashed. Motor vehicles have a particularly bad history in this regard, and the future global picture looks even worse. As noted in Chapter 1, current estimates by the World Health Organization are that motor vehicle fatalities worldwide are running at about 1 million, with injuries in the 70 million range. Forecasts for the future are even more pessimistic.

In this chapter we review the history, historical trends, and the nature of the accidents as well as costs of these accidents to society. The focus is on motor vehicle-related accidents, since this is the dominant transport mode today and it also accounts for 94% of all transportation-related fatalities. There is not a great deal that planners can do alone to decrease motor vehicle accidents, but we examine the tools that do exist.

THE EARLIEST FATALITIES

According to Fallon and O'Neill (2005), the world's first automobile fatality occurred in the Irish Midlands in 1869. The victim was one Mary Ward, an artist and naturalist of some renown at the time. The vehicle involved was a steam carriage from which Ward fell and was subsequently run over.

In the United States the first generally recognized automobile-related fatality was apparently the death of one Henry Bliss of New York City. Mr. Bliss was a pedestrian, and he was struck by an automobile as he stepped off a "surface car" (streetcar) at Eighth Avenue and 74th Street. The accident occurred on Wednesday, September 13, 1899, and Mr. Bliss was rushed to Roosevelt Hospital but died the following day (*New York Times*, 1899). There may have been earlier fatalities, but if so they occurred in more remote areas not as well covered by the news media of the day.

THE FATALITY TREND IN THE UNITED STATES

In 1900 automobile fatalities claimed the lives of 36 individuals in the United States. By 1925 the annual death toll from motor vehicle accidents had reached 20,771. The annual figure was to remain above 20,000 for each successive year in the 20th century, peaking in 1972 at 55,600. The trend in fatalities attributable to motor vehicle accidents over the years since 1900 shows this trend responding to major events of the time, with fatalities going up when driving, and therefore exposure, was highest and decreasing when driving decreased (see Figure 6.1): the rapid increase in fatalities during the early decades of the 20th century, the chaos of the stock market crash and depression of the 1930s; there were declines during the war years of the 1940s when gasoline was rationed and much of the automobile and steel industries' productivity went into the war effort; economic recessions of the 1950s were followed by growth during the 1960s and the decrease in travel due to the oil shocks of the 1970s and early 1980s; and, finally, in the mid-1980s decreases in fatalities as we began to see some safety improvements. During the last 10 years (1998–2007) for which data are available the number of fatalities ranged from a low of 41,059 in 2007 to a high of 43,510 in 2005. During the 20th century there were 3 million people killed in motor vehicle-related traffic incidents in the United States.

Some commentators note that the most important factor is not the total fatalities but the fatality rate per unit of distance traveled. The standard measure is fatalities per 100 million miles of travel. On the basis of this rate, fatalities have been dropping since the early 1900s, but this calculation can be misleading. If the number of miles driven is increasing substantially, you can have a decrease in the rate even though total accidents are increasing; this is what occurred during the period 1997–2007. The rate was 1.64 fatalities per 100 million vehicle miles driven in 1997, and this figure had dropped to 1.36 by 2007. During this same time period total fatalities decreased a lesser amount, from 42,013 to 41,059, but vehicle miles traveled increased substantially, from 2.562 trillion to 3.030 trillion; so, the drop in the rate is

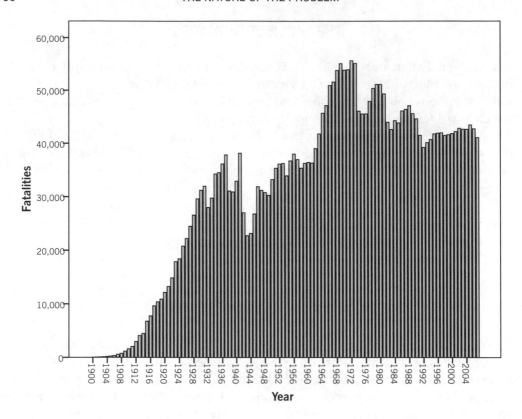

FIGURE 6.1. U.S. motor vehicle fatalities (1900–2004). *Source*: Data from FHWA, 2008.

due in large part to growth in the miles driven (see Figure 6.2). This would suggest that this rate may not be the best measure to use.

Dr. Leonard Evans, a research scientist at General Motors from 1967 to 2000, looked at the trend in fatalities over the years using three different indicators: total fatalities, fatalities per registered vehicle, and fatalities per some measure of distance traveled. He then compared these trends over time with those of Canada, the United Kingdom, and Australia (Evans, 2006). He concluded that U.S. traffic safety policy was a "dramatic failure" in comparison to that in these other countries. In each of the comparison countries total fatalities decreased proportionately more, as did traffic fatalities per registered vehicle. Evans believed that the United Kingdom was the only country with reliable statistics on the amount of driving, and it also had a comparatively greater decrease of the four countries in fatalities per 100 million vehicle miles driven than the United States. The author attributes this to the fact that U.S. policy emphasizes making accidents more survivable rather than attempting to eliminate them altogether. We will return to this point later.

In addition to the fatalities we cannot overlook the injuries resulting from motor vehicle transport. In 2007 estimates suggest that about 2.49 million people are injured annually in motor vehicle-related accidents in the United States. Of this number, 2.24 million were occupants of motor vehicles, 103,000 were motorcyclists, 70,000 were pedestrians, and 43,000 were bike riders. Based on 2003 data, motorcy-

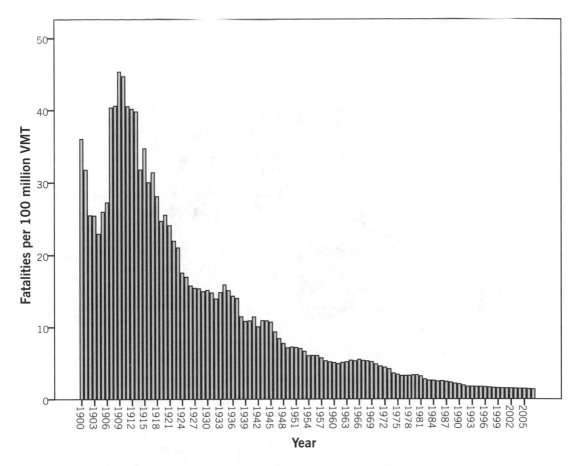

FIGURE 6.2. U.S. motor vehicle fatality rate per 100 million VMT (1900–2005). Source: Data from FHWA, 2008.

clists have the largest number of injuries per hundred million passenger miles, with 555. Automobiles are second, with 69, and light trucks (including SUVs) are third, with 51.

Preliminary data for 2008 show that the number of fatalities for each month from January through October was substantially lower than for 2007 (NHTSA, 2008). This consistent decline is more than likely a result of the downturn in the economy, which tends to reduce the amount of travel taking place. However, even the fatality rate was lower, at 1.28 per 100 million vehicle miles traveled, in comparison with 1.36 for 2007.

THE COST OF MOTOR VEHICLE ACCIDENTS

The human costs of motor vehicle accidents are staggering, but there are also economic costs associated with these fatalities. Estimates for the United States suggest that the largest cost is in terms of market productivity, with 27% of the total costs;

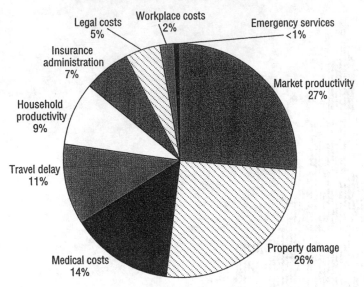

FIGURE 6.3. The components of accident costs in the United States. *Source:* NHTSA (2002).

this is followed by property damage, with 26% of the total costs. Figure 6.3 illustrates the distribution of these costs across the various components.

Total costs of accidents in the United States vary widely. The National Highway Traffic Safety Administration (NHTSA, 2002) estimated that these accidents entailed costs in the area of $231 billion in 2000, while other sources (MacKenzie et al., 1992; Miller & Moffet, 1993) suggested the figure was closer to $300 billion a decade earlier. As for the distribution of these costs by "cause," we find that, of the $231 billion, $51 billion was attributable to alcohol-related events, $40 billion to speeding, and $26 billion to failure to use seat belts. These costs end up being covered by government, the injured parties, or insurance companies, in that order.

WHO HAS ACCIDENTS?

The most accident-prone segment of the population consists of males between the ages of 19 and 24. Women in the same age category are the second most accident-prone segment, but males' accident incidence is always higher than females' in every age category. In addition, the accidents of males are more serious than those of females.

Subramanian (2006) has looked at motor vehicle crashes in the United States by age groups and found such accidents to be the leading cause of death for children ages 4–7, children ages 8–15, youths ages 15–20, young adults ages 21–24, and adults ages 25–34. If we add in motor vehicle fatalities occurring other than on public highways (e.g., in one's driveway), they are also the leading cause of death for toddlers ages 1–3. Because so many young people are involved, motor vehicle crashes rank third among all causes of death in terms of years of life lost. This is a concept that considers age at death and the number of years remaining in life based on actuarial tables at the time of death.

After age 34, motor vehicles are the third-leading cause of death for those of ages 35–44, and the eighth-leading cause of death for those of ages 45–64. Concerns about elderly driving and accidents are not without foundation, but motor vehicle crashes are not among the top 10 leading causes of death for those of ages 65 and older.

THE CAUSES OF ACCIDENTS

It has long been recognized that motor vehicle accidents are attributable to three groups of factors. The first set of causes relates to human error, which would include alcohol-related incidents, driving while tired, driving without experience, driving aggressively, distractions inside and outside the vehicle, and driving too fast. The second broad category of causes is environmental factors, which could include everything from fog to blizzards. The final group of factors is what we refer to as "design factors," which might include vehicle design problems or highway design problems. Anyone who has ever fought the steering wheel as he or she negotiated a curve is familiar with highway design problems. The factors are not necessarily mutually exclusive; for example, beginning a trip during an ice storm and selecting a hazardous route to your destination would include both environmental factors and human error.

Survival or Prevention?

As noted earlier, Evans (2006) believes that U.S. policymakers pay far too much attention to decreasing fatalities from a crash and not enough to preventing them from occurring in the first place. While not opposed to technological improvements that could save lives, he does not necessarily accept all of these. For example, he believes that seat belts were a major safety improvement but air bags were not.

Nevertheless, researchers continue to try to improve motor vehicles with the idea of increasing survivability. Ross et al. (2006) see various opportunities for making safety improvements, including making the passenger compartment stronger, improving occupants' positions in the vehicle when an accident is imminent, and redesigning front ends to increase the vehicle's structural integrity on impact. Zobel (1999) has listed the various innovations and regulations in order of their importance for improving motor vehicle safety as (1) seat belts, (2) passenger compartment integrity, (3) electronic stability control, and (4) air bags.

Among the regulatory mechanisms that are needed if we are to prevent crashes from occurring are laws that mandate the use of seat belts, better enforcement of speed limits, and stronger laws against drunk driving. The one thing that researchers and policy analysts clearly agree upon is the mandatory use of seat belts.

Sweden's government passed a resolution in 1997 stating that as far as road traffic was concerned no one should be killed or seriously injured in motor vehicle crashes. The program was referred to as Vision Zero. Exactly how the government intends to prevent all motor vehicle fatalities is discussed later in the section title "What Local Planners Can Do."

In 2004 U.S. Secretary of Transportation Norman Mineta set a somewhat more modest goal of reducing fatalities to 1.0 per 100 million vehicle miles by the year 2008 from the then current level of 1.44. This might appear to be about a reduction of one-third, but bear in mind that total fatalities might continue to increase since total vehicle miles of travel normally continues to increase. We have not performed a separate analysis here but it was anticipated that fatalities might fall to about 31,000 annually, were Mineta's plan to succeed (Friel, 2005). Most highway safety experts expect that it will be a hard goal to reach (NHTSA (2009). Note that the rate reached 1.27 per 100 million vehicle miles, and total fatalities were 37,261 for 2008.

The Role of CAFE Standards

There is another body of literature that addresses the role of the Corporate Average Fuel Economy standards on fatalities. The argument is that when the CAFE standards were introduced in 1985, the automobile industry in the United States was compelled to make their vehicles more fuel efficient. The standard was set at 27.5 miles per gallon (mpg) for automobiles and at about 20.2 miles per gallon (later 21.6) for light trucks (including SUVs). The standards will change in response to the Energy Independence and Security Act of 2007, which sets a goal for the CAFE of 35 miles per gallon by 2020.

The initial response of U.S. automobile manufacturers in the 1980s was to make vehicles lighter. In the decades preceding CAFE the vehicles had a substantial amount of iron and steel in their bodies. Suddenly we began to see plastics replacing certain bumper parts and aluminum being used in various places. Some argued that making vehicles lighter in this way actually made accidents less survivable for vehicle occupants. The National Highway Traffic Safety Administration (NHTSA) estimates that as many as 2,000 fatalities per year are attributable to the lighter vehicles.

Those who would like to increase the CAFE level today are often met with the argument that this will only result in lighter vehicles and more fatalities. Ross et al. (2006) approach the question from the point of view of physics and suggest a major problem is that lighter vehicles have been designed as though larger vehicles did not exist. The reality is that larger vehicles, from SUVs to 1-ton pickup trucks, significantly increase the probability of a fatality for the occupant of the lighter vehicle. However, it is possible to improve the safety of lighter vehicles with new materials and composite materials that offer high absorption of crush energy per kilogram. However, requirements for the use of these types of materials do not exist at this time.

WHAT LOCAL PLANNERS CAN DO

The Vision Zero program of Sweden, in setting the goal of zero fatalities, initiated a series of actions intended to assist in working toward that goal. These actions along with some others listed below are representative of what local areas can do to reduce severe injuries and fatalities. These measures include:

1. Attempt to separate different road users—pedestrian walkways, biking trails and routes, and automobile users.
2. Review speed limits throughout the locality and reduce those that seem too high.
3. Install roundabouts at fringe intersection areas where accidents occur.
4. Install cable guard rails where needed, as opposed to conventional guard rails that may redirect a vehicle back into the traffic stream.
5. Remove all rigid barriers (boulders, trees, telephone polls, etc.), or if this is not possible use guard rails in these locations.
6. Require vehicle inspections, and set safety standards for automobiles.
7. Require the installation of seat belt reminders in automobiles.
8. Require that motorcyclists use helmets.
9. Be prepared to offer faster help to the injured at collision scenes, and train professional drivers (who are on the road the most) in emergency medical treatment.
10. Use cameras as a way of deterring speeders; these also have a traffic calming effect.
11. Require companies delivering goods and people to have exemplary safety records.
12. Have companies require good safety records of their drivers.
13. Install traffic calming devices that require vehicles to move at slower speeds.
14. Encourage or require driver education classes and possibly even retesting of licensed drivers.
15. Install median guardrails where streets are narrow and the possibility of accidents is high.

An MPO or local planning agency may not be in a position to initiate some of these actions, particularly when the actions require legislation However, these agencies can support legislation at the state or federal level to require concrete actions. Most of the actions are local in nature, and planners should attempt to work with engineers, the city administration, NGOs and local groups to encourage the other steps suggested.

In the Swedish case input from individuals is particularly encouraged. That is, whenever an individual sees a potentially dangerous situation, he or she is asked to report it to local officials so that it can be remedied.

Of course, one solution is not mentioned above because it is even less popular than some of the ones that are listed, namely, congestion. It is true that congestion tends to increase the number of accidents; however, these accidents tend to be minor, rarely resulting in fatalities or severe injuries. Economic interests will argue that congestion results in a loss of income to businesses and transport firms as well as others. The work of Nadiri and Mamuneas (1998) supports this notion since they demonstrate a clear economic "bump" resulting from the construction of the interstate highway system in the United States and, in effect, the removal of some major urban congestion bottlenecks. However, their analysis did not factor in the human costs of fatalities and severe injuries resulting from use of the interstate highway system. What have been the savings resulting from construction of the interstate highway system once we factor in those costs? We will discuss congestion later in this volume. Suffice it to say that allowing congestion to exist in some locations should not be ruled out as a way of decreasing fatalities and severe injuries.

CONCLUSIONS

We have suggested that a sustainable transport system would ideally have *no* fatalities. However, one must ask the question of whether this is an achievable goal. If all envisioned safety devices were installed in vehicles, if all of the improvements in transport infrastructure were undertaken, and if all of the regulations were enforced, would we have zero fatalities? Probably not. There will always be the unanticipated event or behavior that leads to a fatality. At the same time, if we move in the directions suggested in this chapter, we will see a more sustainable transport system in terms of fatalities than what exists today.

CHAPTER 7

Congestion and Sustainability

> Therefore my advice to American drivers stuck in peak-hour traffic is not merely to get politically involved, but also to learn to enjoy congestion. Get a comfortable air-conditioned car with a stereo radio, tape player, a telephone, perhaps a fax machine, and commute with someone who is really attractive.
>
> —ANTHONY DOWNS (1992)

Writing in 1956, Wilfred Owen stated: "The problem of urban congestion has become so great that many communities are coming to the conclusion that there could never be sufficient highway and parking capacity to permit the movement of all people in private cars." It has literally taken a half-century for most transportation experts to fully appreciate this basic statement of fact.

Lewis Mumford (1957), writing at about the same time, said: "Since the war, and especially in the last few years, every town in Europe (like every town in the United States) has become clogged with motor traffic. The old market squares, which once or twice a week were cluttered with peddler's carts and stands, are now cluttered every day with motor cars, since they are the cheapest of central parking lots." Mumford went on to suggest how automobiles should be dealt with before they make "city life first unendurable and finally impossible." His solution involved:

- The vigorous restoration and improvement of public transportation within the city.
- Replanning of both the central and residential neighborhoods to allow for pedestrian movement and restriction of automobile access.
- Designing of small electric cars to run on batteries and restrictions on over-sized cars in the city center.
- Relocation of industry, business, and administration to outlying subcenters, leading to cross traffic as opposed to movement to the city center.

While it is clear that the problem of congestion was recognized for most of the last century, it is not apparent that the solutions offered by Mumford would have solved the problem either then or now, although today we have advocates for mass transit solutions, "new urbanism" solutions, neighborhood electric cars, and, even some who favor decentralized activities that border on sprawl, with all of these actions implicit in his solution.

In this chapter we examine the problem of congestion as it affects sustainability, first defining and measuring it. We look at some actions (tools) that would be part of any set of contemporary solutions to this problem. We have come to understand that controlling vehicle density is part of the solution, but in all honesty this is nearly impossible to achieve. Later we also explore the future of congestion, recognizing that successfully controlling congestion will require a multifaceted solution. Much of this chapter is drawn with some modifications from Black (2003).

CONGESTION DEFINED

The European Conference of Ministers of Transport (ECMT) has described congestion as a "traffic condition in which vehicles are constantly stopping and starting and in which vehicle concentration is high while flow speeds are low" (ECMT, 2000). It is not simply low speed, nor is it just a high concentration of vehicles; it is a high concentration of vehicles with respect to the capacity of the roadway, but even this does not quite convey what we want. This same ECMT report adopted the definition that "congestion is the impedance vehicles impose on each other, due to speed–flow relationships, in conditions where the use of the transport system approaches its capacity" (p. 29). This definition would appear to be one of the better ones, and it describes "congestion" as we will use the term here.

Transport congestion is far from new in our major metropolitan areas; it was clearly evident in London and New York during the late 19th century. Assuming that travel time gives us some indication of the level of congestion, it should be noted that the average length of the journey to work in Europe is 20 minutes; for Paris this travel time is 27 minutes. According to the U.S. Department of Transportation (USDOT, 1994) the average length of the journey to work in the United States was 21.7 minutes in 1980 and 22.4 in 1990. These data suggest that congestion may not be getting much worse in the United States, if travel time is any indicator.

In a study of 300 metropolitan areas of the United States in 1990, Banninga (1999) found that travel times varied considerably across the country. In general travel times were lowest in the cities of the West North Central states and highest in the cities of the Middle Atlantic states (see Table 7.1).

Types of Congestion and Other Causes of Congestion

The earlier definition of congestion actually refers to recurring congestion of the type that many commuters encounter each day. There is also nonrecurring congestion, which may be attributable, broadly speaking, to four types of events. First,

TABLE 7.1. Average Journey to Work Travel Times for Cities by Census Region (1990)

Region (states)	Travel time (minutes)
New England (Maine, Vermont, New Hampshire, Massachusetts, Rhode Island, Connecticut)	19.76
Middle Atlantic (New York, Pennsylvania, New Jersey	25.01
South Atlantic (Maryland, Delaware, West Virginia, Virginia, North Carolina, South Carolina, Georgia, Florida)	20.56
East North Central (Wisconsin, Michigan, Illinois, Indiana, Ohio)	20.17
East South Central (Kentucky, Tennessee, Alabama, Mississippi)	18.03
West North Central (North Dakota, South Dakota, Minnesota, Iowa, Nebraska, Missouri, Kansas)	15.90
West South Central (Texas, Oklahoma, Arkansas, Louisiana)	18.89
Mountain (Montana, Idaho, Wyoming, Nevada, Utah, Colorado, Arizona, New Mexico)	18.67
Pacific (Washington, Oregon, California)	22.09

Source: Data from Banninga (1999).

there is the traffic incident, which may involve anything from a vehicle simply stalling in the traffic stream to a major accident involving loss of life. Second, there is the congestion caused by work zones, which may result from the closing of lanes for maintenance or rehabilitation or speed restrictions for highway worker safety. Third, there is the congestion associated with weather-related road maintenance. Fourth, there is the congestion related to special events ranging from sports events to concerts (see Cambridge Systematics, 2005). Though the first three of these types of nonrecurring congestion can be handled with traffic management techniques, there is not a great deal that can be done about the congestion related to a special event. Of course, it could be handled in many cases by constructing additional arterials in the vicinity of stadium, hall, or auditorium, but this would usually result in excess capitalization in the system since such events are irregular or seasonal.

MEASURING CONGESTION

Over the past decade there has been a considerable amount of effort expended in trying to measure congestion. Lomax et al. (1997) have identified several measures, or indices, of congestion, among them:

1. Travel rate (minutes necessary to traverse 1 mile).
2. Delay rate (actual minutes per mile less acceptable minutes per mile).
3. Total segment delay (delay rate of two times the vehicle volume on the segment).
4. Corridor mobility index (the passenger volume × the average speed) divided by a normalizing factor (25,000 for streets and 125,000 for freeways).

5. Relative delay rate (the delay rate divided by the acceptable travel rate).
6. Delay ratio (the delay rate divided by the actual travel rate).
7. Congested travel (in vehicle miles, the congested segment length times the traffic volume summed for all segments).
8. Congested roadway (in miles, the sum of all congested segments).

Included as well is a measure of accessibility that probably does not quite get to the point. Lomax et al. also note that there are certain other aspects to the situation that should be considered, including duration (how long does the congestion last?), extent (how many people or what size area is affected?), intensity (the total amount of congestion), and reliability (the variation in the amount of congestion). These will obviously vary across different roadways, corridors, and the entire network.

One of the measures that has received the most attention is the Roadway Congestion Index (RCI) developed by Schrank and Thomas (2009) of the Texas Transportation Institute. The RCI takes the following form:

$$RCI = \frac{(FwyVMT/Ln\text{-}Mi) \times FwyVMT + (ArtVMT/Ln\text{-}Mi) \times ArtVMT}{(13,000 \times FwyVMT) + (5,000 \times ArtVMT)}$$

where FwyVMT/Ln-Mi is the freeway daily vehicle miles traveled per lane miles, FwyVMT is the freeway daily vehicle miles traveled, ArtVMT/Ln-Mi is the principal arterial daily vehicle miles traveled per lane mile, ArtVMT is the principal arterial daily vehicle miles traveled, 13,000 is the capacity per lane on freeways, and 5,000 is the capacity per lane on principal arterials. What the index tries to capture is the volume of traffic and divide it by the capacity of the system under analysis. The use of volume/capacity ratios, V/C ratios, has a long history in transport planning and engineering. In general, when the V/C ratio is greater than 0.77 (that is, volumes are 77% of capacity), the facility is viewed as congested. The RCI is a little more precise as a measure and can be applied to an entire urban network if desired.

Table 7.2 presents the RCI index for 12 cities in the United States over the period 1982–2007. One may make a few observations based on these data. First, congestion has gotten worse over the time period for each city covered. Second, the level of congestion appears to have stabilized somewhat during the 1990–1996 period and for a few cities even longer, dating back to 1986, but there is no ready explanation for this topping off of congestion.

The RCI index appears to be a reasonable indicator of congestion. At the same time, it might be worthwhile to undertake some empirical studies to explain why the index varies as it does. Since capacity doesn't change significantly today, the only factors that influence the RCI are vehicle miles of travel on freeways and principal arterials. Something is keeping the congestion down in several of the cities examined here, so the question becomes, What is doing that? Meyer (1994) notes that the index was the highest in large cities and those with the greatest population density. Further analysis may suggest answers to the question of how to control

TABLE 7.2. The Roadway Congestion Index for 12 Selected U.S. Cities

| City | \multicolumn{7}{c}{Roadway Congestion Index} |
	1982	1986	1990	1994	1998	2002	2007
Atlanta, GA	0.83	1.00	1.02	1.18	1.31	1.35	1.31
Boston, MA	0.81	0.92	1.05	1.05	1.10	1.10	1.09
Chicago, IL	0.81	0.91	1.03	1.03	1.17	1.23	1.18
Cleveland, OH	0.73	0.71	0.83	0.89	0.94	0.89	0.89
Detroit, MI	0.91	1.02	1.06	1.12	1.16	1.22	1.23
Indianapolis, IN	0.80	0.86	0.94	1.11	1.17	1.19	1.09
Los Angles, CA	1.21	1.32	1.57	1.49	1.53	1.55	1.58
New York, NY	0.73	0.83	0.91	0.93	1.02	1.08	1.15
Philadelphia, PA	0.83	0.89	0.95	0.94	1.01	1.09	1.11
Pittsburgh, PA	0.67	0.71	0.76	0.73	0.76	0.79	0.78
San Diego, CA	0.83	1.01	1.23	1.21	1.23	1.37	1.37
Washington, D.C.	0.83	1.07	1.05	1.21	1.25	1.31	1.34

Source: Copyright 2009 by the Texas Transportation Institute. Reprinted by permission.

congestion, but we do not know whether the findings can be usefully generalized to other cities, given the key role of size. Let's look at some possible tools for dealing with congestion.

CONGESTION MITIGATION TOOLS

Since the problem of urban traffic congestion has a long history, as noted earlier, there has been no shortage of proposed solutions. Several of these appear in Table 7.3, which is based in part on work performed in the early 1990s by the Urban Land Institute (Dunphy, 1991). Let's examine some of the proposed solutions and assess their potential for contributing to future policies that work.

TABLE 7.3. Actions to Relieve and Reduce Traffic Congestion

1. Traffic signal improvements
2. Expanding the road system
3. Provisions for suburban transit
4. Prompt motor vehicle crash clearance
5. Carpooling and flexible work schedules
6. High-occupancy-vehicle lanes
7. Provisions for light rail transit
8. Land use strategies
9. Intelligent vehicle highway systems and intelligent transport systems
10. Telecommuting/teleworking
11. Congestion pricing and toll roads
12. The do-nothing alternative

Sources: Dunphy (1991) and the author.

Traffic Signal Improvements

One of the oldest solutions to the problem of congestion at the intersections of the urban street grid has been the use of traffic signals. In some cases these have been set to allow traffic to move in various directions for a set period of time, often called a phase. For several decades it has also been common to control access to freeways and motorways with traffic signals that also consider existing traffic levels on the facility prior to admitting additional traffic to it. These controls continue to exist today, and their importance has not diminished. Improvements have been derived from intelligent transport systems (ITS), which have made the signal phases a function of traffic volume. To be sure, this technology is not widespread, but it is found at key intersections in most metropolitan areas in the United States.

One change in the traffic signal arena came about in 1976 through federal legislation that allowed drivers to turn right on a red signal if there was no traffic approaching the intersection. This provision was enacted because it was thought that motor vehicles were wasting fuel while they sat idling, waiting for a signal to change, at intersections that had little traffic. The provision was immediately popular with the driving public, although many drivers appear even now to be unaware that this is a nationwide law. During the law's subsequent history it has become evident that such turns are often unsafe for the motorist as well as the pedestrian (Insurance Institute for Highway Safety, 1980); nevertheless, the law is so popular that no one wants it repealed. A similar regulation exists for left turns under special circumstances (usually from a one-way street to another one-way street), but fewer individuals seem to be aware of its existence, as there are fewer situations where such turns may be made.

Expanding the Road System

In the United States the primary response to highway corridor congestion during most of the 20th century was to expand the road system through the addition of more lanes or the construction of entirely new highway links. It is easy to be critical of this capital-intensive approach to the problem today, but it should be recognized that in many cases the additional capacity was necessary since highway planners of the 1960s and 1970s had not fully anticipated the number of vehicles the network would have to handle.

At some point during the closing decades of the century environmentalists began to question the merits of additional construction. By the 1990s even highway planners had begun questioning the logic of highway expansion. As a result, we appear to have arrived at a point where more highways are not necessarily viewed as the answer to congestion problems. This does not mean we have stopped building highways to solve congestion problems, but other alternatives are considered as well. On occasion, the solution to a congestion problem may still be additional lanes or perhaps a new arterial highway.

In the United Kingdom a similar change in attitude has occurred, but the highway emphasis was never as central there as in the United States. In the United States many public projects are evaluated using cost–benefit analysis, that is, in order to be selected the highway project must generate benefits that exceed its costs. It is not uncommon for the 2–3 minutes of travel time that might be saved per driver per day if the project were undertaken to be expanded by annual multipliers. This annual time saved is then multiplied by the time value over the life of the project (the number of years the project improvement will last) to yield total user benefits. This is a questionable process since the reality is that a few minutes of travel time saved does not necessarily have more than marginal real economic value. Nevertheless, this approach to project selection continues to be popular in the United States and the United Kingdom.

Provisions for Suburban Transit

As recently as 1994 in the United States there were arguments for transit expansion as a way of combating highway congestion. Statistics released since that time have made it clear that this alone may not be the wisest use of financial resources. Transit ridership in general was falling in U.S. cities during the 1995–2005 period in spite of substantial transit investment at nearly all levels of government. Ridership then increased substantially during the period of rapid increases in the price of gasoline, from 2005 to 2008. It was not that riders were attracted to transit so much as that the price of gasoline pushed them out of their cars. It remains to be seen whether the new transit riders will continue to favor that travel mode if fuel prices moderate and remain reasonable. If we look at the figures more closely, it appears that some systems have been able to maintain ridership levels, but these have been chiefly in the major metropolitan areas.

The situation is less encouraging in areas with bus transit. Suburban transit is essentially bus transit, but, additionally, bus transit in areas of very light density in terms of potential riders. One need only look at the major components of transit ridership—the elderly, the young, the handicapped, and the poor—to realize that some of these are not found in great numbers in suburban areas. Those that are found there are not sufficient to support a viable transit service. Should the service be viable? Should it cover its costs? Or should suburban transit be provided as a social service for the aforementioned population groups? The latter should probably be the case, but it should not be viewed as a solution to urban traffic congestion.

Prompt Motor Vehicle Crash Clearance

Many traffic jams on U.S. arterial highways are attributable to minor traffic incidents. In such situations traffic must funnel from two or three lanes down to one or two lanes, and this compression automatically results in traffic slowing and backing up. Part of the problem is that crash scenes generally cannot be cleared without police being present to prepare reports on the circumstances of the event. California has instituted a program of "jam busters," officials in roving vehicles that have authority to clear such crash sites. These have been shown to be effective in removing bottlenecks due to crashes and in reducing resultant congestion.

Some urban areas have begun monitoring critical points on the metropolitan highway network (usually with television cameras) for evidence of traffic incidents. Whenever the screen indicates congestion or the complete absence of traffic, an officer is dispatched to determine the cause of the problem and, if necessary, assist in resolving it.

Carpooling and Flexible Work Schedules

An obvious method of decreasing traffic congestion is to reduce the number of vehicles on the highway during peak hours. Various ways of accomplishing this end include carpools, vanpools, and flexible time requirements for workers' arrival and departure. In most cases the carpools and vanpools result from the voluntary efforts of commuters or the organized efforts of employers. Some municipalities have set up carpool systems in order to meet air quality standards, but these new initiatives have not stemmed a more general decline recently observable in carpooling nationally.

Exactly why carpooling has lately decreased nationally in the United States is unclear, but it is often discussed in tandem with decreases in transit ridership as being related to the increased personal use of automobile by individuals. Of course, most carpooling was first started and most heavily advocated during the 1970s largely in response to OPEC's (Organization of Petroleum Exporting Countries) oil embargoes, beginning in 1973. The ensuing decades have seen large numbers of workers retire or move on to other positions. In other words, the educational and organizational efforts of the 1970s were not sustained, and the riders simply moved on. Carpooling must be continually advocated and facilitated since the workforce is constantly changing positions, residences, vehicles, and so forth.

Instituting flexible schedules for workplace arrival has significantly reduced the level of traffic congestion in numerous cities. For example in Indianapolis (the state capital of Indiana, with a population of 731,327 in 1990) during the 1990s, the city's chief employer, the state government, allowed its workers to arrive at half-hour intervals from 7:00 A.M. to 9:00 A.M. and to depart from 3:30 P.M. to 5:30 P.M.. This staggering of work hours had the effect of stretching out the morning and evening traffic peaks but nonetheless decreasing the height of the peak and thereby reducing congestion. In short, the program in Indianapolis was successful in reducing congestion. An unfortunate consequence, however, was that occasionally government agencies were understaffed at critical hours of demand, which resulted in the program's termination in 2000.

Similarly, flexible time may not be a good notion for certain businesses. Generally, consumers expect businesses to be open with sufficient manpower to serve them at the house they prefer. It wouldn't pay most businesses to have little help at periods of peak demand and peak employment at times of little demand. So, the flexible work schedule is not appropriate for certain service-oriented businesses.

High-Occupancy-Vehicle Lanes

The use of high-occupancy-vehicle (HOV) lanes dates back to the 1960s and 1970s in various U.S. metropolitan areas. In many cases a new lane has been specifically constructed for the use of carpool vehicles, buses, or similar vehicles. In other cases existing lanes are designated as HOV lanes through the use of pavement markings and signing. In general these measures are efficacious in that they allow vehicles using these lanes to move at higher speeds, and this advantage may draw commuters to bus transit or carpooling. It is not clear what overall impact HOV lanes have had in countering the negative trends evident in transit ridership and carpooling. One conclusion is inescapable, namely, that if the HOV lanes are not used they should be made available to other traffic, thereby enhancing overall capacity.

Provisions for Light Rail Transit

Light rail transit is a descendant of the streetcars of the early 20th century. It is seen as a way of reducing congestion in central cities, but some argue that it is not successful at doing this since the systems are so fragmentary, as the old reaching relatively few destinations and having little impact on congestion.

This raises the natural question, Why should urban areas expend large sums on constructing light rail facilities if they are not going to have much impact on congestion? While, typically, these systems cost roughly $21 million per mile, the answer would appear to be that many municipalities view them as attractive (see Table 7.4). The systems in the United States and Canada indicate that the city has entered a higher echelon of modernity, striving for user-friendly transit that minimizes pollution, but not necessarily contributing to a higher level of service. Of course, in Europe these systems have reached much higher levels of maturity and provide a clear alternative to the automobile in such cities as Amsterdam, Berlin, and London, where they contribute significantly to reduced traffic congestion.

Land Use Strategies

It has become popular for planners to talk about specifying land uses in such ways as to minimize the need to travel. This criterion often dictates locating residences, retail establishments, and employment opportunities close to one another so that interaction can take place with minimal transport effort. Examples of such new types of urban planning exist (with Seaside and Celebration, Florida, often cited), but they are not abundant. There is no doubt that such communities could replace future growth on the urban periphery in some cases, but they would work less well in areas where land uses are settled and well established. In effect, we are faced with suddenly changing land uses that by design kept different functional uses from being located next to one another. It was not originally preordained that land uses should minimize travel, but that is exactly what is expected of them now. We will likely be disappointed (as we discuss further in Chapter 11).

TABLE 7.4. Light Rail Systems in the United States and Canada

City	Length in operation	Under construction[a]
Baltimore, MD	30.0 route miles	double tracking
Buffalo, NY	6.2 route miles	
Cleveland, OH	31.2 route miles	
Pittsburgh, PA	25.3 route miles	
Minneapolis, MN	None	11.6 route miles
St. Louis, MO	17.0 route miles	17.4 route miles
Dallas, TX	20.0 route miles	23.7 route miles
Denver, CO	14.0 route miles	1.8 route miles
Salt Lake City, UT	15.0 route miles	2.5 route miles
San Diego, CA	53.4 route miles[b]	
Los Angeles, CA	6.3 route miles	13.7 route miles
San Jose, CA	28.4 route miles	1.9 route miles
San Francisco, CA	39.9 route miles[b]	5.4 route miles
Sacramento, CA	20.6 route miles	12.1 route miles
Portland, OR	33.0 route miles	11.1 route miles
Seattle-Tacoma, WA	NA	22.0 route miles
New Orleans, LA	13.1 route miles[b]	
Boston, MA	28.0 route miles	
Newark, NJ	6.7 route miles[b]	
Toronto, ON	97.7 route miles	
Edmonton, AB	7.8 route miles	
Calgary, AB	7.8 route miles	

Source: Middleton and Wolinsky (2001).
[a]Does not include extensions that are planned unless ground has been broken.
[b]Figures are drawn from Weiner (1992).

There are numerous examples in North America where the central districts of major metropolitan areas have been revitalized. Some commentators view this urban revitalization as demonstrating how trip lengths can be reduced. We have no argument with this perception, but the overall impact on congestion does not seem significant. Nevertheless, when coupled with other congestion reduction strategies, it could be significant.

Intelligent Vehicle Highway Systems or Intelligent Transport Systems

The concept started as "intelligent vehicle highway systems" (IVHS), but then someone recognized that this was hardly an unbiased term vis-à-vis mode of transport. The result is that we now have "intelligent transport systems" (ITS), which makes public funds available to all modes, although the bulk of the funding continues to go to highway uses. This operational advantage for highways reflects not only the early history of such programs but also the fact that nearly all transport takes place over the highway network in the United States.

ITS can facilitate the movement of traffic and reduce congestion in several ways, mainly through better signalization, the transfer of real-time information to motorists that enables them to reroute their vehicles, and detecting incidents more quickly that create congestion. ITS could well help solve much of the congestion problem in the years to come. One might envision the convoying of vehicles in some electronic fashion that would enable not only higher speeds but also less space between vehicles. For example, a car today in a group of cars traveling at 50 miles per hour will be about 80 feet from the vehicle in front of it; this means that we can have about 52 or 53 cars per mile, assuming the distance between vehicles is 18 feet (the car length) plus a car length for each 10 miles of speed. We now need 98 feet of highway lane for each vehicle. Rounding upward, we have 100 feet per vehicle, or 52.8 vehicles to the lane mile. If we can use ITS to electronically connect vehicles in a convoy in such a way that the vehicles are only 2 feet from one another (i.e., 20 feet per car), we could get 264 vehicles into the same space taken up by 53 vehicles today, a factor of 5:1. While this may be a possible solution to the congestion problem sometime in the next three decades, it won't necessarily help us very much soon.

Telecommuting/Teleworking

Obviously, congestion would be considerably less if there were fewer drivers on the highways. If we can't get today's drivers to use mass transit of some sort, can we get them to stay at home perhaps? Advances in telecommunications have made this tantalizing possibility a commonplace reality. We now have thousands of workers gainfully employed at remote locations from their employer, sometimes at home and sometimes in a televillage close to their home where they can congregate and perform their normal workday functions; these are commonly referred to as telecommuters or teleworkers. This trend toward telecommuting has already lessened the number of vehicles on the highway, although its other merits are questionable.

Telecommuting is not the simple all-purpose answer that it might at first appear to be. In addition to questions regarding the actual decreases in travel that may occur (Mokhtarian, 1997), there are social questions that need to be addressed (Giuliano, 1994). Suffice it to say that the decreases in travel may be offset by the disadvantages of the employee's being made more remote from his or her place of work.

Congestion Pricing and Toll Roads

As is true of much of the terminology in transport, "congestion pricing" is a misnomer. It isn't really congestion that is being priced upward but rather the absence of it. In other words, what are you willing to pay to use a transport facility that is *free* of congestion? So, perhaps we should refer to this phenomenon as "congestion-free pricing" or, if we are talking of highways, perhaps it should be called a mobility tax or an accessibility tax, because if you are unwilling to pay the tax then you cannot have access to the facility. Oddly enough, people working in this area have changed the name of congestion pricing to value pricing, which is one of the poorer alternatives that could have been selected. As a practical matter, we will use the term "congestion-free pricing" here.

Functionally, there is very little difference between toll roads and congestion-free pricing in terms of their impact, in that each involves the payment for use of a road or highway. In the first case, we may be using these payments to help cover the initial construction costs and/or the maintenance costs of the facility. In the second case, there is also a payment that may be used to help cover some initial construction costs, or maintenance costs, but the objective of the payment or fee is primarily to reduce use of the facility, thereby permitting users to be free of congestion. While this result may also occur with toll roads, if the tolls are sufficiently high, that end is not the primary objective.

In the case of certain highway projects, we have seen that congestion-free highways may be constructed by private entrepreneurs in the United States (e.g., SR-91 in California, see Fielding, 1994). The tolls or fees charged are used to cover all costs as well as to provide a return on investment for the investors. This blurs the distinction even more between fees paid for the use of toll roads and fees paid for the use of congestion-free highways.

Perhaps the major difference between the two types of facilities is the relative size of the toll charges as compared to the fees. Tolls are generally vehicle-specific and are relatively fixed over a year or more, while fees paid on congestion-free facilities may vary by time throughout the day. The higher the level of congestion on parallel facilities, the higher the fee for use of the congestion-free facility. Or, the higher the level of traffic for a given time of day (e.g., the morning or evening peak hours), the higher the fee for using the less congested facility.

Although fees paid for congestion-free facilities are sufficient to achieve their aim of keeping traffic moving, it is doubtful that they will see wide adoption for two reasons. The first relates to geography, in that congestion-free lanes are worth paying for only when all parallel routes are congested. Rarely is this the case except where the physical geography (mountain ranges, water masses, and the like) limit alternative routes between selected points of origin and destinations (as in California). The second factor limiting adoption is that there is no strong constituency advocating for more congestion-free facilities. Certainly the great majority of the population does not favor such facilities since most people believe that their tax dollars have already paid for sufficient facilities. In effect, without a strong body of support for congestion-free facilities or toll roads, we are unlikely to see many more.

Wachs (1994) has argued that there are political risks associated with what we call congestion-free pricing and that no political constituency will fight for it. "Advocates of congestion pricing will have to settle for smaller victories during the foreseeable future. Eventually many small victories could add up to a new approach to highway management and finance, but don't count on it happening any time soon" (Wachs, 1994, p. 19). While this sentiment may be somewhat dated, the reality is that congestion pricing still does not have a major political constituency willing to fight for it. It is selected only when no other alternative seems to be available or affordable.

The Do-Nothing Alternative

Certain transport researchers argue that, every time we take a major step to solve congestion problems, the result is an increase in travel (because travel is made easier) and the congestion problem continues, but at a higher and less tractable level. While purely conjectural, this idea has some substance because these improvements do indeed stimulate travel.

As a result, a growing number of researchers assert that it may make more sense *not* to try to solve the congestion problems affecting our highways. Their argument is that if we do nothing the problem may in part resolve itself as people decide not to travel at particular times or if they must travel at certain times they will seek out alternative noncongested highways or corridors. Does this argument sound plausible? To some extent it does if we stop to consider our own driving behavior in the face of an obvious congestion situation.

The same argument can be made for most transportation planning. That is, we develop many transit plans in anticipation of future problems. One of these problems is congestion, and we believe that we can prevent it if we know it will occur at a given point in the absence of steps taken to avoid it. The argument in transportation policy is typically not that the problem will not eventually resolve itself but rather that there are significant social and economic costs in allowing the problem to resolve itself. Therefore, if we forecast future conditions and plan to resolve problems before they occur, we will prevent these significant social and economic problems. However, we have never quite quantified the savings that result from planning a solution as opposed to allowing it to occur on its own.

Perhaps a step beyond the "do-nothing approach" is what could be called the "shut-it-down approach." A 1998 report titled "Traffic Impact of Highway Capacity Reductions" (summarized in *Traffic Technology International*, 1998a, 1998c) suggests that removing lanes from existing road facilities results in a general loss of traffic. The report was prepared by a team from the University College of London in behalf of London Transport. This report noted that "reducing road space for general traffic causes some traffic to 'evaporate,' on average by a quarter of the original flow on the affected road." The report suggests that for a road closed due to the addition of a bus lane there was a decrease in traffic of about 41%, with less than half of this traffic reappearing on alternative routes. This conclusion suggests a net reduction of about 25% of the original traffic. While a loss of 1–2% might be reasonable as some discretionary travel is canceled or combined with other trip chains, we are frankly skeptical of the suggestion that one-quarter of the traffic volume on any road is discretionary or that it was possibly diverted to public transit. We would suggest that the team repeat the research in a controlled situation rather than base its findings on "case studies from 15 countries."

ANOTHER APPROACH

There are very fundamental relationships that exist in the field of transportation engineering that are worth reviewing here since they clarify a dimension of the congestion problem (see Figure 7.1). The first of these is the relationship between the volume of traffic on a highway and the density of vehicles. As can be seen from Figure 7.1a, the relationship is positive and curvilinear, with volume increasing along with density until some optimal speed is reached. After the optimal speed is reached, the relationship becomes negative and curvilinear. What is happening is

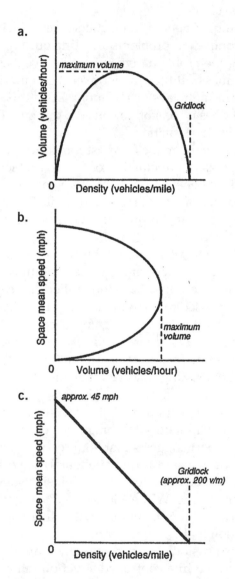

FIGURE 7.1. Basic relationships between traffic volume, speed, and density. *Source*: Data from Wohl and Martin (1967).

the density is becoming so great that the volume begins to fall. As indicated, grid-lock occurs at maximum density, whereupon volume drops to 0.

Figure 7.1b depicts space mean speed and volume. As the volume increases, we see an increase in speed up to some optimal speed. Beyond that speed the amount of space needed to stop the vehicle increases, and as a result the volume on the highway begins to drop. The implications are that high speed actually increases congestion, an observation that has been noted on experiments on the M-25 beltway encircling London.

The final relationship explored (shown in Figure 7.1c) is that between speed and density. Speed is at a maximum when the roadway is virtually devoid of other vehicles (i.e., with density approaching 0). On the other hand, density is at a maximum (i.e., gridlock occurs) when the space mean speed drops to 0. This describes the maximum packing of the highway space, with vehicles bumper to bumper.

Garrison and Ward (2000) have taken the volume density relationship and added to it lines representing speed (see Figure 7.2). At about 50 miles per hour we seem to reach a flow of 2,200 vehicle per lane mile, which corresponds to a density of about 50 vehicles to the mile. Note that increasing the speed, for example to 70 miles per hour, increases the necessary distance between vehicles (and lowers the density of vehicles) on the highway. Decreasing the speed initially does not have much of an impact on flow, and if the speed is greater than 20 miles per hour, we can still maintain flow in excess of 2,000 vehicles per lane mile. From these relationships the

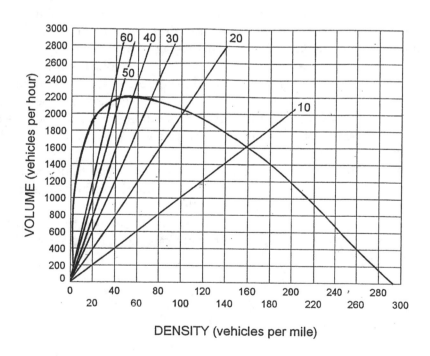

FIGURE 7.2. A highway capacity curve for uninterrupted flow. Reprinted by permission from William L. Garrison and J. D. Ward, *Tomorrow's Transportation: Changing Cities, Economies and Lives,* Norwood, MA: Artech House, Inc., 2000. © 2000 by Artech House, Inc.

authors conclude that it should be possible to control congestion by controlling the density of vehicles on the roadway. Unfortunately, this is not as easy as it sounds; the authors suggest metering the on-ramps to control the number of vehicles on the roadway at any one time.

It should be apparent that the on-ramps could very well become congested, and the question then becomes whether the driver wants to drive in congested conditions or instead wait in line for an opportunity to access the roadway. Garrison and Ward note that ITS could be used to enable drivers to know the state of the system each morning before they leave for work. This foreknowledge could result in drivers changing departure times if they had the flexibility to do so. This approach is obviously not a complete answer to the congestion problem, but it is a step in the right direction that could possibly lessen the impact of congestion in the near term.

CONCLUSIONS

One thing that is relatively certain is that we will not eliminate corridor congestion anytime soon as a major transport problem. Lave (1990) has argued the opposite. His point is that we have approximately one driver for every registered vehicle in the United States and that, although the national fleet may increase, there will be no one to drive these new vehicles since no driver can drive more than one vehicle at a time. This has been dubbed the "saturation" argument. The argument has received some support from the National Personal Travel Survey (Rey et al., 1991), which agrees with the saturation argument with regard to men. However, women are continuing to join the labor force in increasing numbers, as they have over the past two decades, and currently (in 2008) represent 59.5% of labor force participants compared to 44% in 2000 (U.S. Department of Labor, 2009). As newly trained drivers they can add significantly more vehicles to already congested facilities. While this argument also assumes some uniformity in automobile ownership across income groups that may be overstated, if incomes continue to rise, we will doubtless see additional motor vehicles.

Perhaps most disappointing to our aspirations for congestion-free driving is a study for the Federal Highway Administration (Cambridge, 2005) suggesting that, since congestion is so common and apparently endemic, we should simply factor it into our travel times estimates. Reliability in estimating arrival times should not be based on travel time alone but rather on travel time plus time delays attributable to congestion.

PART II

POSSIBLE SOLUTIONS

CHAPTER 8

An Introduction to the Range of Possible Solutions

The domain of the policy-making unit must be congruent
with the domain of the causes and effects of the problem
with which the policy deals. This is often called the
principle of subsidiarity.
—HERMAN E. DALY AND JOSHUA FARLEY (2004)

We begin with the statement by Daly and Farley, above, simply to acknowledge
that not all of the problems of sustainable transport can necessarily be resolved by
policymakers in the employ of local, state, or national governments. Therefore in
this chapter we give an overview of the solutions that are possible, understanding
that not all of them can be implemented at every policy level or geographic location.

Considering the enormity of why our transport systems are not sustainable,
including global climate change, substandard urban air quality, diminishing petroleum reserves, motor vehicle fatalities and injuries, and congestion, we must recognize that the vast scale of these particular problems requires that they be addressed
at different levels. The one major exception is global warming or climate change,
which rightfully demands a global solution, or at least the consensus of key nations
on how to attack the problem.

The other problems are susceptible to solutions propounded at different levels
and aimed at various scales. For example, one might address the problem of motor
vehicle fatalities as a global problem, but in practice a national program, or even
state or local program, might be most effective in stemming the level of fatalities
and injuries. Diminishing petroleum reserves probably can't be reversed through
actions at any governmental level, but the development and use of alternative fuels
can certainly be prompted by both nations and localities, as shown in numerous

historical instances. Similarly, air quality problems and congestion are often most effectually handled at the scale as well as local and state levels. So, although attacking these problems globally might be admirable, it would be naive to believe they would be resolved through concerted action at that scale. So, in the chapters that follow we examine the various ways and scales at which these problems can best be addressed.

POLICY SOLUTIONS

The first set of proffered solutions we offer are pricing solutions, which in turn, are divided into two types. The first entails getting the true costs of using various transport modes—in particular, motor vehicles—reflected accurately. If we can get even some of these indirect costs into the price of gasoline, that price will more closely resemble its actual cost to society. The second set of pricing solutions has to do with congestion-free taxing and the use of tolls. We will examine some of the approaches that have been used in this area.

Land use and how it factors into various solutions are also examined in the chapters to come. Land use planning does not directly address any of the major problems of transport sustainability, but if we can control the activity space over which driving occurs we can materially affect emission levels, fuel use, and traffic congestion levels. This undertaking is not as easy as it sounds since there are fundamental disagreements regarding land use planning, such as whether compact cities are better or worse than dispersed cities.

Yet another approach to sustainability in the transport sector relates to indicator-based planning, also referred to as benchmarking. This is a very different approach to planning than that typically followed in the United States. It involves identifying specific variables related to sustainability—or, more accurately, nonsustainability—measuring these, and then attempting to improve on the values obtained. For example, for any given city, we might calculate how many minutes it takes the average resident to get to work (as a measure of congestion), or the vehicle miles traveled as well as other variables, and try to set targets as to what these values should be. Determining exactly how these targeted goals could be achieved would entail implementing specific policy initiatives.

Our next set of solutions, based purely on policy, involves examining a wide range of programs that run the gamut from encouraging greater use of bicycles and more walking by individuals to large-scale global solutions to some of the problems. Specific examples of these programs and how they have been implemented are provided.

One specific set of policies to be examined involves speed and speed limits. These may be set at various governmental levels ranging from municipalities and localities to states or provinces. In some cases these speeds have been set by governmental units without any clear understanding as to exactly what implications they have for fuel consumption, emissions, or accidents. We do not believe that these are necessarily capricious policies, although the manner in which they are sometimes set suggests this possibility.

Certain countries have approached sustainability at the national level, developing specific plans and agendas to improve the situation within their own borders help to solve the global problem. We examine such plans in the cases of the Netherlands and Israel. Other countries that have also undertaken such plans, most notably Canada and the United Kingdom, have met with mixed success. The United States, on the other hand, has not been very aggressive or resourceful in this area. The actions of the first Bush administration during the late 1980s verged on outright opposition, while those of the Clinton administration were little better, being voluntary for the most part. The George W. Bush administration took office bitterly opposed to the Kyoto accords and ended its tenure little changed in its attitude, based even on ingrained skepticism of the scientific case for global warming.

The broad area within transportation planning (and engineering) generally referred to as "travel demand management" consists almost exclusively of policies and actions that will make transport more sustainable. We refer to this area as "sustainable travel demand management" (STDM) and focus our discussion on the policies and actions that offer the most credible approaches aimed at developing sustainable transport solutions.

Next we look at the potential role of education in this entire area. To a certain extent we have been educating the population in the United States to partake in enjoying all of the mobility they could possibly desire. While this may have been the mindset for most of the 20th century, when we gave unfettered encouragement to the automobile industry to vigorously promote the use of gas-guzzling cars. Now we must convince the public that this is not necessarily a good idea. Changing directions so radically will not be an easy undertaking.

These various policy solutions and educational approaches are more likely to be found in European countries than in the United States. In the United States we have always relied heavily on the idea that there is a technological fix for nearly every problem. This is one of the truly interesting differences between these two regions. We will examine the various technological solutions that exist in this particular area, of which there are four major categories.

TECHNOLOGICAL SOLUTIONS

The first set of solutions relates to the information and communications technology area. The principal solutions we will look at are telecommuting or teleworking, the various communications substitutes for travel, and finally the role of e-commerce as it affects business-to-business transactions and business-to-consumer transactions. Communications has always been closely related to transportation, and up until the development of the telegraph nearly all communications over significant distances required transportation.

A second set of solutions involves the introduction of alternative fuels. Many of these are already in use, and we will examine their use. It is unlikely that planning organizations will be involved in developing new fuels, but they can be very influential in the adoption of some of these by cities, states, or other governmental units for use in their various vehicle fleets. We will examine the merits of each of the fuels and their potential as a long-term solution to the problem of diminishing petroleum reserves.

A third set of solutions is more technical and is included more for background than for implementation. This is the area of different vehicles (including hybrids), fuel cells and their use in transport, and the probable change in the future role of catalytic converters. We will also discuss the role of electric vehicles even though these have nearly disappeared from our toolbox of sustainability solutions.

The last set of technological solutions, namely, intelligent transport system technologies, is found almost exclusively in urban areas. Nearly every city has implemented something in this area in an attempt to better manage the flow of traffic. At the same time, some of these technologies do not directly address sustainability issues. Most of them involve mechanisms that will facilitate the flow of traffic, and in that sense they will reduce the costs of congestion, namely, travel time, fuel consumption, and emissions. Some others offer the promise of decreasing fatalities from accidents. However, there are many technologies in this area that do little for sustainability, for example, fare collection systems or passenger counting systems for transit operations. We focus our discussion on those that have the most relevance to the sustainability problems addressed here.

CONCLUSIONS

Before closing this short chapter we should note that we need to see some very basic changes in human behavior. It is difficult to itemize everything that is necessary, but attempts to minimize discretionary travel would certainly be a good start. It would not hurt for individuals to simply ask the question "Do I need to make this trip today?" Certainly, we all have to get to work and school, but could we call a friend instead of driving over to see him or her? So, you forgot to pick up a pound of coffee—can't you drink tea today? We have all gotten to the point where driving to pick up a Sunday *New York Times* or some other newspaper has become a timeworn ritual. We do so many things without ever stopping to think about the transport or other cost ramifications—and why not? We have all long known that petroleum is a finite resource—we just choose to ignore that fact. Certainly accidents happen, but I'm a careful driver, so it won't happen to me. I'm just driving one car—congestion isn't *my* fault. My car is in good shape—I'm not the major contributor to pollution. In point of fact, all of the sustainability problems we encounter today are created by those who perceive their actions as perfectly innocuous. Therein lies the problem.

It is the "tragedy of the commons" all over again. We all use the roadways, but none of us believes that he or she is responsible for the problems of that use. We all expect someone else to take responsibility for the problems generated by our use, and to some extent various levels of government do. They try to solve the problems we create with the solutions explored in the remainder of this volume, but wouldn't it make far more sense not to create the problems in the first place?

We have seen such altruism in the past. When President Jimmy Carter urged people not to drive unless it was necessary during the energy crisis of the late 1970s, there was an immediate 10% drop in total vehicle miles nationwide. An active citizenry will respond if they understand the problem in response to informed and persuasive leadership.

PRICING

CHAPTER 9

The Full Costs of Transportation

> Many believe that the price of gasoline should be much
> higher to account for oil spills, leaking storage tanks,
> pollution, global warming, energy dependence, and
> other unpaid extraction, transport, and combustion costs.
> —DANIEL SPERLING (1995)

The costs of transportation have long been viewed as consisting of very traditional elements such as the cost of fuel, the cost of lubricants, insurance costs, and so forth. Over the past several years there has been a growing recognition that many other costs are generated by transport vehicles and systems, but these never find their way into a total costs accounting scheme. These new costs, often called externalities or external costs, have the potential of completely altering public policy toward this sector. In this chapter we look at some of the recent literature and identify the full costs of transportation.

Many view the cost of transportation as the price of gasoline to keep automobiles running. Others may add to this cost the price of lubrication and oil for the vehicle, but the need for these occurs so infrequently today that many dismiss these latter costs. While we know that transport actually costs more than the prices of fuel and lubricants, we often act as though the daily out-of-pocket cost of transport is the cost of transportation.

Obviously, there are other transportation costs that represent very significant outlays for individuals. Included in this group would be the cost of parking, the cost of insurance, and the price of the vehicle itself. Parking has also become less important today. Companies often provide parking for their employees, while shopping centers and malls offer "free parking" to attract customers. In reality, the cost of free parking is included in the cost of operating such facilities, and it is absorbed in the price of the goods or services we purchase and as a result is completely unrecognizable to us. Even central-city shopping hubs often eliminate charges for parking in an attempt to attract businesses and customers back from the suburban malls and shopping centers. In this case, the city uses other revenue sources to provide parking-related services once covered with parking meter revenues. So, indirectly we continue to pay for parking, although we may not be able to put a clear-cut price on it.

The cost of automotive insurance is a very real cost, often paid for by the quarter-year or semiannually. As such, it is not a cost that we have to think of often, and it is less on our mind than the monthly rent or mortgage and certainly of little concern when we decide whether to use the car to accomplish some task.

We also don't think much about what vehicles cost to purchase when we drive. To be sure, when we need to purchase a new or used vehicle, we are very much aware of—often even shocked at—the price of vehicles that may meet our needs, but we rarely take that price and consciously distribute it across the miles driven to determine the vehicle's capital cost per vehicle mile.

The costs of operating an automobile are calculated periodically by the U.S. Department of Transportation or annually by one or two of the major automobile rental agencies. These agencies all consider the costs above, except for parking, and the media often report the value derived. These "costs of operating an automobile" are interesting to most drivers, but they remain somewhat artificial in their minds. Nevertheless, these are the direct costs of operating an automobile.

While drivers may not take a realistic view of automotive operating costs, over the past two decades transport researchers have begun to move beyond what are often thought of as the traditional accounting costs. This change has resulted in a willingness to look at the indirect or external costs of transportation, that is, the externalities. Such externalities include the environmental pollution costs generated by different transport modes, the medical costs not covered by insurance, the costs of urban sprawl, the cost of noise, and several others. Including these additional costs results in a redefinition of the costs of transportation and spatial interaction, particularly if the price of fuel is increased to incorporate them.

A voluminous body of literature has developed over the past several years in the area of full transportation costing. As it is impossible to summarize or review all of the literature, we must limit our review in this chapter to five recent studies. These studies are distinctive in that they examine comprehensive transportation costs, not just one or two components of these costs. The first is the 1992 report *The Going Rate*, prepared for the World Resources Institute (MacKenzie et al., 1992). Researchers with the Natural Resources Defense Council prepared the second study that is reviewed here; titled *The Price of Mobility—Uncovering the Hidden Costs of Transportation* (Miller & Moffet, 1993), it was published in 1993. The third study is *The Costs of Transporting People in the British Columbia Lower Mainland*, prepared for TRANSPORT 2021, transportation a long-range plan for Vancouver (Van Seters & Levelton, 1993). The fourth is the Apogee (1994) report on *The Costs of Transportation*, prepared for the Conservation Law Foundation. And the final study reviewed here is *Transportation Cost Analysis* (Litman, 1995), prepared by the Victoria Transport Policy Institute. We examine each of these studies and the costs they identified later in this chapter.

During the mid- to late 1990s three other noteworthy costing studies were produced. The first, from the United Kingdom, was *The True Costs of Road Transport*, produced for the Centre for Social and Economic Research on the Global Environment (Maddison et al., 1996). While not adding any new cost items to those enumerated in the studies reviewed here, it does operationalize several of these, providing case studies of Sweden, North America, the Netherlands, and, of course, the United Kingdom, which is the primary focus of that volume. The second volume addresses the sometimes neglected subject of freight transport. A TRB (1996) publication titled *Paying Our Way: Estimating Marginal Social Costs of Freight Transport*, operationalizes certain costs treated here and also discusses various costing approaches and ways of implementing full costing. The final study, *The Full Costs and Benefits of Transportation* (Greene et al., 1997), is an edited volume of papers on the title subject. Focusing on such costs, as accidents, congestion, and air pollution, it differs from the other studies in that it also discusses the benefits of transport. It is a more balanced and rigorous treatment of this subject than has appeared heretofore.

The reasons for undertaking a comprehensive examination of the costs of transportation are numerous. There may be an interest in influencing transport development policy, either nationally or locally, by pointing out that the actual costs may be significantly higher than the perceived costs. Note that the agencies funding several of the studies are what could be described as "national environmental" organizations. Local policy can also be influenced by an examination of the total costs of transport if the favored solution is found to have a "total cost" far greater than some alternatives. Rarely are those who are interested in "full costing," CPAs or financial analysts, intent on making the accounting more rigorous, rather, many proponents have an interest in simply slowing or stopping a transport project.

THE FULL-COSTING STUDIES

The Going Rate

Not unlike the situation with the other studies reviewed here, the authors of *The Going Rate* (MacKenzie et al., 1992) sought to identify what some of the hidden costs of our motor vehicle-dominated transportation system were with the specific intent of influencing policy. They assert that the costs of this transport system are much greater than generally recognized, and to illustrate this point they note that in the United States only about 60% of the road construction, rehabilitation, and maintenance costs derive from user fees and taxes, while the remaining 40% comes from general revenues. They also highlight the costs of highway services, accidents, and air pollution, among other items. Table 9.1 identifies the major cost components that they believe should be addressed, or at least recovered in some way. The authors point out that it might be logical to generate revenues for these costs by increasing fuel taxes. They suggest a tax of "well over $2 per gallon," with the increase being phased in over a decade.

Of the costs included, there is little argument that most of these should be included in a "full-cost" transport study. We see some problems with including a couple of the "costs" identified. One of the items included by the authors is what

**TABLE 9.1. Cost Components
of *The Going Rate* (1992)**

Market costs
    Roadway capital outlays
    Roadway maintenance
    Highway services
    Parking

External costs
    Costs of air pollution
    Risks of climate change
    Security costs of importing oil
    Congestion costs
    Motor vehicle accidents
    Costs of noise
    Damage from vibrations
    Land loss

they refer to as "the rising risks of climate change." We take issue with this item as such. There has clearly been a significant increase in the amount of carbon dioxide entering the atmosphere. We would go further and state that this will in all probability lead to what some have called a "forcing" of the greenhouse effect, resulting in continued warming of the planet. At the same time, no one knows what the resulting increase in temperature will be. In addition, we do not understand the feedback mechanisms at work in terms of the interaction of atmospheric carbon and oceans. The general circulation models in use today are unable to replicate what has occurred in the past 100 years, thus, how can we believe they will be more accurate at forecasting the future? (see GAO, 1995). In addition, it is almost impossible now to assess the financial aspects of global warming. Its negative impacts on one sector or region may be offset by positive impacts on other sectors or regions. Until we have a clearer picture of these impacts, incorporating the costs of halting transport's share of global warming emissions does not appear to have much merit.

Another cost examined by this study was the security costs of importing oil. These costs are based on the idea that since the United States expends a large amount ($101 billion annually, according to the report) maintaining a military presence in the Persian Gulf to ensure access to Middle Eastern crude petroleum. The author would like to see half of this cost borne by transport users, as opposed to the public. We disagree. Our rationale for excluding this cost is that the United States, as the dominant world power, would most likely have to maintain a military presence in areas that have even a minimal strategic value to this country. As a result, it is not appropriate to enter this item into the costs of transportation.

There are some other costs included with which we have some problems as well, including congestion costs, noise costs, vibration costs, and the cost of land loss. We agree congestion costs should be included, but not explicitly. In other words we would look at the impact of traffic delays on the value of time lost for individuals, on the level of emissions, fuel use, and related items. Noise and vibration costs are almost impossible to estimate in any meaningful way unless we know the location of the impact. In many cases these costs are nonexistent outside of urban areas. The cost of land loss is the result of a somewhat myopic view of land values and their relationship to transportation. While land is lost to transport, transport significantly increases the value of nearby land by making it more accessible. As a result, devoting land to transport may actually result in a net gain in the value of land, even after factoring in the value of the land "taken" for transport.

A final point is that this study examined primarily motor vehicle costs on highways, streets, and roads. It did not get into the costs of the various other transport modes, nor did it attempt to integrate the costs identified into an estimate of total "operating" costs.

The Price of Mobility

In *The Price of Mobility*, Miller and Moffet (1993) attempt to estimate the full costs of car, bus, and train travel in the United States. They note that most federal programs require a comparison of the costs of different transport modes, but this comparison is rarely done in a satisfactory way. They seek to make such comparisons possible, approaching this objective by using costs per passenger mile of travel (pmt) measures derived from aggregate national statistics.

Miller and Moffet divide transport costs into 17 components (see Table 9.2), most of which have been discussed earlier, but they add a few others that have not been discussed thus far. One of these is what could be called the secondary costs of energy use, such as the energy costs of producing transport fuels and vehicles. The argument here is that the actual process of manufacturing these products uses energy that would not have been used otherwise. This is undoubtedly a societal cost, but it is presumably also a cost recovered by the price of fuel or the price of the vehicle. We believe incorporating these energy costs would lead to some double-counting.

TABLE 9.2. Cost Components of *The Price of Mobility* (1993)

- Personal costs (vehicle cost, insurance, fuel, maintenance, etc.)
- Capital and operating costs (highway construction, repair, etc.)
- Local services (traffic control, policing, driver education, etc.)
- Energy (fuel production, vehicle manufacturing and repair, etc.)
- Congestion (increases in travel time costs, emissions, etc.)
- Parking (excessive land needs, indirect automobile subsidy, etc.)
- Accidents (portions not insured, productivity loss, life value)
- Noise (medical related ailments)
- Building vibration damage (deterioration of structures)
- Air pollution (acid rain, global warming, aesthetics)
- Water pollution (runoff, underground tank leaks, oil spills, etc.)
- Wetlands (loss due to highway construction)
- Land loss (due to highway construction)
- Historic buildings and archeological properties
- Property values (increasing value and minimizing use)
- Transportation equity (poor impacted by lack of access)
- Urban sprawl (inefficient use of land and higher costs to serve)

Air pollution costs, such as acid rain, global warming, and aesthetics, are also considered by the authors. Global warming was discussed earlier, but we have not discussed the costs of acid rain. Most researchers who have analyzed this problem (which chiefly affects New England and middle Atlantic states) attribute the acid rain to the burning of high-sulfur fossil fuels by electricity generating plants in the Midwest. The exhaust from these plants is transported great distances in the upper atmosphere, due in part to the very high smoke stacks at these sites. In the Midwest there is little evidence that ground-level transport emissions contribute to acid rain at present, though convectional activity or the movement of warmer air to higher elevations, may play a small role. As for aesthetics, it is difficult to value independently of some more concrete variable.

Miller and Moffet (1993) also examine water pollution. Many petrochemicals get deposited on streets and highways by motor vehicles and find their way to streams, lakes, and reservoirs after rainfall. Salts used for snow removal in some states and various de-icing agents follow a similar path. These all contribute to water pollution, but quantifying the amount is difficult.

Negative impacts on historic buildings and archeological properties are also noted by Miller and Moffet, though transport damages to these sites are difficult to quantify. There are numerous instances of historic structures being destroyed by the construction of highways in the United States, far more prior to than after the Historic Preservation Act of 1966 and subsequent executive orders requiring an environmental impact assessment of projects affecting them. If historical and archeological losses persist, given these changes, it reflects mainly lack of oversight or a flaw in some sector other than transportation.

Transportation equity issues are also raised by Miller and Moffet. Any government that has made the automobile its country's major mode of transportation, as the United States has, essentially disenfranchises anyone who is unable to operate such vehicles due to disabilities, age (too young or too old), or the lack of income to acquire the vehicle. Once again, we don't disagree with the importance of this element, but we see no way of operationalizing it.

Urban sprawl is also noted as a cost resulting from transportation. The logic of this argument is that transportation results in a level of mobility that enables at least some members of society to live at increasing distances from the denser parts of our urban areas, and therefore the costs of such sprawl must be viewed as a component of transport costs. Urban sprawl exists in the United States because transportation has enabled individuals to take advantage of the complete lack of land use control that exists in most parts of the country. We do not advocate rigid land use zoning and control, but we do recognize what happens when it is lacking.

The Vancouver, Canada, Study

The study of transport costs in the British Columbia Lower Mainland (Van Seters & Levelton, 2003) estimates the total cost of transporting people in that area in 1991 and "goes on to calculate the average cost 'per unit' of travel, by different modes, for

TABLE 9.3. Cost Components of the Vancouver Study (1993)

Direct user (operating) costs	Time
Fixed vehicle costs	Personal
Variable vehicle costs	Commercial delays
Parking fees and fines	
	Urban sprawl
Indirect parking costs	Infrastructure
Residential	Loss of open space
Commercial	Future transport options
Government	
	Environmental and social impacts
Transport infrastructure	Unaccounted-for accident costs
Road construction	Air pollution
Road maintenance	Noise pollution
Roadway land value	Water pollution
Transit land value	
Protection services	

urban peak, urban off-peak and suburban travel." The study incorporates many of the same components examined in the other studies (see Table 9.3). It includes parking costs, for example, but goes further, breaking these down into residential, commercial, and governmental costs. The residential component may be viewed quite simply as that portion of residential space that is used for parking. If you live in a home valued at $170,000 on a $30,000 lot and the house has a garage that represents 20% of the space and a driveway that occupies 10% of the lot, then the residential costs of parking are $37,000 ($34,000 + $3,000). This is a simplified calculation, but it gives you the gist of the idea. If you have no garage and park your car in the street, you avoid these costs.

Governmental parking addresses the question of the costs to the government of providing parking for its employees. Obviously, parking must be available somewhere, and there are some who believe that parking should be provided on lower-valued land on the periphery of urban areas and transit should be used to move workers to employment centers. Others believe that the parking should be taxed as a fringe benefit. This is unlikely since nearly all employers provide parking of some type to their employees. Even those that pay for the parking generally only pay a token amount to help defer operating costs for the parking facilities.

While this project examined 20 separate components of transport costs, we have discussed many of them previously. Several more are discussed in the analyses later in this chapter.

The Apogee Study

The Apogee report of 1994 sought to develop a method of comparing various transport modes for policy analysis. To this end, the researchers also reviewed the literature, set out an analytical framework for comparing costs based on passenger miles of travel, examined the transport systems for two cities (Boston and Portland, Maine), and derived some findings.

This study examined most of the components of what could be called personal costs—depreciation, insurance, taxes and fees, gasoline and oil, repair parts and tires (see Table 9.4). Tolls, transit fares, and parking are also included. User tax receipts, which were originally included, were later removed from the government expenditures to eliminate double-counting. Transit fares were examined by the other studies, usually with personal costs since they represent the user's operating costs for that mode.

Accident costs are also examined, as are travel time costs. The costs of providing capital, maintenance, and operating funds for transport were included here as well. One difference in the Apogee report is its explicit recognition that the cost of motor vehicles should also reflect operation of the state motor vehicle bureaus and agencies. The costs of the police, fire, and justice systems are also included here, as are government expenses related to research on fuels and energy related to transport.

Pollution costs for all major pollutants (volatile organic compounds, carbon monoxide, nitrogen oxides, carbon dioxide, sulfur oxides, and total suspended particulates) are also included on a dollars-per-gram emitted basis. Noise is also included among the costs examined by the Apogee study.

Sometimes government fails to invest funds in its transport system because of financial difficulties. Deferred maintenance results in a distorted picture of what the maintenance should be. In this study these costs are included. The approach was basically to look at forecasts for maintaining the current system and see to what extent current expenditures fell short of the estimate.

Importing petroleum has an impact on the U.S. balance of payments as well as inflation in some cases; fewer funds are available for domestic investment, savings

---

TABLE 9.4. Cost Components of the Apogee Study (1994)

- Depreciation and financing (on vehicle used)
- Insurance (for automobile)
- Registration and taxes (title, license, excise tax, inspection, etc.)
- Gasoline and oil (including taxes)
- Repairs, parts, tires
- Tolls
- Transit fares (out-of-pocket costs)
- Parking (nonresidential and residential)
- Accidents (cost per type by rate)
- Travel time (value of time and commuting share)
- Federal/state capital investment (right of way, construction, etc.)
- Federal/state operations and maintenance (patching, snow removal)
- Local capital, operations and maintenance (local streets and roads)
- Department of motor vehicles (administrative costs)
- Police, fire, and justice systems (portion allocable to transport modes)
- Energy supply—governmental (research and subsidies)
- Air pollution (governmental and societal by pollutant)
- User tax receipts (net after deducting costs paid by users)
- Deferred investment (in transport facilities by government)
- Energy supply—trade effects (balance of payments)
- Noise (stress, annoyance, and loss of property values)

decrease, and so forth. Apogee estimated this cost to be between $2 and $124 per barrel.

Transportation Cost Analysis

One of the most recent efforts in the area of full transportation costing is the volume written by Todd Litman of the Victoria Transport Policy Institute titled *Transportation Cost Analysis: Techniques, Estimates and Implications*. Published in 1995, this work goes beyond most of the previous studies reviewed here by discussing the implications of improper pricing, problems of transportation equity, and several related ideas (see Table 9.5). Litman's earlier work was cited extensively in the Vancouver study, reviewed above. Although most of the costs identified by Litman have been discussed earlier, a couple of items could use some clarification.

Roadway land value is assessed as an opportunity cost. That is, if the land were not used for a road, what would be its highest-valued and best use? We asserted earlier that roads provide easier access, which is a major determinant of the value of land. In addition, most road right-of-way is purchased at average land values for the area where it is located. If the land can be shown to have a higher value, then one always has access to the courts for redress of underpayment. Therefore, we do not see this as a major component of costs, although it may have more significance in Canada or Europe.

Resource consumption and waste disposal both refer to automobiles. In the consumption context, automobiles consume significant resources as they are manufactured. In general, these are nonrenewable resources, and therefore perhaps they should be priced with this loss of resources in mind. Automobile disposal is another problem. It is believed by many that these vehicles should be made in such a way that they can be disposed of easily or recycled indefinitely. There is evidence of significant ongoing recycling of vehicles. When an automobile is no longer functional

---

TABLE 9.5. Cost Components of *Transportation Cost Analysis* (1995)

- Vehicle costs (purchase or lease cost, operating cost, etc)
- Travel time costs
- Accident costs
- Automobile parking costs
- Congestion (incremental congestion costs)
- Roadway facility costs
- Roadway land value (opportunity cost of roadway land)
- Municipal services (police, fire, courts, corrections, etc.)
- Transportation equity and option value
- Air pollution (attributable to motor vehicle use)
- Noise (sound and vibration)
- Resource consumption (by automobile manufacture and use)
- Barrier effects (to movement via nonhighway modes)
- Land use impacts (external costs caused by traffic)
- Water pollution (from automobiles, roads, and parking)
- Waste disposal (costs of automobile disposal)

---

as a transport vehicle, it is usually broken down into its components and sold as parts or recycled as scrap if it has no higher value.

In 1999 the European Union countries approved a law that requires automobile manufacturers to accept their old vehicles back without charge and to recycle the parts. The law applies to all cars sold in the EU after January 1, 2006. Automakers will have to reuse and recover 95% of the vehicle on a mass basis and recycle 85% of it (Ferrã & Armaral, 2006). This is not an unreasonable requirement since the weight of iron and steel (68%), nonferrous metals (8%), and lubricating and other fluids (9%) typically accounted for 85% of the weight of a 1998 car, on average. Nevertheless, European automakers fought the legislation, perhaps fearing that the 85% figure would be boosted over time. There are also requirements for automobiles manufactured earlier than 2006, but these are less stringent.

Barrier effects are caused by at-grade highways being built around urban neighborhoods. The highway becomes a barrier to walking, biking, and other activities. This was a common problem for U.S. interstate highway construction during the 1960s, but it is less of a problem today, given the requirement for environmental impact studies prior to construction and the concern for community cohesion in those studies, as well as the generally lower level of new construction.

Litman (1995) has also produced a major bibliographic undertaking related to transportation costing. That bibliography, which is periodically updated, currently exceeds 1,100 citations.

THE COSTS OF TRANSPORTATION

In the previous sections, we introduced some of the individual costs that have been recognized in the literature as components of the full costs of transportation. Some of these we find to be acceptable, while others we find to be wanting. Whether a particular cost should be included in a costing framework often depends on the use to be made of that framework. On a certain philosophical level we might include a number of different costs. However, in a practical application where we might be looking at alternative solutions to a given transport problem, many of these appear unmeasurable and irrelevant. In this section we will reexamine these costs and note which of these we believe should be considered in situations where alternative routes or projects are being evaluated. In each case we will identify our rationale for this decision.

Before we look at each of these costs, something should be said about my own position on transport costs as they apply to this particular type of assessment. The intent here is to evaluate these costs as a way of evaluating alternative modal solutions for transport problems. In such an assessment one must ask whether the cost is real or perhaps merely judgmental. If the cost is more the latter than the former, we will suggest it is not relevant in project evaluation. This does not mean that it is irrelevant in other policy types of assessments. Even if the cost is a real cost, it may not be appropriate to incorporate it in an analytical framework that reflects our particular costing perspective.

The costing approach used here makes use of what is often referred to as avoidable costs. If the facility were not constructed or the service were not provided, what costs would be avoided? An illustration of this approach may be instructive. If a small regional railroad opts not to provide freight service on a branch line, it will avoid incremental operating and maintenance costs on the line—these are some of the avoidable costs. At the same time, there are also unavoidable costs. Unavoidable costs might include the salary of the president of the railroad, the secretarial staff, and so forth, that would be necessary whether the branch line were operated or not. These costs would have to be covered independently of the line extension or extra service. This is what is meant by avoidable and unavoidable costs.

In the present instance, these concepts are being used to examine the cost of various components of total transport costs, or to determine whether they will be used at all. We believe such systems should rely very heavily on costs that are incurred primarily by the provision of the transport service. Let us now examine some of the costs enumerated in Table 9.6. This table brings together all the different costs that have been cited in the literature as components of total transportation costs. As the reader can see, the list is extensive. If we count only the major categories of costs, they number 19. The table presents the components in alphabetical order, and that is the order in which we discuss them.

Accident Costs

Transportation accident costs are incurred when a vehicle incident occurs that results in personal injury or some loss of property. The chief causes of these events are generally human error, vehicular or roadway design defects, or environmental conditions, but we will not concern ourselves further here with causal factors (Institute for Research in Public Safety, 1975). Instead, we try to examine what types of accident-related costs should be incorporated into any comprehensive definition of full transportation costing.

While one's first impulse might be to total up all accident costs in a full-costing approach, this action would be incorrect. The primary reason why we cannot do this is that we generally have insurance as one of the major components of operating cost. Insurance may cover medical costs or property damage costs, depending on the level and types of insurance purchased. Including all accident costs along with insurance costs would obviously result in double-counting of this cost item.

At the same time, not all costs are covered by insurance. For example, most motor vehicle insurance programs have deductibles (base amounts that must be paid prior to receiving insurance coverage of costs above this deductible level) or ceilings on coverage. In addition, it is arguable whether insurance beneficiary payments are consistent with certain assessments of the value of a human life, from either a willingness-to-pay or productivity perspective. Therefore, while insurance costs may rightfully be placed with operating costs, those accident costs not covered by insurance must be included here.

Since insurance costs are covered as a component of operating costs, the logical thing to do is include in our framework that portion of medically related costs

TABLE 9.6. Transportation Costs

Accident costs
  Deductibles
  Productivity Losses
  Value of Life

Capital costs
  Highways, streets, runways, tracks
    Planning
    Land acquisition
    Preliminary engineering
    Construction
    Deferred investment
  Terminals and garages
  Vehicles (motor vehicles, aircraft, buses, etc.)

Congestion costs (see Time costs; Energy costs; and Pollution)

Fares

Highway-related governmental services
  Police
  Fire
  Criminal justice

Land-related costs
  Archeological sites
  Historic buildings
  Loss of open space
  Loss of wetlands
  Urban sprawl

Loss and damage

Macroeconomic costs
  Balance-of-payments position
  Inflation

Maintenance costs
  Grass cutting
  Snow removal
  Patching

Manufacturing and refining
  Energy costs
  Resource use

Military security for petroleum shipments

Operating costs
  Insurance
  Fuel, oil
  Registration
  Licenses

Parking-related costs
  Fees
  Fines
  Governmental (subsidized)
  Private residential

Pollution
  Air
    Air quality
      Nitrogen oxide
      Carbon dioxide
      Carbon monoxide
      Suspended particulate matter
      Sulfur oxide
    Urban ozone
    Acid deposition
    Stratospheric ozone depletion
    Climate change
    Long-term health
  Noise
  Structural
    Vibration damage
  Water
    Marine (spills)
    Runoff

Property values

Repair and rehabilitation
  Vehicles
  Facilities

Subsidies

Time costs
  Commercial
  Personal

Transportation equity

that are not covered by insurance payments. That value is estimated to be roughly 50% of the total accident costs, or approximately $ 0.016 per vehicle mile of travel for motor vehicles in 1983 (Kanafani, 1983)—$0.03 per vehicle mile in 2007 dollars. The Bureau of Transportation Statistics (2004) estimates that about 9% of this latter cost is covered by governmental units, which is another way of saying taxes. For transport modes other than motor vehicles, one could calculate medical costs using industry averages for these modes, assuming none of these costs is covered by medical or personal accident insurance.

There is also the question of the value of human life. As noted above, one approach to valuing human life assesses the productivity of the individual, that is, how many more years could the person have contributed to society and what value would we place on that contribution? In this case, it is assumed that the product of average annual wages and years of lost work are an indication of the productivity value of individuals. One can also value human life through some contemporary assessment of the willingness-to-pay argument as conducted by panels. A traditional estimate of the value of a human life today is $1.5 million. This calculation stems primarily from the traffic accident analysis literature (NHTSA, 1989). For valuing the benefits and costs of transport projects, Caltrans (2006), the California Department of Transportation, uses a value of $3.1 million, which is fairly close to the 1989 NHTSA figure as adjusted for inflation. The economics literature generally places a value between $2.3 and $4.9 million on each human life (Smith, 2000).

Capital Costs

As indicated in Table 9.6, capital costs have three major components: the costs of highways, streets, runways, and tracks; the costs of terminals, garages, maintenance facilities, and other structures; and the costs of vehicles, whether these are motor vehicles, aircraft, locomotives, streetcars, bicycles, or any of the other numerous transport vehicles in use today. It is difficult to generalize about these components because of the complexity of the modes available, but no one would argue against the use of these capital costs as components of full transport costs.

The question is, How should these costs enter the accounting system? The cost of the physical facilities through which a transport mode operates or where it is stored and maintained are often considered as part of the mode's total operating costs if the system is privately owned. If the facilities are publicly owned or held, then their costs are often covered by taxes. For example, highway construction is often covered by tolls, motor vehicle fuel taxes, or user taxes. In some cases parts of the costs are covered by public and private funds, as in the case of railroad grade-crossing improvements. There are numerous costs included within the costs of providing this physical plant. These would include planning costs, land acquisition costs, preliminary engineering costs, the cost of materials, and the cost of construction of the facilities. These are also generally included in operating costs for private operators, but care must be taken to assure that they are covered on the public side.

One caveat worth noting here is that deferred maintenance is often practiced by both public and private transportation units. States often do not have the funds to assure that all highways or bridges are maintained, and this shortfall in funding results in deferred maintenance. Some 40 years ago several railroads on the verge of bankruptcy deferred maintenance on their roadbeds. One might prefer to ignore this practice were it not for the fact that any public or private operator that engages in it is giving a misleading picture of the true cost of the mode. We believe a normalized maintenance program should be assumed.

The costs of structures are generally reflected in operating costs for private entities or user taxes for publicly provided facilities. In some cases these costs are also shared.

Just as some of the accident costs above are covered by automobile insurance, which is a component of automotive operating costs, the price of an automobile and its depreciation are also components of those operating costs. Since these are covered by motor vehicle operating costs, they should not be included here. Capital vehicle costs are generally included in operating costs for the mode.

One should attempt to include all of the costs above that are generally considered as capital costs and at the same time be cognizant of the potential for double-counting some of these if we have included taxes (that may be used to cover some of these costs) as a cost elsewhere.

Congestion Costs

Congestion costs are one of the most popular topics in the field of transportation research and policy today (TRB, 1994a). However, to be precise, there is no such thing as congestion costs, except as a catchall phrase for several other costs that vary with congestion, such as increases in travel time, fuel use, pollution costs, and so forth. Consequently, we believe these costs should be considered as they are incurred, but not explicitly under the label of "congestion costs."

Fares

Fares are not costs as such, except perhaps to the consumer. Rather, they are fees levied by the public or private sector to recover costs incurred in providing the service. Presumably, the fare should be set at a level sufficient to recover the operating costs for the mode in question. This is generally the case for private operations but not necessarily for the public sector (e.g., public transit and Amtrak), where governmental subsidies sometimes make up the difference.

There are numerous ways that these can be handled in a full-costing framework. It seems logical to look at the operating costs of the modes, recognizing implicitly that someone must cover these costs through fares or subsidies, although we don't care who in this case. To do otherwise would result in double-counting of the costs.

Highway-Related Governmental Services

This services-related cost component is a recent addition to the literature on transportation costing, and there are those who believe that these costs should properly be incorporated into any full-costing analysis. We agree that much of the time of police personnel is spent in transportation or traffic safety, regulation, and enforcement. Similarly, firefighters are generally involved in controlling the risk of fire at traffic accidents, providing emergency medical services, and extracting victims from wrecked motor vehicles. And the courts are heavily involved in assessing penalties for traffic violations, ranging from the rolling stop to fatalities attributable to driving under the influence of alcohol. An argument could therefore be made that all such costs are transport-related. But is it reasonable to assume that a single project would increase or decrease the need for such services? This is the test that must be passed.

In addition to these functions we often have a number of state, federal, or local government employees who have transportation systems planning, administration, or regulation as the primary component of their position. Should the salaries of these individuals be allocated to the various transport modes?

Bearing in mind that the objective here is to develop a system for assessing transportation alternatives, then one must ask whether the construction of a specific transport facility or the provision of a transport service will significantly affect the magnitude of the costs of any of these highway-related governmental services. Using the avoidable cost criterion, will *not* providing the facility or service result in a decrease in the need for any of these functions or activities? We think not. Indeed, highway violations and accidents are more closely related to the size of the population served, not the size of the network. Closing even a major highway will not significantly decrease the cost of any of these governmental services. Therefore, we will not incorporate them here.

Land-Related Costs

Land-related costs actually include the construction impacts on historic or archeological sites, the costs that result from the loss of land being used for specific transport-related purposes, and the costs of urban sprawl. Although these are all land-related costs, the manner in which we treat them may be quite different.

Archeological Sites or Historic Structures

It is not at all uncommon to have highway construction halted when engineers realize that they are infringing on a prehistoric settlement or burial ground. Usually, academics are then asked to visit the site and evaluate its importance. If the site is adjudged as significant, then the roadway may actually be rerouted around the site. The same outcome does not always apply to historic structures for the simple reason that these are more difficult to assess. Obviously, in the United States if the site or structure qualifies under the National Historic Preservation Act of 1966 (or Executive Order 11593), an impact assessment has to be undertaken prior to development. However, if the site or structure does not qualify for inclusion in such an inventory, then it may be legally demolished for a transport project.

During the late 1960s in the town of Brownsville in western Pennsylvania there was a three-story red brick structure that had been built between 1810 and 1820. The house was quite majestic, with a cast iron railing above two semicircular stone stairways leading to the second floor; it had been owned originally by a riverboat captain named Adam Jacobs. Although it was 150 years old, the house was not considered unique, and when a ramp was being constructed for a new bridge on route U.S. 40 across the Monongahela River, the house was demolished.

How should we value such sites and structures? This is a difficult question. Let us assume that an archeological site completely changed our understanding of the Indians who inhabited an area. Let us similarly assume that the demolished building discussed above was the *first* of its type built west of the Appalachian Mountains. Its uniqueness would still not help us to value it in a full-cost project accounting. In effect, all such sites are specific to a given project, and therefore we do not believe they should be included in any *generalized* costing system. Planners should be aware of their existence and attempt to incorporate them individually in analysis as appropriate.

Loss of Open Space and Wetlands

The construction of transportation facilities results in a new use for land, and some land preservation advocates are concerned that such land use results in a general cost that should properly be attributed to the transportation sector. In some cases the land is open space on the fringe area surrounding our cities, but in other cases it may be scarce wetland acreage that should be preserved.

The amount of property used for transportation purposes totals roughly 2% of the land area of the United States, a substantial but not overwhelming proportion. But there is something else at issue here. Most land increases in value when it is made more accessible; conversely, land that is inaccessible is not of much interest to society as a whole. If we wish to claim that certain land loses value because of the construction of transportation facilities, then we must also acknowledge that many proximate parcels gain significant value from the additional access provided.

With regard to specific new land uses that impinge on much-valued wetlands, an environmental impact assessment or analysis would surely identify the current land status, and we see little way that such a project could move ahead without minimizing anticipated environmental impacts. If the concern, however, is with undeveloped land that may be developed for transport purposes, then the owners of such land are reimbursed for its going market value. In the latter case, the land cost is properly considered part of the capital cost of a transport project and is included elsewhere in our costing.

Urban Sprawl

Urban sprawl is the growth of residential areas beyond the current spatial limits of compact urban development. Such sprawl necessitates that urban services and utilities be provided to areas where the population density remains low, thereby resulting in excessive costs being borne by city taxpayers or on other customers of the utilities that are required to serve these areas. Burgeoning urban sprawl may even require the city or utility to purchase additional equipment.

The use of this land beyond the urban area for housing or economic activities is made possible because of a lack of land use controls. If the land were zoned for nonresidential or noncommercial activities (e.g., agriculture or open space), then there would be no sprawl. In effect, although transportation is usually held responsible for urban sprawl, transportation facilities (specifically highways) only allow movement to or from areas beyond the periphery of our cities. Transportation in and of itself does not create sprawl, but transportation without land use control may facilitate it.

Conclusion

We do not view most land-related costs as costs that should properly be included in the generalized transport cost system being developed here, the one exception being the market value of land used during construction of a transport facility. In most other cases, the costs would be nearly impossible to estimate in a full-costing framework. The costs generated by a lack of land use control may be properly viewed as the costs of urban sprawl or as the costs of not having effective zoning ordinances in the county or city of interest, but they are not transport costs.

Loss and Damage

Transportation firms occasionally lose or damage the products they are transporting. When this occurs, the carrier must usually reimburse the shipper or receiver for the loss or damage. Such claims are so common that they are actually viewed as a component of operating costs. Including them here would result in double-counting, and therefore these costs are ignored.

Macroeconomic Costs

There is little doubt that certain aspects of transportation have macroeconomic effects. One of the most obvious examples of this is the macroeconomic impacts of changes in the cost of petroleum imports on a nation's balance-of-payments position and inflation rates. The first of these results from a pronounced imbalance in trade if one country purchases far more petroleum from petroleum-producing countries than they in turn purchase in goods from that country. Inflationary tendencies result from the price of a product increasing without any real change in the quality of the product being purchased. For example, when oil-producing nations agree to increase the price of this fuel, those increases (if substantial enough) may have wide-ranging inflationary impacts.

Is it logical to place the costs of these macroeconomic tendencies on transportation, or should such phenomena more broadly be viewed as the result of a failed national energy policy? We believe the latter. On the other hand, increases in fuel prices are already factored into the price of the fuel and including them again as a cost item here would result in double-counting once again. As for balance-of-payments problems, in this case the imbalance results in certain countries having what are often called excessive petro-dollars. Once again, this problem exists because some countries are unable to live within the limits imposed by their own natural resources and because they have not pursued vigorous enough programs of identifying and developing alternative fuels.

Maintenance Costs

The costs of removing snow from highways and streets, cutting grass and weeds from the roadway medians and shoulders, and patching cracks or potholes in the roads are examples of maintenance costs for the highway sector. Alternative transport modes also have comparable maintenance costs, but since such costs are typically included in overall operating costs, they should not be double-counted here.

Operating Costs

Operating costs apply to all transport modes and include everything from the price of fuel to the cost of washing the vehicle. Lubricants, registration, and licensing fees are also components of operating costs. In some cases operating costs include the wages of workers involved in performing the transport process. In the case of private transport by family members, the value of time is often treated as a separate cost item. Operating costs are standard costs for the operation of all transport modes and should be included in any full-cost accounting scheme.

Manufacturing and Refining

Energy is used in the manufacture of automobiles and other transportation vehicles. This energy resource is depleted in the process, and some would argue that the cost of this energy should be an "indirect cost" of using the transport mode. Others note that the cost of fuels (primarily petroleum) consumed by our transport sector represents only the direct energy costs. Since petroleum is also used in the refining of petroleum as well as in its physical distribution, some believe that the additional fuel used in these processes should also be included in the cost of transportation.

We believe these costs are already reflected in the cost of the final product—vehicles or fuels—and including them here would again lead to some double-counting. On the other hand, there may be some merit in including certain environmentally related costs for such activities if these can be clearly identified.

Military Security for Petroleum Shipments

Some believe that U.S. military forces are maintained in the Middle East primarily to assure that the flow of petroleum will continue without interruption. As a result, they believe that the cost of maintaining a military presence in the Middle East—even the costs of the wars fought in Kuwait in 1991 and Iraq more recently—should be charged to the price of fuel derived from petroleum imports from this area.

Others argue that the natural responsibilities that accompany being a world power militate against this accounting interpretation. In this view, aggressive actions of one country against another (e.g., Iraq against Kuwait) is something that the international community cannot condone and therefore must undo. While this type of reasoning may not extend to preemptive attacks, as in the case of the United States versus Iraq, the line between internal civil conflicts versus flagrant human rights abuses is sometimes difficult for the international community to discern objectively. Our view is that military security costs, even in behalf of secure petroleum shipments, should not be viewed as a component of total transport costs.

Parking-Related Costs

Most parking costs are components of transportation costs. While their significance has become less prominent over time, they still exist. Daily parking charges still apply widely in the downtown districts of major metropolitan areas, while smaller municipalities sometimes waive or minimize them in an attempt to compete effectively with suburban shopping centers and malls. Fines for illegal parking are also very much a part of life in areas subject to metered parking.

Business and industry typically provide parking for their employees. So well ingrained is this practice that employees of most companies would probably initiate a labor stoppage if they were told that they would have to pay to park at their place of work. Government, hospitals, and universities also normally provide parking for their employees at no cost. Occasionally employees may have to pay a nominal annual fee for parking, but it is rarely sufficient to cover the cost of maintaining the parking area, let alone the value of the land used. In Washington, DC, hotel parking spaces are valued between $6500 and $9100 per year. Few government employees would be willing to pay the $25 to $35 per workday to cover this cost, assuming government parking would be valued in the same way. As a result, it is often viewed as part of the cost of doing business or running the government.

As was noted in the introduction to this chapter, parking costs may also relate to maintaining a vehicle at home, whether in a garage (attached or not) or even in one's carport (including the value of the land and roof extension so utilized). Even if no such structure is provided, the cost of one's driveway should be considered as a transportation cost. While parking at the curb may entail no direct transportation costs, further research may shed some light in this area. For our part, we suggest that the analyst be aware of all parking costs and include them if measurable and applicable.

Pollution-Related Transportation Costs

It has been recognized for several decades that transportation is a primary source of air pollution. Initially, the concern was that certain motor vehicle emissions decreased air quality and posed a health risk to the public. The result of this concern was the Clean Air Act of 1970 (as amended) and the National Ambient Air Quality Standards (NAAQS) that set the guidelines for managing air quality in most U.S. cities today. Our knowledge of the impacts of air pollution have broadened in the past several years so that some researchers today regard urban ozone, acid rain (or acid deposition), stratospheric ozone depletion (holes in the ozone layer), and long-term climate change (global warming) as primarily attributable to motor vehicles, or the burning of fossil fuels by motor vehicles. In the subsections below we will look at each of these major atmospheric problems and assess whether they should be incorporated as constituent costs here.

There are several other types of pollution that should be considered in this context, namely, noise, water, and structural pollution. Noise pollution should be apparent to anyone who has stood near an underpass, a rail line, or in a busy intersection downtown in a large city. Water pollution from transportation sources is multifaceted, affecting fresh water bodies and even the oceans of this planet in numerous ways. Structural pollution is actually damage to buildings resulting primarily from vibrations. Each of these will be discussed in greater detail later.

Air Pollution: Air Quality

In the United States the ambient air quality standards in effect today seek to regulate the levels of emissions in our urban areas. These emissions have been found over time to contribute to several atmospheric problems discussed below. The components of these emissions are nitrogen oxides, sulfur oxides, carbon monoxide, hydrocarbons, and particulate matter (also called suspended particulate matter, SPM, or total particulate matter, TPM). Exposure to these atmospheric pollutants can result in numerous medical ailments, ranging from eye irritation to heart disease, cancer, and death. Although attempts have been made to control these emissions, they continue to represent very real cost components for our transport modes.

Researchers more than 20 years ago struggled with how to measure and cost the various emissions. Approaches varied from disaggregating total national damage (a top-down approach) to assessing the technological cost to reduce each of the pollutants emitted (a prevention cost approach). We believe estimates of these costs should be included where possible.

Air Pollution: Urban Ozone

Urban ozone is in large part a product of motor vehicles. This type of ozone is formed by the combination of hydrocarbons and nitrous oxides in the presence of sunlight. If we could reduce the level of urban ozone's component emissions, then we would certainly decrease the amount of urban ozone. This is desirable since urban ozone is believed to be implicated in numerous respiratory and eye ailments afflicting individuals. We implicitly examine urban ozone as a result of the pollution created by the individual air pollutants previously cited.

Air Pollution: Acid Rain

Acid rain emerged as a recognizable environmental problem during the mid- to late 1970s. In general, acid deposition, or acid rain, consists of either nitric acid or sulfuric acid, which in turn derives primarily from nitrogen oxides or sulfur oxides. The nitrogen oxides may emanate from either internal combustion engines or manufacturing processes. Sulfur oxides may also derive from motor vehicles burning fossil fuels, but more often than not they originate in the emissions from electric utilities or manufacturing plants burning coal that is high in sulfur content. Once the emissions are airborne, they are transported by air currents to areas of the country (notably the northeastern United States) that are unable to handle the resulting acid deposition. The soils of the Northeast are generally thinner (in depth) than elsewhere and naturally acidic in many cases. As a result, acid deposition makes the soils even more acidic.

The primary impact of acid rain appears to be on trees and the fish population of lakes and streams. The greatest damage to trees results from the acids disturbing their metabolism, thereby increasing their vulnerability to parasites, pests, and drought. Fish populations are reduced by the acid's deadly impact on insects, a major component of their diet. In other cases, the acids in runoff catalyze aluminum in the soils, which once deposited in lakes and ponds can lead to the formation of fungus on fish gills, which in turn eventually suffocates the fish.

Additionally, the human health impacts from acid rain include respiratory problems for the very young and the very old (i.e., those with developing lungs and those whose lungs are less able to withstand exposure to such acids). While relatively uncommon, these health impacts, result most often from acid rain in the form of mist (i.e., acid fog).

Damage to property is also caused by acid rain, chiefly in the form of acid "burns" on metal surfaces or the dissolving of limestone on the surface of statues, cemetery markers, or buildings. The author has been told that the undercoating placed on new cars in the United States today is specially formulated to guard against rusting attributable to exposure to acid rain. Older structures that contain copper in their roofing are also susceptible to leaks when exposed to acid rain.

Despite the significance of the acid rain problem, we do not believe it should be included as an *explicit* component of transport costs—based primarily on two considerations. First, it is uncertain precisely how much of the acid rain problem may be properly attributed to the transport sector. Motor vehicles emit sulfur oxides, which rise due to convection currents and are transported long distances by air currents, but the overwhelming evidence suggests that power plants are the chief generator of acid rain. Second, the Clean Air Act Amendments of 1990 seek to reduce the levels of nitrogen oxides and sulfur oxides emitted. In all likelihood, the problem of acid rain in the United States may soon be ameliorated by existing legislation if it is implemented strenuously enough.

We do believe that sulfur oxide and nitrogen oxide emissions should be considered as components of full transportation costing, recognizing their contribution to several other environmental problems. However, of the two, nitrous oxides are clearly the more troublesome pollutant.

Air Pollution: Stratospheric Ozone Depletion

This planet is surrounded by a layer of ozone, sometimes called stratospheric ozone to distinguish it from urban ozone. This layer of ozone protects the planet and its inhabitants by decreasing the amount of incoming ultraviolet solar radiation that reaches the surface. It was recognized some 30 years ago that certain anthropogenic gases had the capability of damaging this protective layer of ozone. By the mid-1980s it became evident that the level of ozone was significantly dropping in the spring and that a "hole" was developing in the ozone layer over the southern polar region. In addition there appears to be a general thinning of the ozone level, which may or may not be related to the formation of the hole.

The primary gases involved in damaging the ozone layer are chlorofluorocarbons (CFCs) and halons. CFCs were used for several years as propellants in spray cans, but their use for this purpose was halted in the United States in 1978. Butane and propane are often used as propellants today. However, CFCs (specifically, Freon 11 and Freon 12) continued to be used as coolants. Halons are used primarily in fighting fires.

In 1987 more than 30 nations convened in Montreal to discuss limiting the levels of CFCs being produced. The agreement reached, referred to as the Montreal Protocol, sought to freeze production at 1986 levels. It was soon realized that this level would not halt the damage, and as a result subsequent agreements forged in London and Copenhagen ultimately succeeded in halting all CFC production by the end of 1995 and phasing out halons by 2000 (with a couple of exceptions).

There are essentially two sets of problems that may occur unless continued damage to the ozone layer is eliminated or reversed. The first is a human health problem. Humans exposed to excessive ultraviolet radiation often develop skin cancers, cataracts, and retinal damage. The second problem is that increases in ultraviolet radiation could potentially destroy plankton (or phytoplankton) populations in the polar oceans. The impact of this destruction would be a complete disturbance of the food chain of the oceans and the potential elimination of large populations of marine life, and the loss of these food resources to humans.

While this is a significant problem, corrective actions appear to be under way. However, we may very well have to live with the problem for many years to come since the chemical reactions already unleashed in the stratosphere may not soon abate. In addition, the HCFCs that are being used as replacements for CFCs are also detrimental—just *less* detrimental.

We will not charge this problem to the transport sector, since it is difficult to determine the extent of the damage that has occurred or will occur. Certainly at this time the impacts are not yet overwhelming. There is a strong possibility that the problem will continue into the future, but it appears likely that (at least in the United States) CFC and halon emissions will cease altogether.

Climate Change

The phenomenon referred to as "climate change" today is more frequently called "global warming" in the popular media. To understand global warming (see the earlier discussion in Chapter 3) one must be aware that this planet is surrounded by gases sometimes referred to as "greenhouse" gases, and their impact on the planet, sometimes referred to as the "greenhouse effect," is such that it makes the planet warm enough for human life. By now, most scientists have concluded that we are fast adding far too many greenhouse gases to the atmosphere. Most environmental scientists further believe that these additional gases will cause a "forcing" of the greenhouse effect, which would result in a discernible warming of the planet. The major scientific question is not whether the planet will warm—that is taken as a given—but rather *by how much* it will warm.

Of the gases that contribute to this problem, the transport sector is responsible for generating enormous quantities of carbon dioxide, methane, carbon monoxide (which converts to carbon dioxide), nitrogen oxides, some sulfur oxides, and some residual chlorofluorocarbons. So, there is some basis for believing that the transport sector should be held accountable for some of the damage attributable to this problem.

What types of damage are we talking about? While several studies address the specific impacts that are anticipated, it is difficult to say conclusively whether "climate change" will be primarily negative or positive, on balance (Black, 1990). Certainly a warmer environment in North America would increase some growing seasons and shorten others. Rainfall patterns would change, but we don't know where and by how much (although some progress has been made on this question, as noted in Chapter 3). While it would be easier to warm certain portions of the continent during the winter it would be more difficult to cool other portions during the summer. Crop production areas might shift with temperature changes. Warming would cause some melting of the polar ice caps and mid-latitude glaciers, which would result in an increase in the sea level, as would thermal expansion attributable to the oceans warming, but massive flooding would not necessarily ensue. Sea surges during storms are of far more concern, like those experienced in hurricane Katrina in 2005 in the Gulf Coast region of the United States. We know little more so far about the net impacts of global warming.

The past couple of years' experience has convinced many members of the scientific community that government will probably not take much action to try to reverse global warming until its adverse consequences are more obvious. Unfortunately, if one waits that long, it may then be too late to ameliorate the situation. For this reason, the scientific community appears to be moving away from sole concern with abatement and toward ideas about adaptation.

While the Kyoto protocols conversely, are a stark testament to abatement strategies, specifically targeting emission reductions by the developed nations of the world, the U.S. Senate—at least prior to the Obama administration—was little inclined to ratify the treaty. Nevertheless, other countries are actively involved in reducing their emissions of carbon dioxide.

Returning to transport costing, our position is that we do not know for certain yet whether global warming will generate more costs than benefits. Absent that degree of certainty, we see no reason to regard it as a clear cost to the transport sector. Nevertheless, we do believe that a full costing framework should attempt to value and cost several greenhouse gas emissions, though not necessarily for their greenhouse role.

Other Types of Pollution

Noise Pollution

Noise in excess of 50 decibels is generally annoying to individuals and may cause stress, headaches, and other physiological disturbances. For some individuals, noise may affect their housing decisions, and as a result it is believed that excessive ambient noise levels reduce the value of housing. In general this perceived difference in housing values in the presence of varying noise levels has been used as the basis for valuing the cost of noise.

There are undoubtedly situations where noise is intolerable—for example, an apartment next to an elevated railway—but such instances are the exceptions rather than the rule. Inhabitants in certain areas may actually notice the *absence* of noise more than its presence. It is usually only in urban areas that noise is bad enough that it would constitute a component of transport cost. In general, we would not include noise in our system because of the difficulty in valuing it and the fact that it is not encountered in most areas as a significant cost item.

Structural Pollution

What is called "structural pollution" here is more often referred to as "vibration damage." In general, trucks are believed to be the major cause of vibration damage. Usually, it is not the passage of a truck that creates the vibration but rather the presence of a pothole, or similar road deformity, that results in a sudden drop of the bed of the truck. The clattering impact is what causes the most significant structural pollution. One exception may be found in the Swiss Alps, where the tremendous number of trucks en route from Germany to Italy seem to be causing structural damage to very old housing. Huge trucks passing through the streets of a city like Rome can also cause significant vibration damage. Anyone who has lived within 1/8 of a mile of a rail freight line has also encountered intense vibrations in their homes; it may be only a light rattling of glassware in a cupboard, but it is nonetheless unmistakable. The question is, How significant are such vibrations in terms of total transport costs.

In certain situations vibrations may be highly significant, but typically to assess damages we need information on far more variables (surface conditions and heavy truck volumes by highway segment) than are normally available. For most of the transport system, we do not believe structural pollution is significant enough to bother including here.

Water Pollution

Runoff from streets, roads, and runways into our streams, rivers, lakes, and coastal waters represents a major source of water pollution today. The transport sector is responsible for disseminating such contaminants as rubber, asbestos, gasoline, an array of petrochemicals used as fuels or lubricants, as well as pesticides used for weed control and chemicals used to melt ice and snow. There is no question about this—the only question is how to go about valuing this pollution.

Water treatment facilities are generally able to handle these pollutants as part of their general treatment of all waste water. Using our avoidable cost criterion, one should ask if the absence of transport-generated pollutants would significantly affect the manner in which waste water and sewage are treated. If this could be answered with any consistency from one location to another, then we might have a basis for valuing water pollution attributable to the transport sector. Since there is no research on this question, we will ignore water pollution.

Property Values

In theory the presence of transport facilities increases the value of property by increasing its accessibility. Locating economic activities along major highway corridors is an example of this. There are situations, however, where the value of property may decrease due to the construction of transport facilities. A limited-access, at-grade highway such as an interstate highway within a metropolitan area may actually decrease local accessibility. In certain cases transport facilities may create noise and thereby damage property values. An obvious example would be the construction of an airport in such a way that the runway approaches are immediately above residential areas. Sometimes the houses most affected are purchased by the airport authority since it is recognized that the airport has negatively impacted the value of the housing.

In general, however, we believe that greater transport access increases, rather than decreases, the value of property. While not universally true, it describes the most usual outcome. Therefore, we do not consider transport as creating a cost for the housing or residential property sector.

Repair and Rehabilitation

The costs of repairing and rehabilitating our vehicles, streets, roads, and highways are legitimate costs of the transport sector. The repair of personal vehicles is a component of operating costs, and since these are covered elsewhere they will not be examined here. Aircraft, locomotives, rail cars, and other privately held vehicles have their repair included as part of their operating costs as well.

Repairing or rehabilitating highways and publicly owned facilities is covered through taxes, fares charged, or subsidies. These are generally considered as part of the operating costs as well, and we will not examine them as a separate item here. However, if some administrative unit must use general funds for this purpose, this portion should be considered a cost.

Subsidies

Several transport modes are subsidized in the United States today. The ones with which we are most familiar are probably urban transit and Amtrak, but there are indirect subsidies that go to several different modes in the form of state and federal government grants. Included would be low-interest loans, airport capital grants, and the dredging of rivers and ports by the U.S. Army Corps of Engineers. In the United Kingdom subsidies to the many corporate descendants of British Rail would also be included. Some might also include certain academic research in this category, but to the extent that this research is covered through highway taxes, it is probably already counted. We would include the cost of operations and facilities as operating costs for the different modes of transport. We would not necessarily concern ourselves with whether fares plus subsidies cover the cost of transit operations—our focus is on the costs, not whether profits are realized.

Time Costs

Our time has value. As a society we generally try to make the best use of our time, and this is why we value it. We know that time spent in travel also has value and that this value varies in our society as a function of earning power or productivity. We don't know exactly who is driving or traveling at any given time, and as a result we simply calculate the average value of time for an area and say that this figure applies to all individuals. In general, this value is related to the average manufacturing wage in the area, approximating one-half of that wage level.

This calculation is obviously an underestimate in the case of commercial travel. In that case, the driver and others in the vehicle are being paid at a rate closer to the average manufacturing rate. When commercial vehicles are slowed by congestion, there is a very real cost to these economic activities. We therefore value the time of commercial truck occupants at the level of the manufacturing wage in the area.

Transportation Equity

Our automotive-oriented society has created problems for all those who lack ready access to this mode of transportation, namely, the elderly, handicapped, and poor. We have not included the young since they often have access to transport from their parents, unless the parents are poor. Is it reasonable to assign a cost to this equity issue, and if so, how do we place a precise value on it? Let's say that there is an equity issue involved here. Let us go a step further, however, and say that we attempt to correct this policy error on the part of government by providing public transit. Let us also say that the cost of public transit is the cost of transportation equity. Therefore, the cost of transportation equity will be indirectly considered as the cost of public transit, and we see no need to include it as a separate cost component. If a community does not have public transit, it presumably views any equity question as insignificant, and so would we.

MEASURING THE EXTERNAL COSTS

During the past two decades researchers have sought to measure several *external* costs related to transportation (see Friedrich & Bickel, 2001; Quinet, 2004). One must applaud those efforts because such measurements are needed to help inform objective decision making. At the same time, it is sometimes discomforting to see such components as military security costs and global warming costs included in these discussions. There must be some point where, having included the most important costs, the rest can be set aside. Table 9.7 lists the costs included in a U.S. research project that developed ALTERNAT, a computer program for evaluating the costs of alternative modal solutions in various geographic contexts (see Black et al., 1995; Black, 1999). This list is significantly shorter than the one reviewed in this chapter, but the ALTERNAT methodology sought to incorporate only those costs that are realistically viewed as contributing to the overall cost of transportation, that is, the ones that are not avoidable.

In certain cases, some of the costs noted earlier but not incorporated in the methodology developed, may be significant. For example, noise pollution costs were not

---

TABLE 9.7. Costs Included in the ALTERNAT Study

- Accident costs not covered by insurance
- Capital costs (not covered through transport taxes)
- Maintenance costs for facilities (highways, bridges, etc.)
- Operating costs of vehicles (locomotives, airplanes, motor vehicles, bicycles)
  - Insurance (or loss and damage for self-insured)
  - Fuel
  - Oil and lubrication
  - Licenses
  - Repair and other vehicular maintenance costs
  - Taxes (state and federal)
  - Purchase price and interest
- Parking costs (fines and fees)
- Pollution costs
  - Nitrogen oxide
  - Carbon dioxide
  - Carbon monoxide
  - Sulfur oxide
  - Suspended particulate matter
  - Hydrocarbons
- Rehabilitation costs
- Value of time (personal and commercial)

included in our assessment. This is not to say that they are unimportant—they are just not very significant in most cases. In those cases where such costs are important for planning, then planners should include them in their analyses.

CONCLUSIONS

The costs reviewed in this chapter are the major costs that one encounters in examinations of full costing of transportation. A number of the costs cited in the literature have been dismissed, and justifications for doing so have been offered as appropriate. Undoubtedly, some will disagree with these judgments, and they are certainly free to include whatever costs they view as relevant in their studies.

Another point that should be emphasized is that this chapter examined only costs. It did not examine benefits explicitly, nor did it explore the methodology known as cost–benefit analysis. Nevertheless, those who are eager to include several *external* indirect costs in their project assessments should recognize that, down the road, someone will inevitably advocate the inclusion of external indirect *benefits* as well.

CHAPTER 10

Pricing and Taxation

Any policies or strategies to reduce the problems
of transport without strong pricing components
will only produce weak results.
—LEE SCHIPPER (1996)

There is no need here to get into the economists' approach to pricing as it applies to road traffic, but those who have such an interest should consult the works of Pigou (1920), Vickrey (1969), and others (see, *inter alia*, Button, 1984, 1993a; Morrison, 1986) for classic treatments of the subject, or a more current introduction to the same by Rouwenthal and Verhoef (2006). The last source is intended as an introduction to this broad area for those who are not trained in economics.

For our purposes, it should be understood that increasing the price of a good or service without increasing or improving any other aspect of that good or service tends to make it less attractive to us. Therefore, if we take transport as a service and increase the price without any other changes, we generally use it less. On the other hand, if we are offered something more attractive at a higher price, we may find this acceptable, assuming we can afford it. In effect, this is what it is all about. We are going to try to alter travel behavior using such pricing approaches.

We begin this discussion with a review of congestion-free pricing, followed by examination of such proposals as parking charges, fuel tax increases, VMT (vehicle miles traveled) taxes, and emissions fees. Each of these is intended to cut down on travel or decrease the attractiveness of motor vehicles as a mode of travel.

CONGESTION-FREE PRICING

The goals of congestion-free pricing are the same as for other types of travel demand management techniques, namely, to reduce congestion by encouraging drivers to use other routes, transport modes, or times of day for their trips. In some cases drivers may alter their destinations or even decrease the number of trips taken either through trip chaining (taking care of several trips with a single itinerary that links destinations "chained" together) or by canceling discretionary trips altogether.

As these are rather broad goals, some specific objectives may be used to evaluate the level of success of the pricing strategy employed. One of these is clearly reducing the number of points of congestion along the road system, and another is minimizing the length of individual queues that do form. If we get the reductions anticipated, we should see relatively smooth traffic flow with improved fuel economy and reductions in emissions.

In practical terms, congestion-free pricing involves charging a fee for using certain lanes of roadways that experience congestion, thereby discouraging many from using those lanes and keeping them free of congestion. Early on, academic commentators suggested that the fee would work best if it varied with the level of traffic, but that approach was viewed as not technologically feasible in the 1950s and 1960s. Today with the technological constraints having all but disappeared, such fees are typically based on average traffic volumes for different times of the day. Of course, various drivers may value trips quite differently, and one's level of income may significantly affect one's use of particular roadways but planners and policymakers naturally are well aware of these drawbacks.

Corridors that have implemented congestion-free pricing generally are located where alternative routes are scarce or offer considerably longer trip times (e.g., along the California coast). Some also offer free travel for high-occupancy vehicles, which may include buses, carpools, vanpools, and vehicles with more than the driver in the vehicle. The crucial attribute of these facilities is the presence of one or more free-flowing lanes for those paying the fee.

In general, users of the facility create an electronic account that covers their fees. Vehicles using the facility typically are equipped with a transponder located near the front windshield, and each time the vehicle passes through the scanner the driver's account is billed. This process is much like that for the toll collection devices located on toll roads throughout the United States and elsewhere. The major difference between these congestion-free pricing roads and toll roads is that the latter do not provide a free-flowing lane and their revenues typically go to cover original construction, maintenance, or reconstruction costs for the facility (though they may be used for other purposes). Two of the better-known congestion pricing highways in the United States SR 91 and Interstate 15, are located in California. We will discuss each in turn.

SR 91 Express Lanes, Orange County, California

The SR 91 project is a 10-mile-long highway with four lanes of express toll located in the median of the larger highway. The system operates continuously, 7 days a week and 24 hours per day, with tolls ranging from $1.00 during the late night to $4.75 during the evening peak period. Fees are assessed automatically and may be paid electronically only.

This operation is typical of the types of systems described earlier. There are free-flowing lanes, but there are also free lanes for vehicles with more than one occupant. This highway is actually operated by a private transportation company under a lease arrangement, with the state of California retaining title to the land used.

I-15 Hot Lanes, San Diego County, California

The I-15 project is an 8-mile-long system with two reversible lanes in the middle of an eight-lane freeway. Vehicles with two or more occupants pay no toll. The tolls are dynamic and vary from $0.75 to $4.00 in most cases but can reach $8.00 in very congested periods. Toll collection is based entirely on an electronic payment system.

In general both of these projects are very successful. There are numerous other projects around the United States that follow similar models, as described by Sullivan (2003).

CONGESTION-FREE AREAS

The preceding discussion focused primarily on congestion-free roadways that were made so through the use of congestion-free pricing. Normally it is a very straightforward situation: you get on the highway and remain on it until you leave it. The problem becomes more complicated once you start including numerous other roads, or more specifically a whole area. Two such situations that have internationally received considerable media attention are the "London Congestion Charging Scheme" in the United Kingdom and the "Area Licensing Scheme" in Singapore. Let us examine each in more detail.

London

The British Parliament gave the Greater London Authority (GLA) the power to charge for road use in 1999, and in 2003 the GLA implemented the London Congestion Charging Scheme, an area licensing scheme covering central London, or at least 22 square kilometers of that area; in 2007 this area was expanded to include parts of West London. All vehicles entering, leaving, driving, or parking in the area when the charge is in effect (7:00 A.M.–6:30 P.M.) must pay a congestion charge. As of 2008 the charge was £8 or ($14.93 U.S.), with failure to pay resulting in a fine of £60 ($111.98 U.S.) if remitted within 14 days. The monitoring of vehicles is accomplished through a system of cameras. There are exemptions for motorcycles, bicycles, and mopeds, vehicles used by the disabled, buses, and taxis. Various government vehicles are also exempt, as are some alternative-fuel vehicles if they pay a £10 ($18.66 U.S.) annual registration fee. Vehicles of residents who live inside the zone also are assessed only an annual registration fee (Santos, 2005).

The scheme would appear to be responsible for an 18% decrease in vehicles entering the congestion-free zone. Of these, it is believed that about half of these trips have been diverted to public transport. About one-quarter of the vehicles have been diverted around the zone, not passing through it, and about one-eighth of the trips were diverted to another mode—taxis, walking, and so forth. The remainder appear to have been diverted to times not covered by the congestion fee, or perhaps the trips were discretionary and were not made at all.

The London program is generally viewed as a success, and other cities may eventually adopt similar schemes (New York City briefly considered that idea in 2008). The GLA has considered extending the zone to include other neighborhoods and/or increasing the fee to discourage even more trips.

Singapore

Singapore's Area Licensing Scheme (ALS), originally begun in 1975, was made more systematic and comprehensive by the Road Pricing System in 1995 and Electronic Road Pricing (ERP) in 1998. We will focus our discussion on the ERP program. Covering traffic in the central business district from 7 A.M. to 7 P.M. and expressways and outer-ring roads from 7:30 A.M. to 9:30 A.M., this system utilizes smart-card technology extensively. When the vehicles enter areas covered by the program, charges are assessed via a transponder and a specific amount is deducted from the driver's account. Transponders were placed in 97% of the city's vehicles at no charge prior to the beginning of the program. The amount charged for use of specified areas varies by vehicle type and time of day, failure to pay resulting in fines of approximately £10 ($16.44 U.S.).

It is difficult to assess the relative success of the Singapore program because several programs were already in place prior to the ERP programs inception. It is well established that vehicle entries into Singapore declined by 70% under the original ALS program. Initiation of the ERP program resulted in an additional 15% decline in traffic volumes. Prevailing vehicular speeds were generally kept in the optimum range of 20–30 kilometers per hour (Santos, 2005).

In general, both the London and Singapore programs appear to have worked quite well. This does not mean these programs have no critics—such is not the case. But from a sustainability point of view it has to be noted that both the London and Singapore programs have been quite successful.

As noted already, the success of these programs led New York City to consider such a scheme for portions of Manhattan. A congestion-free pricing program actively promoted by Mayor Michael Bloomberg during 2007 and early 2008 died in April 2008, mostly as a result of active opposition within the New York state legislature. Such a program may well be enacted in New York during the next decade, but if so it will require much more groundwork and adroit political sponsorship before that occurs.

PARKING CHARGES AND TAXES

Parking charges work in a more indirect manner, comparatively speaking. While not constituting a direct tax or surcharge on the trip, they make the trip more expensive at the destination end and in this way increase overall trip costs. Initial attempts to place prohibitive taxes on parking levies in the United States met with some resistance in the courts (the argument being that it is unconstitutional to target specific economic activities with particularly onerous taxes). But this argument generally gave way to more specific proposals related to urban development, and these measures were found to be acceptable.

Momentarily leaving aside pricing mechanisms as such, we sometimes find that cities may zone an area for parking only by local residents, in effect adding the cost of a traffic ticket to parking in those areas. The goal obviously is to get people to not use the automobile for making a trip and to decrease local traffic in specific areas, and to some extent it succeeds. But it is not always a very popular solution; for example, local residents become upset when their parents or children are unable to park in the zoned areas.

Still and Simmonds (2000) note that (1) changes in the provision of parking and its price can alter the cost of travel, the convenience of travel, the mode selected, and the timing of trips through the day; (2) parking changes can also affect the attractiveness of destinations; (3) the use of space for parking prevents it from being used for other purposes; and (4) fees for parking can be a significant revenue source for urban areas.

Regarding whether parking fees lead to changed transit modes and decisions not to make certain trips, it can be noted that the former generally occurs. In particular, higher-priced parking leads in some cases to increased use of mass transit. As to whether it influences the decision to make a trip, the evidence is less clear (Shiftan & Burd-Eden, 2001).

While increases in parking fees attributable to taxation and other causes are not particularly popular with the driving public, they are particularly opposed by retail businesses that view them as making other destinations with low-priced parking more attractive. Those areas with the lowest fees or no fees are usually the local shopping malls. To ensure the viability of central-city shopping areas and to remain competitive with suburban retailers, municipalities have often removed parking meters and allowed free on-street parking.

Feitelson and Rotem (2004) have suggested that a flat surface parking tax based on the amount of land the parking covers might be most equitable overall. Their concern, however, is more with the proper use of urban space than with attempting to control trip making and transport mode choices.

POLLUTION/CHARACTERISTICS TAXES

Economists have long had an interest in taxing vehicles based on the pollution that they produce and its detrimental effects on urban air quality. This section addresses some of the more problematic aspects of implementing this idea, focusing in on some very real practical problems with such a tax.

Since all pollutants are not equally damaging, determining the correct level of the potential tax that might compensate for damages is not a clearcut decision. For example, the damage done by urban-based ozone depletion is significant, but weather conditions as much as the absolute level of nitrogen oxides and hydrocarbons radically affect the depletion rates. Assuming we could estimate these values, we would still have problems with the levels of emissions. Depending on how you drive, how well you maintain your vehicle, and how much congestion you encounter, the levels of emissions for different pollutants can be quite different even from the same vehicle. So, this is generally viewed as a very difficult tax to determine and to implement.

Johnstone and Karousakis (1999) have advocated a vehicle characteristics tax, a tax on the attributes of the vehicle that are thought to be closely related to emissions, such as vehicle weight, age, fuel used, horsepower, and the type of fuel injection system. Such taxes have already been implemented in Denmark, France, Italy, the Netherlands, Spain, and Germany (Fergusson & Taylor, 1999). While this approach deals with some of the problems, one must still demonstrate that taxing the vehicle's attributes ultimately diminishes the level of emissions. The tax could easily enough be administered through existing sales or registration taxes that are common across the United States.

Kavalec and Setiawan (1997) carried out a simulation study of the potential impacts of implementing a pollution fee based on per-mile emissions of reactive organic gases and nitrogen oxides. Based on the three separate simulations undertaken, the fee would result in reductions in pollution, vehicle miles of travel, and gasoline demand. The simulations suggested that new vehicle sales would increase as drivers shifted toward more efficient vehicles. They also noted that the tax would likely be regressive, as the oldest and least efficient vehicles were disproportionately owned by lower-income individuals. One should bear in mind, of course, that this was just a simulation study, not an empirical analysis.

FUEL TAX INCREASES

The first state-level gasoline tax was enacted in 1919, and by 1929 every state had adopted such a tax; One could say: "Never before in the history of taxation [had] a major tax been so generally accepted in so short a period." Of course, people wanted better roads at the time and thus could see a clear personal benefit from the tax. The fact that the Federal Highway Act of 1921 provided matching grants to the states for highway construction also helped sway public opinion in favor of fuel taxes since the states had no other dedicated source of the matching funds. Interestingly, some 40 years later many states were slow to accept federal urban mass transit capital funds for lack of specific matching funds (Smerk, 1991).

In spite of its rapid acceptance initially by states, the motor vehicle fuel tax is not easily increased at the state or federal level. Both levels of government assess such a tax on fuel. As of 2009, the federal tax was $0.184 per gallon of gasoline, and the average state tax was $0.185 (API, 2009). Although we have seen significant price rises in gasoline costs during the first decade of the 21st century, there is a general reluctance to increase this tax by even 1 or 2 cents. This blanket reluctance to raise taxes—perhaps the artifact of mindless political posturing—is all the more unfortunate because the current level of taxes from this source is clearly insufficient to cover maintenance costs on the existing highway system.

The federal gasoline tax became a hot political issue briefly during the 2008 presidential campaign, with some candidates urging temporary suspension of the tax during the summer, given the inordinate increases in gasoline prices that consumers had lately had to bear. This was a silly idea in reality since the price was fluctuating comparable amounts or more on a *weekly* basis and the funds were definitely needed for the existing highway and transit infrastructure.

Minor increases in the fuel tax at the state or federal level would not likely have any impact on fuel consumption, given that substantial increases during the 2007–2008 period are only now beginning to have real impact on travel demand. Some changes of mode observed, have been mainly from automobile travel to mass transit, but these were in response to nearly a dollar's increase in average price per gallon.

Aside from highway maintenance and reconstruction costs increasing, while fuel taxes remain the same, there is also the problem of whether fuel economy has increased sufficiently that it may also be contributing to the problem. If we play this scenario out, then there has to be genuine concern down the road for large numbers of hybrid vehicles since these could potentially use much less fuel and thereby extract lesser revenues as tax.

This problem has been largely anticipated, and research is currently under way to evaluate the feasibility of a system of taxation that would monitor vehicles remotely and assess taxes based on total miles driven on various levels of roadway. The system was initially conceived as one relying on satellites and transponders, but instead it may eventually involve the use of microwave towers and transponders.

CONCLUSIONS

Over time we will likely see more and more cases of congestion-free pricing on U.S. highways. The most recent comprehensive federal highway legislation gave states permission to establish tolls on existing interstate highways. How far this trend will go currently remains uncertain, but such projects as well as other types of pricing must ultimately enjoy the long-term support of those affected by them, and this prospect does not seem likely (see Schade & Schlag, 2003).

Congestion-free pricing along the lines of the London or Singapore model may increase as well, as local areas see fewer and fewer options in terms of limiting vehicles in central areas. Although there are undoubtedly U.S. cities that would like to try such approaches, this is not likely to happen in the near term. A key element in London and Singapore's success was the presence of a high level of public transit. It is questionable whether many U.S. cities have the requisite level of transit service to go congestion-free successfully. Cities that might are on the eastern seaboard, like New York, whose trial balloon in that direction was, as noted, relatively quickly deflated.

The United States does use parking charges and taxes, and these are likely to continue. Care must be taken not to damage the viability of central shopping districts, however, if there is continued movement in this direction. What would make the most sense as a way of limiting urban traffic would be an increase in fuel taxes, but these initiatives are typically so politically unpopular that, if recent experience is any guide the tax increase would have to be both substantial and closely paired with the public's desire for energy independence for it to have a significant impact on traffic or emissions.

Pollution can be curtailed somewhat by a decrease in traffic volumes attributable to any of the foregoing actions. There is nevertheless something attractive about a pollution tax itself. Since we are not in a position to price this very well at present, we are probably best advised to consider a characteristics tax (in its stead) that seeks to contain total pollution generated.

PLANNING

CHAPTER 11

Urban Form
Planning for Sustainability

> Land/travel linkages are both multidimensional and difficult to
> deconstruct, and little if any hard evidence indicates how the built
> environment can reliably manipulate travel behavior. The best advice
> might be to keep expectations low until more is known. The risks of
> doing otherwise go beyond disappointment, and include unintended
> consequences such as worsening traffic problems.
> —RANDALL CRANE (2000)

It has long been recognized that urban form, the shape and geographic area occupied by a city, can influence the length of virtually every trip made in the urban area
and as a result the total travel in a city. If we wish to decrease fuel use, congestion,
pollution, and crashes, which also increase with travel, it is desirable to reduce the
factors that increase the travel needed in a given environment. We begin with the
influence of various classic urban shapes on the amount of travel needed; this is
followed by a discussion of the influence of models in this area and some notions
from new urbanism planning as well as an evaluation of the merits of compact cities
in the transport sustainability area. A general discussion of land use control in the
United States concludes the chapter.

It should not surprise the reader to find that changes in land use offer little
toward making existing urban areas sustainable, generally because these areas are
already well established. We may be able to have some impact on land use at the
fringes of cities, but not enough to seriously alter major transport sustainability
problems. Internal changes in existing cities will take far longer than North American and European cities can afford to wait, but the ideas may be of value to rapidly
motorizing cities in the developing world.

This chapter also examines urban sprawl, one aspect of urban land use that has
always been viewed as a contributor to nonsustainability in the transport sector.

Some of the emerging literature in this area that views sprawl from a somewhat different perspective will also be explored. Before we move on, it is important to understand a personal bias of the author that overshadows nearly all that follows in this chapter. We will simply refer to it as a caveat.

A CAVEAT ON THE LINKAGE BETWEEN TRAVEL AND LAND USE

In a very real sense, transportation planning began during the middle of the 20th century. The rapid growth in automobiles that occurred during the post-World War II period began creating congestion that was having a negative impact on the economy. There was a need for some type of metropolitan area transportation planning, which then arose in several cities (Detroit, Chicago, Pittsburgh, Philadelphia) during the 1950s. Early efforts to understand urban travel were crude, and the modeling was experimental.

There were two flow models that had seen some use in the social sciences, primarily in migration studies, namely, the intervening opportunities model of Stouffer (1940) and the gravity model of Stewart (1942). A variation of the former was used in the Pittsburgh Area Transportation Study (PATS), and the latter was suggested for use in several areas. Details of the operation of these models are not necessary here. Suffice it to say that both of these models make large areas (in terms of population or other measures of size) attractive as destinations, particularly if they are located at short travel distances. However, urban travel is not migration. There are many reasons why one might want to travel a short distance to a large city where there naturally would be more employment opportunities. Much of urban travel is repetitive, particularly the journey to work, and one might believe—as early planners believed—that individuals would want to keep these distances short as well. After all, movement was difficult in many parts of the United States, given the street systems that had been built, in many cases prior to the automobile.

Planners soon realized that the important constraint on travel was not distance but travel time. They believed it was possible to construct our way out of congestion by building more and longer urban highways that increased the length of urban trips but decreased the travel time involved. Bypasses were built in many urban areas with this in mind. These were followed by (usually interstate highway system) beltways (or ring roads in Europe) around most of the major metropolitan areas. In other cases arterials were built from the suburbs directly into the central city.

The gravity model became the dominant model for transportation planning by the mid-1960s. We now use travel time factors in the models, as opposed to distance, and trips are assigned to destinations, which, other things being equal, place a heavy emphasis on trying to go to the nearest places in terms of travel time. The question is, How many of our trip purposes are truly satisfied by the nearest place that can "satisfy" such trip purposes? Probably none of them. If this is the case, then when we do such planning studies we are seriously underestimating the amount of travel that actually takes place; but that is not our primary concern here.

Planners have embraced the operation of the gravity model as an accurate model of reality. But, if the model truly reflects reality, then wouldn't it be desirable to try to have all of the common trip purposes located near the population? In effect, the entire field of new urbanism planning is trying to decrease travel in this manner, but we don't necessarily go to the nearest place that will satisfy the purpose of our trip, no matter how close it is; and attempts to alter land uses and decrease trip lengths with this in mind are not likely to succeed. Our reality is far more complicated than the gravity model.

An idea related to this has been proposed by Wegener (1995). He has noted that, for many urban areas, we have what can best be described as "ubiquitous accessibility," in which it is fairly easy to get just about anywhere. If this is the case, then most of the theory regarding urban movement and land use begins to fall apart. We won't go that far here, but we do believe that current theory may have far more value in teaching concepts than in planning cities. One might well suggest that, were travel to become more difficult, then the old theoretical ideas might have greater value. That may be, but we have seen some major changes in travel fuel costs during the new millennium, and indications thus far are that it has had only a minor impact on travel and travel behavior and probably no impact on destination choices.

A somewhat similar caveat has been offered by Boarnet and Crane (2001) with regard to research in this area. They note that many of the models in this research area "assume that causality flows from land use and urban design to travel behavior. That assumption is commonplace in the recent literature; studies often leap from the observed correlations between urban design and travel behavior to the conclusion that design changes can cause changes in individual travel" (p. 842). Such thinking overlooks the complexity of urban travel and its apparent link to land use. Crane (2000) has gone further, stating that "little verifiable evidence supports the contention that changes in urban form will affect travel as intended at the scale proposed" (p. 3).

Giuliano and Narayan (2003) found different results in their comparative study of travel in the United States and Great Britain, concluding that "differences in daily trips and miles traveled are explained by differences in both urban form and household income" (p. 2295). At the same time, differences in urban form are defined by these authors primarily as differences in metropolitan area size and population densities, perhaps not the best measures but ones often requisite for such national comparisons.

Badoe and Miller (2000) undertook an examination of several different studies of the interaction of transportation and land use. They concluded that "the findings of these studies are mixed, with some suggesting that land use policies emphasizing higher urban densities, traditional neighborhood design, and land use mix do result in declines to auto ownership and use, while enhancing patronage of the more environmentally friendly modes of transit and walk. Other studies find this impact to be at best very weak" (p. 235). These authors further recommended the use of an integrated urban model that would take fully into account the various variables and interactions that drive the urban system.

In the remainder of this chapter we review some ideas related to land use and urban form and their influence on urban travel. The reservations noted earlier are necessary because we have rushed into believing that changes in land use are the key to urban travel reduction. For decades this was not questioned, but there are limitations to the relationship and more recent research literature demonstrates this. The reader should be aware of these limitations. The material discussed below is generally accepted knowledge.

CLASSIC URBAN FORM

The form an urban area takes can have a significant effect on energy consumption and environmental impacts. To some extent, the city's form, or shape, is dictated by physical geography. Thus, we see elongated cities located in valleys or along coast-lines, or crescent-shaped cities surrounding a bay, lake, or port facilities, or circular cities reflecting the absence of any of these barriers to growth. Most of the classic location theory literature assumes that there are no physical barriers and that cities will develop in a circular fashion. Under those circumstances, "Urban form evolves as the outcome of location decisions of many thousands of households, firms, and public sector agencies" (Anderson et al., 1996, p. 7). This form can also be influenced by land use and transport policy, but often the agencies in charge of land use may not coordinate their activities with those in charge of transport planning, and the potential synergistic benefits are lost.

Urban transport planning officials completed some major transport projects of the 1950s and 1960s without explicitly recognizing that traffic flows influence the density of land use and that greater density stimulates greater traffic flow. Oddly enough, a classic work in urban transport planning had appeared during the mid-1950s that made this point in its title, *Urban Traffic: A Function of Land Use* (Mitchell & Rapkin, 1954). While we recognize these things more readily today, we still seem to be unable to incorporate them into our planning decisions very effectively. Private and public structures are often built without any apparent recognition of the fact that many of the decisions made will increase average daily trip lengths in a city or generate sprawl that in many cases does the same thing.

Increases in trip lengths—unnecessary travel—is a form of inflation where more travel is "spent" while few if any additional needs are satisfied. In that sense, it is little different from economic inflation. In the latter case, we spend more for goods and receive no additional products for our currency. But travel inflation is, in a sense, worse even than economic inflation since it leads not only to additional travel but also to additional pollution, fuel use, accidents, and deaths. Therefore, it makes logical sense that if we want to decrease excess travel we must attempt to control land use and urban form. This has led to proposals from the new urbanism planning school.

Research on the linkage between urban form and the amount of travel is extensive, with the work of Newman and Kenworthy (1989) most notable in the literature.

At the same time, that line of research has been roundly criticized by others working in the area. Van de Coevering and Schwanen (2006) provide a good summary of these criticisms.

"NEW URBANISM" LAND USE PLANNING

There is much discussion of the possibility of creating "new towns" that would enable their residents to satisfy most of their travel needs—that is, work trips, shopping trips, and recreation—by walking or biking within the town and thus decreasing vehicles on the highway, air pollution, and motor vehicle accidents and injuries. There is considerable research that suggests that residents of such communities do substitute walking trips for driving trips (Khattak & Rodriguez, 2005). On the other hand, there is also the possibility that individuals who move to such areas were disproportionately interested in driving less to begin with (Boarnet & Crane, 2001).

Planning for such communities is sometimes called "the new urbanism"—though the specific label doesn't really matter. There is certainly nothing wrong with the underlying ideas conceptually, but the reality is that people cannot live truly full lives within the strict confines of such towns as these, which nonetheless continue to be created. Three "new urban" towns that have received much fanfare are Seaside, in Florida; Kentlands, in Gaithersburg, Maryland; and Celebration, in Florida.

The new community of Seaside, Florida, attained some fame and notoriety with the theatrical release in 1998 of the Jim Carrey motion picture *The Truman Show*, which was filmed there. Much of the architectural homogeneity apparent in the community is attributable to a building code that is considered by most as strict (some might say "overly rigid"). The code requires all houses to have a front porch of a specific size, 16 feet from the street. There must also be a white picket fence in front of each house. The community has public spaces that foster interaction: parks, gazebos, sidewalks, and the like. Streets are narrow, and the pedestrian rules, as opposed to the automobile.

Kentlands is a community within Gaithersburg, Maryland. The development has a commercial district, open space and parks, playgrounds, swimming pools, jogging trails, schools, and similar user-friendly land uses. All of these amenities are located within walking distance of the residences. Initial construction of this community started in 1989 and continues even today. Kentlands is generally considered one of the most successful of the new urban communities.

Celebration, Florida, is yet another example of the new urbanism. In this case it is a village built by the Walt Disney Company on the southern edge of its Walt Disney World property on the outskirts of Orlando. The concept is that one can both live and work within the same community. The community occupies nearly 5,000 acres, and the average sales price of its homes was $275,000 during the late 1990s (a price that would hardly encourage a wide variety of income levels). Several key functions are located away from the city center, including the town's office center and its health center. In addition, most of the homes have two- or three-car garages, which casts some doubt on how little this community actually relies on the automobile. Some general criticism of Celebration is available in Frantz and Collins (1999).

There are numerous examples of sustainable communities throughout the world. von Weizsacker et al. (1998) focus specifically on the Bremen-Hollerland area of Bremen, Germany, the Village Homes area near Davis, California, the Laguna West area near Sacramento, and Haymount in Virginia. A few towns of this type in European and North American countries will not accomplish much in terms of the travel and traffic problems that exist on these continents. Neither will the idea help to solve problems in other developed countries. Is there a place where such a planning approach offers some potential? Two areas seem to be worth consideration in this regard. The first is in the so-called edge cities developing on the outskirts of large metropolitan areas in North America and Europe. The second is in the suburban areas of the rapidly motorizing cities of the developing world. However, people in either place will not likely wish to be told where they must work and where they must live, which raises the question of exactly what can be done though land use options to make transport more sustainable.

LOCAL LAND USE CONTROL

Perhaps the most fundamental role of land use policy is to control the placement of activities. Such control enables urban areas to shape expansion, development, and construction while reducing sprawl. Of course, that is the optimistic side of the picture. In the United States the ability to do what you want with the land you own is in the same category as the right to bear arms, the pursuit of happiness, and other fundamental rights. Nevertheless, on occasion a local governing unit—perhaps the city council or the city planning commission—will reject a development proposal due to its potential traffic or environmental impacts on neighboring areas. However, there are legal mechanisms that permit individuals to petition for reconsideration, or a variance, to the ordinance, law, or ruling. In many cases the petitioner can change his or her request sufficiently to have the use he or she desires permitted. In effect, land use controls in such environments are little more than bureaucratic barriers that in time can be scaled by those who wish to do so, in most cases.

Of course, there are other problems as well. One of these is the division of administrative authority over parcels of land, particularly in the United States. Cities usually have their own land use controls. These controls may extend into the urban fringe, an area within 2 miles of the city, and they may have control over land uses in these areas as well. Beyond this 2-mile fringe, counties may have control of land use, but county land use controls are considerably weaker than city controls and, in most cases, ineffective as a way of controlling development. Most states in the United States offer little oversight of such local plans, and state land use plans are novelties where they do exist. One possible exception is the Oregon urban growth boundary program of 2007, which was intended to prevent urban sprawl. The Oregon legislature gave its state planning group the power to require coordination of regional and local plans for any area adopting an urban growth boundary, as well as consistency between local plans and regional and state land use planning goals.

FEDERAL CONTROL OVER LAND USE

While most land use decisions are in the hands of local or state officials, the one major exception involves the location of industries and activities that may generate emissions that pose dangers to air quality. Control in that case is lodged not at the local or state level but rather at the federal level.

Enactment of the National Environmental Policy Act (NEPA) of 1969 marked the beginning of a series of laws that sought to control where certain types of activities could be placed, or what Hagman (1975) has referred to as the "quiet federalization of land use controls." NEPA required the preparation of environmental impact assessments for all projects funded or regulated by the federal government, including all types of activities, ranging from highway construction to the building of power plants. If, after intensive study, the project was deemed environmentally detrimental, then the problems of the project could be shown to the responsible agency, and in most cases the latter would be empowered to alter the offending location or change the nature of the project. Passage of the Clean Air Act and its amendments along with the Clean Water Act also extended federal control over various environmental concerns and activities. An extensive review of these is not possible here, but the point is that the federal government has the power to "shut down" or prevent many types of land use activities that may be inconsistent with sustainable transport.

However, sustainable transport is not just improved air quality, and federal statutes can only do so much. There is no federal agency on the transport side that rushes forward with an objection to a new high school being built in a part of the county that has the lowest population density. There is no agency that points out that the 1,000 students bused 7.5 miles one way per day represents 15,000 passenger miles a day, or nearly 2.7 million passenger miles during the school year. These numbers do not even take into account the athletic and extracurricular activities at the school. Our hypothetical school may generate 2.7 million passenger miles per year, and this is only one school. Perhaps some agency should review these decisions from a sustainable transport perspective.

URBAN SPRAWL

It should be apparent that uncontrolled growth in an area results in some areas being developed at low density and other areas being passed over altogether. This phenomenon is generally referred to as sprawl, and historically it has been viewed as undesirable because it generates unnecessary travel and costs associated with the delivery of urban services (utilities, policing, busing, transit, and so forth). A review of such costs may be found in the report of the Transportation Research Board titled *Costs of Sprawl—2000* (Burchell et al., 2002). The undesirability of sprawl has been the prevailing wisdom for most of the 20th century, as noted by Ewing (1997), and that judgment remains unchanged. Gordon and Richardson (1997) have controversially asserted that the Los Angeles type of urban sprawl may in reality be a desirable pattern of land use that can be served at a lower cost to taxpayers than can a compact city. While their provocative paper has generated much academic debate, its thesis is correct only if the clusters of development are self-sufficient in terms of goods and services.

If we consider a dispersed pattern of towns spread across the landscape and also assume these to be self-sufficient, then travel will probably be kept to a minimum. If we then move individual settlements toward one of the places that has grown larger (perhaps due to some type of specialization), we then get a clustered pattern that resembles "sprawl." Of course, all the small places are still self-sufficient—or nearly so—so we do not have the apparent inefficiencies of sprawl. It is possible to get a similar geographic pattern with sprawl, but what makes this distribution inefficient is not the pattern but the way the pattern is serviced and where people choose to live in relationship to their work, social, and recreational activities. Sprawl has always been discussed as a problem related to spatial patterns, but it is really a problem stemming from the pattern of transport flows. If flows are localized, these can be efficient, but if dispersed, they can be very inefficient. Because of this it might be best not to talk about sprawl but rather the flow patterns.

If sprawl consists simply of individual housing units without any clear core community center, it is virtually impossible to see any efficient manner of serving these areas. Some municipalities attempt to prevent this type of development by acquiring land for open spaces on the urban fringe, but while this may save green areas, it simply drives such housing beyond these areas and may actually increase total transport and travel cost externalities. Zoning and other land use controls are the answer, but as noted these are not very effective in the United States.

Whether or not Oregon's urban growth boundary program has succeeded in accomplishing its overarching goal of preventing sprawl has received mixed reviews. Lewyn (2002) believes that both the supporters and the opponents of the program have overestimated its positive effects and negative effects, respectively. Since 2002 a referendum passed that was favored by property owners to loosen the controls and allow compensation for what some viewed as a legitimate "taking" of property under the Fifth Amendment to the U.S. Constitution. As the estimated compensation approached $20 billion, however, the state voided the referendum and allowed exceptions to the strict prohibition on housing. The Oregon case illustrates the type of conflict that exists and is increasingly arising between land owners and anti-sprawl environmentalists. Court cases and legislative activity have not resolved the problem there, despite the fact that Oregon's institutional arrangements represent the cutting edge of contemporary land use control.

In this discussion it is probably worth spending a little time on a couple of concepts that have come into the literature over the past two decades or so that seem to be related to sustainable transport, although they may not be. One of these is the notion of wasteful commuting and the other is the idea of spatial mismatch, each of which we briefly examine.

Excess Commuting

"Excess commuting" and "wasteful commuting" are terms that have come into use to describe situations where the actual aggregate travel distances of some segment of the population is compared with what this would be in some type of optimal situation. The optimal situation may be obtained by solving the transportation problem of linear programming or some other system optimization methods. This technique was used nearly four decades ago by Wheeler (1967) to examine work trips of individuals in Pittsburgh, Pennsylvania, using data from the Pittsburgh Area Transportation Study. The shortcomings of the methodology are well recognized, that is, that most individuals are not really interested in system optimization solutions and that all individuals cannot necessarily do any job in the urban area (a plumber cannot do surgery, a waiter cannot teach kindergarten, a contractor cannot serve as a judge, and so on). The concept might be of some interest if employment data were available in sufficient detail, but to assume that someone trained in one craft, skill, or profession could even do any job in that category is simply ludicrous. Unfortunately, most data are not refined enough to examine questions of wasteful commuting, and even if one found situations where the data were available, one would have to question the use of optimization methods that seek a *global* optimal solution. In effect, excess commuting is a concept based on the inappropriate application of a methodology to inappropriate data.

Spatial Mismatch

The term "spatial mismatch" is used to denote the fact that in many cases a sizable portion of the labor force consists of unemployed residents largely "stranded" in inner-city communities. While new jobs are often located on the periphery of many cities, transit is not set up to take inner-city residents to those areas. As a result, one might say that there is some type of spatial mismatch between workers and workplaces. Over the years, there has always been some type of spatial mismatch. For most of the early 20th century suburban whites commuted to the central city. Transit lines were set up with this type of flow in mind. Now we need to reverse the flow on these systems so that they enable central city residents to reach the suburbs. The problem is not quite this simplistic; low incomes and dispersed employment centers in the suburbs make the "reverse commute" problem far more difficult to solve, but existence of the problem is hardly new and novel. It exists because central cities in most cases have gradually been losing employment opportunities. An interesting approach to formalizing the basic hypothesis of spatial mismatch has been offered by Arnott (1998).

Neither wasteful commuting nor spatial mismatch has much to do with sustainable transport. They are mentioned here only because some may think they have relevance to sustainability. They do not.

CONCLUSIONS

There should be no doubt that land use is indeed a major determinant of travel in urban and metropolitan areas. It should also be apparent that we have the capability of altering travel by controlling certain land uses, but often we do not do this. Often we seem to not want to take such action if we would have to give up something in the process. Therefore, it seems as though this is an area that will see few major changes.

The idea of constructing new towns that are more self-contained and less car-dependent is certainly attractive, and there is no doubt that this may be of some assistance for fringe areas of small and medium-sized localities. This trend, however, will not likely be of much help overall in creating a sustainable transport system. In addition, what if the trips that we take are a function of the amount of time we have available (as numerous researchers now believe)? If this supposition proves to be true, then the enclaves created by advocates of the new urbanism will be viewed in the next couple of decades only as monuments to our lack of understanding of the linkage between land use and urban travel.

At the same time, some things *can* be done to make urban areas and their transport systems more sustainable. Newman and Kenworthy (1999) and Van de Coevering and Schwanen (2006) suggest that worthwhile pursuits include revitalizing the inner city; concentrating new development around existing rail service if the city has sufficient rail infrastructure; extending the transit system to allow for cross-city and orbital connections; building urban villages around these rail transit lines; and discouraging urban sprawl. These are all reasonable actions, but they may be very difficult and expensive to implement. Nevertheless, there are certainly key land use changes that would improve the sustainability of transportation in most cities.

CHAPTER 12

Indicator-Based Planning

To measure the performance of something,
it has to be made operational, including
concepts related to transport and mobility.
—HENRIK GUDMUNDSSON (2003)

One might initially raise a question about the title of this chapter, namely, Why would one want to base planning on an indicator? It is not what we traditionally think about when we talk about planning—or is it? Actually, most of the planning of the 20th century was essentially indicator-based planning. The indicator of interest back then was congestion. We went through such a convoluted process—inventory, trip generation, trip distribution, modal split, traffic assignment—to identify future congestion points that we perhaps lost sight of what it was we were trying to do, but the indicator was clearly congestion. Congestion remains a problem today, but it has been subsumed in a broader class of problems generally referred to as the sustainability of transport.

If the sustainability of the transport system of a given urban area, state, or nation were of particular interest to us, we would want to evaluate just how well we were doing with regard to the specific criteria defining "sustainability." We would want to assess the status of the system. Beyond that, we might be actually trying to make the system *more* sustainable, and if that were the case we would want to evaluate the progress that was being made and determine whether existing programs are working or whether something different should be tried. To accomplish this, we would need one or more indicators to help us make that assessment.

In this chapter we identify some of the indicators that have been proposed for assessing sustainability and suggest those that we believe are the most important ones to track. Then we propose how one could use these in assessing the state of the system, whether the system is becoming more or less sustainable, and how different

137

programs can be evaluated that seek to make the system more sustainable. Before we move on, it is important to recognize two problems that will get in the way.

THE FIRST PROBLEM

What is sustainable transport? One would hope the reader would know the answer to this question by now, but if you have randomly turned to this chapter or if you have never seen this book, the question would naturally arise. If you have ever sat in on a planning meeting, you will recognize that vague concepts can be a major stumbling block. Everyone in the meeting has a different idea of what it is you are talking about. Even though the attendees of the meeting may have done a significant amount of reading prior to the meeting, this will not help, since most of the literature is contradictory. Such meetings are often reduced to arguments over definitions, and as a result nothing is accomplished.

If it is virtually impossible to agree on what sustainable transport is, then is it possible to take another tack and identify what it is that makes a transport system *unsustainable*? If we take this approach, can we identify those attributes of the system that keep it from being sustainable—from being able to serve present and future transport needs? If that is the question, then we come back to the five factors that have been referred to several times in this volume—finite fuels, emissions harmful to the global environment, emissions harmful to local environments, fatalities, and congestion. If you disagree with this perspective, that is fine—you will still be able to use the approach in the remainder of this volume for indicator-based planning. You will simply be looking at another indicator.

THE SECOND PROBLEM

A second problem will come up only if you don't agree with the author—that is, if you don't share my belief that there are only five dimensions to transport sustainability. We have noted elsewhere in this volume that many individuals who want to have a more sustainable transport system are concerned about transport's impacts on the biological world. These impacts can be substantial, but they certainly will not prevent transport from being around in several centuries, nor will they result in the elimination of species. If neither of these occurs, then the biological realm is not relevant to the argument. That is not to say that these impacts are unimportant; they are of some concern, as noted by Forman (2000) and the Dean Report (TRB, 1997). They are just not going to be of major concern in making the transport system *more sustainable*.

Another issue that has garnered more attention than it deserves is equity. Some researchers believe the transport system should be fair or just in some sense; otherwise, the system is not sustainable over the long term. Yet, we have never had a truly equitable transport system—Why would we want to burden the concept of sustainability with this mandate? This notion of equity worked its way into sustainability through the notion that the system should be available for use by future generations—sometimes referred to as transgenerational equity—and if that is the case (so goes the argument), it should also be available to all members of the current generation. This is a shortsighted argument. No matter what we have in the future, it will certainly make anything from the current generation look inferior by comparison. I do not miss having a horse and buggy or a "steamer" automobile as my major transport mode.

We should not place too many demands on our attempts to achieve a more sustainable transport system. If we do that, it will burden the concept to the point where even if we were successful we would not be able to identify the success. One is reminded of the attempts during the 1960s to revitalize urban transit in the United States. So much was expected of the Urban Mass Transportation Act of 1964 and later amendments that, even though they succeeded in the basic goals of providing additional transport for the elderly, the poor, and those unable to drive, the legislation was not heralded as a major accomplishment. If we expect more of ourselves than we can likely accomplish in the realm of sustainable transport, we may very well end up walking away from both the idea and the ideal.

THE INDICATOR INVENTORY

Because the concept of sustainability is very broad-based and wide-ranging in the literature, numerous indicators have been suggested to aid in measuring it. One of the leading efforts at isolating useful indicators was made by Heanue (1997) for the National Science and Technology Council's Transportation R&D Committee. He recommended considering:

1. Market penetration of alternatives to petroleum-based fuels.
2. Transport sector emissions of greenhouse gases.
3. Water quality, number of species endangered, and soil protection measures.
4. Number of acres of revitalized urban area and reclaimed brown field sites.
5. Number of trips made and miles traveled (by mode).
6. Amount of reliance on single-occupant vehicles.
7. Amount of access to jobs and services for the transport-disadvantaged.
8. Number of people in areas that attain national atmospheric air quality standards.

Heanue's recommended list included numerous indicators that related to the behavioral aspects of transport and travel, probably reflecting the idea that voluntary actions by drivers will be critical in making the transport system more sustainable, which was consistent with the Clinton administration's philosophy.

Litman (1999b) proposed a different approach to sustainable transport indicators, one based more on personal or household travel characteristics. Included in his list of indicators were:

1. Average portion of household expenditures devoted to transport.
2. Average amount of residents' time devoted to nonrecreational travel.
3. Per capita automobile mileage.
4. Ability of nondrivers to reach employment centers or services.
5. Per capita land area paved for roads and parking.
6. Quality of pedestrian and bicycle facilities.
7. Quality of public transit (frequency, speed, safety, etc.).
8. Special transit services and fares relative to low-income residents.
9. Transit coverage, residents within ³⁄₁₀ of a mile. (½ kilometer).
10. Motor vehicle accident fatalities.
11. Per capita transport energy consumption.
12. Medical costs attributable to transport.
13. Publicly financed transport costs.
14. Residents' role in transport and land use decisions.

These criteria may lead to a more equitable transport system, but they are not necessarily critical in terms of the sustainability of that system. Some factors, such as those intended to reflect the quality of the transit service, have little to do with a sustainable system if the system is not used.

Several European cities have begun exploring and monitoring transport sustainability, among these cities is Berlin, which has identified the following 12 indicators:

1. Level of motorization.
2. 30 kilometer speed limit on main street network.
3. Car sharing.
4. Bicycle traffic.
5. Public transit use.
6. Facilities for disabled on public transit network.
7. Long distance accessibility.
8. Freight transport trends.
9. Number of flights.
10. Air pollution and noise.
11. Accident trends.
12. Revenues from road use taxes in relation to infrastructure costs.

The foregoing lists are typical of some of the indicator sets that have been assembled. Other major studies in this area have been completed by the U.S. Environmental Protection Agency (EPA, 1996) and the OCED (1998).

The Pentad Again: Finite Fuels, Emissions, Safety, Congestion (Global and Local)

In order to make the transport system more sustainable, we must seek to improve a number of areas related to travel and transportation. For example, we could increase the safety of the system and thereby decrease the number of incidents involving personal injury and loss of life. Improving the flow of traffic or decreasing congestion in the system would also increase the system's sustainability. We might also decrease our reliance on finite fossil fuels as an energy source for most of our transport. Doing so might also enable us to decrease emissions that harm human health in local areas as well as affecting global atmospheric conditions. The key attribute in common among these diverse potential initiatives is that they are all a function of the amount of driving that takes place. If we are going to focus on these five factors for planning or monitoring the transport system, then we need to identify indicators for each of them.

Motor Vehicle Incidents, Injuries, and Fatalities

In general, the safety of the transport system can be well assessed by using indicators of the number of incidents, the number of persons injured, and the number of fatalities. All of these indicators are available for the states and municipalities in the United States. The figures are not nearly so reliable for international comparisons since in many parts of the world motor vehicle incidents and injuries are not reported very well. For comparative purposes, the fatalities figure is probably the most reliable indicator (though in certain countries if a person does not die within a specified number of hours after the accident, a different cause of death is assigned.

Congestion

There are numerous indicators of congestion in the transport system (many of which we summarized in Chapter 7). If the RCI index is available, it could certainly be used, but we may want to use something as simple as the number of registered vehicles or a similar measure of the potential for congestion.

Fuel Use

The amount of fuel used by the transport system is highly relevant since the bulk of this supply has its origin in unrenewable fossil fuels. Fortunately, the principal fuels used (diesel and gasoline) are taxed, and therefore the number of gallons sold is available (though not always accessible except as statewide data). We are especially interested in this indicator because it tells us the extent to which we are depleting this resource.

Local Emissions

Local emissions from motor vehicles can be estimated. There are several of these that may be of interest, but we focus in particular on nitrogen oxides, volatile organic compounds, and carbon monoxide. The first of these is a precursor of urban ozone. The second usually contains carcinogens, and the third can lead to blood disorders and may cause death.

Global Emissions

The primary gas emitted from transport vehicles that contributes to global warming is carbon dioxide. Depending on fuel economy measures, motor vehicles may release up to 20 pounds of carbon dioxide for each gallon of gasoline used.

Vehicle Miles of Travel

As was noted all of these indicators are highly correlated with total vehicle miles traveled. Thus, it is worth looking at this indicator for its own contribution to the sustainability analysis as well as for its possible use in evaluating the impact of various policies on travel.

Indicators Not Used

There are a number of other variables that some planners might like to see used. If we are interested in getting people to drive less, shouldn't we also be looking at transit ridership? If the community has a program of increasing transit ridership, one could argue that this indicator should definitely be monitored. This is true. On the other hand, wouldn't we expect to see significant reductions in vehicle miles of travel if transit ridership increased. However, including transit ridership would not give us new information for measuring sustainability of the system.

The number of hybrid vehicles in use in the area is a variable of interest, but it is not an easy variable to obtain in all states; also, we see no reason to believe that hybrids are affecting total fuel use very much so far. If we want to encourage the purchasing of hybrid vehicles through some type of governmental program, then we might want to monitor this variable. Clearly, the greater the number of hybrid vehicles on the road, the less fuel that will be used. We prefer to use the fuel sales indicator as a backdoor approach to measuring the use of hybrids. It is reasonable to assume that as fuel use drops there may be a contribution coming from the use of hybrid vehicles. This assumes the economy has recovered from any recession.

Alternative (nonfossil) fuels are often viewed as desirable. There are several of these available in California, and the Midwestern states have moved toward ethanol blends with some vigor. For most urban areas these data would not be available, but even if they were we would make the same argument: as alternative fuel use increases, fossil fuel use must decrease in the short term, assuming fleet size does not change significantly. As a result, including this as an indicator does not tell us much more than the fossil fuel use indicator.

Overlap in the Indicators Identified

Of the various indicators identified for use above, one thing should be very clear: they are all related to the amount of driving taking place, or vehicle miles traveled. The greater the VMT, the higher the exposure to highway incidents and the associated fatalities and injuries. Increases in VMT also increase fuel consumption and all of the attendant emissions. Congestion as well is related to the total driving taking place.

In order to assess the degree of this interrelationship, data were collected for the states individually, and a principal component analysis was performed on these variables. Principal component analysis is a mathematical technique that yields one or more components that describe all of the variables examined (see Harmon, 1976; Rummel, 1988). In this particular case, one component was obtained. The component loading for each variable may be interpreted by understanding that these values may range from 0 to slightly less than 1. The closer the value is to 1, the more similar the variable is to the component, or vice versa. As Table 12.1 indicates, for U.S. states, VMT is nearly identical to the single component derived, its component loading being .99103.

What this means is that if we want a single indicator to monitor that will give us a fairly good idea of changes in sustainability, then that single variable would be VMT. As it increases, all of the other indicators also increase, and that means that sustainability is getting worse. Similarly, if we can decrease VMT over time, then the system is becoming more sustainable. We would not go so far as to imply that this would be true for the countries and cities of Europe, but it may be; further research would be necessary to establish if that is the case.

This key indicator may appear to be the answer to all indicator planning, but we are not quite there. The analysis above was performed using state-level data for the United States. We may want to look at cities or multicounty areas of the United States, and while these data are available for urbanized areas in *Highway Statistics* (FHWA, 2006), they may not be available for all of the areas that may be of interest.

There may be other indicators easily available. One of these is usually traffic fatalities for the county, metropolitan area, or state of interest. Some governmental authority in the area usually maintains this type of information. There may also

TABLE 12.1. Principal Component Analysis for the Individual States of the United States

Indicator	Component loading
Carbon dioxide emissions	.97648
Carbon monoxide emissions	.95825
Motor vehicle crash fatalities	.97349
Gasoline sales	.98579
Motor vehicle crash injuries	.91868
Motor vehicles registered	.96775
Emissions of nitrogen oxides	.96823
Vehicle miles traveled	.99103
Emissions of volatile organic compounds	.97134

Source: Black (2002).
Note. N = 50, eigenvalue 8.4, variance accounted for 93.7%. Based on data for 1997.

be congestion measurements available for the area, and these can be used to evaluate different projects and programs. Emissions data are less readily available in a usable format for program assessment unless there is a local program or agency to collect the data. It is primarily because of the difficulty of getting data on some of these measures that we suggest using VMT to evaluate most programs.

PROGRAM OR PROJECT EVALUATION: VMT REDUCTIONS

Let us illustrate how we could evaluate a program. At the outset we would identify the goal of the program and what its objectives are. Let's assume that the primary goal is to simply reduce vehicle miles of travel in the area of interest. The objective may be modest: say, a 5% decrease in vehicle miles of travel over the next 5 years. We may have a number of different ideas in mind as to how this goal could be accomplished. We may want to significantly increase the level of public transit service by adding vehicles and decreasing headways (the time between bus arrivals at a given location). We may also want to initiate a park-and-ride system. A marketing program in which the benefits of carpooling could be identified might also be a part of the plan.

We could secure estimated VMT data from local transport planners or possibly from state transport planners. If such data are not available and are not going to be available, then you need to set up a procedure for estimating the numbers. You may simply identify 1,000 drivers from the area of interest and have them regularly insert the mileage accumulated on their car or cars for given time periods on a website. This would then be extrapolated for the number of vehicles registered in the area. To be sure, the estimate you get may bear little similarity to data that may be published later by the Federal Highway Administration or other agencies. That really doesn't matter since what you are most interested in is whether any of your actions have changed the estimated VMT. The data could be collected weekly or monthly or every few months over the 5-year project term.

If your project is successful at reaching a 5% reduction, then you may infer that you have also reduced greenhouse gas emissions as well as emissions of pollutants. One should not really expect to reach the goal in this case. We do not believe that any urban area that has been able to reduce its VMT in the past several years. Perhaps a goal of no change would be more realistic.

PROGRAM OR PROJECT EVALUATION: FATALITY REDUCTION

If your goal is improving the safety of the transport system of some area, this may have the objective of reducing average annual fatalities by a set number or percentage. This will require some monitoring of fatalities for the area of interest. Although those working in the highway safety field dislike the use of the word *accident* (preferring *incident* instead), this writer believes that many fatalities are random in the sense that a vehicle hits you so quickly you have little chance to avoid contact. It is true that most fatalities have causes that can be identified, and this consideration argues against the use of the word *random* in relation to these events. Nevertheless, as one looks at a time series of fatalities, one is often struck by the seemingly random fluctuation that occurs in the series. This is the reason for seeking a reduction in the average, as opposed to a reduction in a specific annual count.

The program to accomplish such a reduction may involve stricter enforcement of speed limits in the locality. It may also involve higher fines on those who exceed the posted speeds. Public-interest television spots highlighting fatalities on the highways might also be of some value. If fatalities are occurring where vehicles are traveling at the posted speed, then it may make sense to lower those speed limits. One could add guardrails to the medians to help prevent head-on crashes, or replace solid guardrails with heavy metal cord that has less of a tendency to deflect vehicles back into the traffic lanes. These are a couple of actions that could be undertaken locally.

Of course, the program may be unsuccessful. The heaviest emphasis today is on making crashes survivable, which generally involves technological improvements in the vehicle itself. Nevertheless, these programs will also help to reduce fatalities.

These are not programs that one should simply walk away from. The tragic human dimensions of fatalities are worth emphasizing again and again so that the public is always aware of them. Similarly, speed reductions should not suddenly be lifted under the misimpression that this action will have little or no negative impact on fatalities.

Some of the programs just discussed could be implemented in different ways. Perhaps we want to set a very clear objective for 5 years from now and then determine what must occur each year in order to meet that targeted goal. While this might be possible for VMT goals, it is less likely to work for traffic fatalities for the reasons previously mentioned.

CONCLUSIONS

In this chapter we have discussed the use of indicators in planning. Numerous possible indicators were identified, but we eventually argued that the five factors identified at the outset of this volume were the primary ones of interest. We concluded that, at the least, one should attempt to monitor vehicle miles traveled since this variable is a reasonably good indicator of all the others. The chapter ended with illustrations of the ways in which two projects or action programs could be evaluated with indicators.

POLICY

CHAPTER 13

A Continuum of Policies

Government policy toward motor vehicles is fragmented
and increasingly misguided, resulting in small
environmental benefits being gained at exorbitant cost.
—DANIEL SPERLING (1995)

Actions to make transport sustainable can be undertaken at just about any geographic scale, but are all of these actions likely to be successful in solving the major problems before us? Probably not, but that does not mean they shouldn't be tried. The actions that are possible run the gamut from very personal efforts to multinational conventions and treaties. We are primarily concerned with global activities since these seem to offer the most promise of success. However, global success will presuppose local activities to ensure that local situations do not become worse. On the other hand, local actions in the absence of global initiatives, while worthwhile, will not resolve the major problems of transport sustainability.

A popular automobile bumper sticker in the United States urges one and all to "Think globally, act locally"—a noble sentiment perhaps but possibly short on logic? One might be better advised to "Act globally *and* act locally"—and at every other level imaginable!

A CONTINUUM OF ACTIONS

Figure 13.1 depicts the continuum along which sustainable transport actions or programs might be developed or implemented. It begins with the individual at one end and moves through community and county initiatives to state and multistate activities; next, national programs are also critical, as are multinational and international or, as we refer to them here, global programs. Let us examine some of these programs and activities at these various institutional levels, or scales.

149

Personal	Local	State	Multistate	National	Multinational	Global
				United States' Partnership for a New Generation of Vehicles		
	Assist public transit			Brazil's ethanol program		
Purchase green cars	Purchase green fleets	State ethanol subsidies			ECMT policies	
Use public transit	Set up auto-free zones	State transit subsidies	High-speed rail compacts	Netherlands' global warming policy	EUCAR	Montreal Protocol
Use bicycles or walk	Parking policies	California-type air quality statutes	California emissions policy	Israel's sustainability policy	European Union environmental goals	Kyoto Protocol

FIGURE 13.1. Continuum of sustainable transport actions.

Personal Actions

We can begin with the individual and his or her personal decisions toward making transport sustainable. Among these personal initiatives might be such actions as (1) using the local transit facility or car pooling, (2) using seat belts for safety, (3) driving in a defensive manner, (4) using bicycles or walking, (5) driving motor vehicles only if mass transit alternatives are not available, (6) purchasing energy-efficient motor vehicles, (7) maintaining a motor vehicle so that it operates at peak efficiency, and so forth. While no one would deny that these actions might contribute to transport sustainability, they are not sufficient to accomplish it simply because they are voluntary and uncoordinated actions, for the most part. With the exception of seat belts (whose use is mandated by law in the United States), the other actions involve a degree of choice on the part of the individual, and for the most part they are *not* chosen.

There are occasions when individual actions may directly contribute toward some sustainability objective and actually be successful in attaining it in the short run. A reasonably good example of this occurred during the OPEC oil embargo of the 1970s. In the United States, President Jimmy Carter encouraged individuals to conserve petroleum and to not travel unless it was necessary. The net result was about a 10% reduction in fuel use that could not be attributed to anything except the "national interest" response of the population. In reality, this was an example of a sustainability initiative at the national level that was implemented by individuals. Unorganized individuals left to their own devices would hardly have been able to accomplish this. Indications are that we may once again see a push toward conservation measures during President Barack Obama's administration.

Local (Town, City, and County) Actions

Small units of government are not usually able to accomplish much in the transport sustainability arena. Among the actions that are open to them are (1) strong control over land use and the prevention of urban sprawl through zoning ordinances; (2) the offering and subsidizing of public transit operations; (3) the creation of car-free zones in certain areas of the community; and (4) the provision of free parking in the central part of the locality.

Some of the foregoing actions are actually in conflict with one another, and the specific ones chosen are a function of the major sustainability problem facing the community. For example, if the community is trying to prevent the suburbanization of retail activities and preserve its central area (i.e., trying to prevent sprawl), free central area parking might be chosen. On the other hand, if congestion is the major problem in the central area, discouraging parking there and creating peripheral parking would be favored. One must know exactly what problem is to being addressed and select measures that are appropriate while recognizing the potential interactions that solution may have with other problems.

In the United States, counties do not have substantial resources, and as a result, they are somewhat limited in what they can accomplish toward sustainable transport. They will typically be the providers of rural, or nonurban, public transit, which should decrease the need for some automobile travel.

State Actions

Although it is easy to discount the importance of states in setting and attaining sustainability goals, that would be, on balance, a misperception. While much has been made of the increased speed limits that certain states enacted in 1995, several other states pointedly abstained from that action, and in the long run they will probably be viewed as more rational and responsible in their transport policymaking. States also produce legislation that enables counties and localities to offer urban and rural public transit service, and they sometimes assist in providing the local matching funds for federal programs in these areas.

In general, a state or province might not be perceived as being able to do much on its own to move a nation or the world toward sustainability in transport, usually owing to their small populations relative to the nations in which they are located. One notable exception, however, is the state of California.

The area that is today southern California has had air quality problems for as long as humans have occupied it. Even early Spanish explorers noted the presence of smoke from Indian campfires that never seemed to dissipate. The basic problem is that breezes coming off the Pacific Ocean produce a layer of cold air near the surface. Warm winds descend on the region from the mountain ranges, producing a layer of warm air. Since the cold air will not rise and the warm air will not fall, the result is an atmospheric inversion that traps whatever pollutants are generated in the area.

This part of California has been plagued with air quality problems from motor vehicle emissions for more than 50 years. Because of this history, California was among the first states to enact legislation to improve atmospheric quality and reduce these emissions, beginning with legislation in 1963 requiring that cars sold in California have positive crankcase ventilation (PCV) systems to reduce hydrocarbon emissions. By 1966 the state was requiring exhaust control devices that would reduce lead, nitrogen oxide, and carbon monoxide emissions. At the federal level, Congress enacted the Motor Vehicle Air Pollution and Control Act of 1965, which resulted in national air quality standards comparable to California's, beginning with the 1968 model year (Flink, 1990, p. 387).

In general, California has long been a trend-setting laboratory (at the state level) for air quality legislation at the federal level, and the national Clean Air Act of 1990 had provisions that applied exclusively to it. Specifically, California has the right to set more stringent emission control standards than those required by the federal government for the rest of the country. These standards called for a phasing in of ultra-low-emission vehicles. Other states were given permission to adopt California's provisions if they so elected, and New York did so almost immediately.

In September 1990 the California Air Resources Board (CARB) mandated that, beginning with the 1998 model year, 2% of all new passenger vehicles and light trucks sold in California would have to be zero-emission vehicles (ZEV), with the percentage increasing to 5% in 2001 and 10% by 2003 (Ogden & DeLuchi, 1993). What has been called the ZEV mandate was later adopted by Maine, Maryland, Massachusetts, New Jersey, and New York (Sperling, 1995). On December 14, 1995, CARB suspended the ZEV mandate for 1998. On February 8, 1996, Governor Pete Wilson of California signed an agreement with General Motors, Ford, Chrysler, Nissan, Honda, Toyota, and Mazda that required the industry to meet the 10% quota set for 2003. This was followed in 1998 by CARB's reducing the ZEV mandate from 10% to 4%, noting that the industry had made progress in the development of alternative fuel technologies. Most other states dropped their mandates, except for New York; the latter state had its mandate overturned by the U.S. Circuit Court of Appeals in August 1998. New York and the other states had followed California's lead, as permitted by the Clean Air Act, but when California dropped its mandate the other states had no "legal" grounds for theirs. We could go on citing numerous other activities of the state of California. It has been by far the most active of the states in the air quality area as it relates to motor vehicles (see Sperling & Gordon, 2009, pp. 179–204).

States have also been instrumental in setting up programs to fund transport alternatives such as high-speed rail systems. Examples here include the Miami–Orlando–Tampa corridor in Florida, the Cleveland–Columbus–Cincinnati corridor in Ohio, and the San Diego–Los Angeles–San Francisco–Sacramento corridor in California. There are also some multistate high-speed rail proposals for corridors in the Northeast and Midwest. Some of these require interstate agreements (compacts) and are therefore less common.

National Actions

For the most part, a nation is unable to do a great deal by itself to solve worldwide environmental problems, such as global warming or stratospheric ozone depletion, or to reduce certain pollutants that are global in their distribution. A nation can be somewhat more successful at attacking problems that are local (national or regional) but globally distributed. For example, in the United States a policy decision was made to reduce the emissions of sulfur oxides and nitrogen oxides that contribute to acid deposition. Provisions of the Clean Air Act amendments of 1990 called for significant reductions in these over long periods of time. These reductions should go a long way toward eliminating this environmental problem in the northeast United States and southeast Canada as well as some other areas of the United States where this is a problem. It will not eliminate the damage already done, although damaged marine life and forest areas should recover naturally over time. It will also not solve this problem in parts of Scandinavia, central Europe, or parts of Asia. Those countries and people will have to enact their own legislation or encourage their neighbors to take similar action.

On rare occasions one country may contribute so much to a global environmental problem that its actions may positively or negatively impact that problem worldwide. A good example is the U.S. decision to remove lead from gasoline sold domestically. The introduction of catalytic converters in 1975 virtually mandated the phasing out of leaded gasoline since the latter would disable the control devices located in the converters. This resulted in the dramatic decline in airborne lead pollution from about 180 million short tons in 1970 to 1,596 short tons in 1994. Because of the massive size of its motor vehicle fleet, the United States was actually contributing so much lead to global atmospheric levels that removing this pollutant from its gasoline resulted in a radical reduction in global atmospheric lead levels. This was an unusual case. Soon afterward, the European Union followed the U.S. action and eliminated lead from their motor vehicle fuel as of 2002. Lead is still found in fuel in some countries of Central and Eastern Europe. It should be noted that 50% of the fuel used in Europe is diesel, which has no lead content (Eurostat, 1999).

In most cases there is not a great deal that one country can do to combat global problems. This does not stop some countries from trying to establish policies that will improve conditions. For example, Gordon (1991) notes that in 1989 the Netherlands set forth a program to reduce its contribution to global warming from the transport sector. Included among its initiatives were provisions to:

- Improve the infrastructure, operations, and funding of public transport.
- Encourage the development of high-speed rail as an alternative to air travel.
- Discourage vehicle use for business and other institutions.
- Improve bicycle facilities.
- Create road pricing systems that would allow variable tolls by the time of day and the day of the week.
- Shift automobile fixed costs to variable cost status.

- Decrease tax breaks for automobile commuters.
- Use land use controls to encourage development near public transit facilities.

Although a single nation's efforts to confront this problem head-on are laudable, the effects are multiplied when other countries join the action.

The Netherlands' policy, for example, had a significant impact on Israel's policy toward sustainability in general and transport sustainability in particular. Israel's policy in the latter area calls for specific actions to be taken on reducing the environmental impacts of the existing motor vehicle fleet, modifying individual behavior and changing attitudes, increasing the cost of using motor vehicles, making public transit more attractive, and better managing mobility and physical planning (Feitelson, 1996).

Other praiseworthy national policies could be noted, such as Brazil's decision to support the development of a large-scale ethanol fuel program. However, the Netherlands' policy appears to have had discernible real impacts beyond its own borders.

Multinational Actions

Several countries working together are sometimes able to make significant strides in combating a global problem. In this regard one could recognize the activities of the European Conference of Ministers of Transport or the research funded by the Organisation for Economic Co-operation and Development. It was the ECMT that proposed a decrease in carbon dioxide emissions to reduce the threat of global warming. Although this proposal failed, it is difficult to estimate how bad things would have been otherwise.

Global Actions

Very few global environmental problems have received the attention that has been given to stratospheric ozone depletion. It was recognized in the 1960s that chlorofluorocarbons being released into the atmosphere could potentially break down and attack ozone in the upper atmosphere. The sudden discovery, through satellite imaging, of the existence of a "hole" in the ozone layer over the southern polar region during the 1980s resulted in this problem being catapulted to the top of the list in terms of environmental problems.

Among the potential problems created by the loss of stratospheric ozone, which results in more ultraviolet radiation penetrating the Earth's atmosphere, were increases in human eye problems (retinal damage and cataracts) and skin cancers along with the destruction of phytoplankton in the polar oceans (which has potentially lethal implications for the food chain in the oceans).

Chlorofluorocarbons have been a major contributor to the gradual depletion of the ozone layer, and a major source of CFCs in the United States has long been the air conditioning units of motor vehicles. Typically, through normal use repeated leakages of Freon 11 (CFC 11) from automobile air conditioners would eventually necessitate the recharging of the unit. Residual CFC 11 in the air conditioning unit would then be vented to the atmosphere prior to the unit's being recharged. In other cases the recycling of motor vehicles would often result in the air conditioning unit's being crushed, whereupon any remaining CFC 11 would then be vented into the atmosphere. There were other uses of CFCs (e.g., as a propellant in spray cans of all types, in residential and commercial air conditioning units, and in cleaning computer boards), but transport was a major source.

It seemed apparent that something had to be done about CFCs. In 1987 a group of more than 30 countries met in Montreal, Canada, with the objective being to cut back on the use of CFCs. An international treaty was signed that called for industrialized countries to reduce their use of CFCs by 50% prior to 1998. It was soon realized that this would not be enough to eliminate the problem. The signatories of the Montreal Protocol along with numerous other nations (93 in all) met in London in 1990 and set the year 2000 as the year for the phaseout of all CFC (and carbon tetrachloride) use. Even this ambitious timetable was eventually deemed too slow, and the phaseout deadline was later moved up to December 31, 1995, for the industrialized nations. Existing stockpiles of CFCs could be sold, but more could not be produced.

It is this type of cooperation, negotiation, and action that must be taken if we are to be ultimately successful in curbing or eliminating undue global warming.

International Global Warming Negotiations

On June 13, 1992, 20 years after the first United Nations Conference on the Environment, an Earth Summit convened in Rio de Janeiro for the purpose of developing a plan to cope with several global environmental problems. One of the chief concerns of the 132 countries represented at the summit was climate change brought on by global warming and the creation of a negotiating mechanism on how to proceed in attempting to resolve this problem. The operative mechanism became known as the Framework Convention on Climate Change, and eventually it was approved by 159 nations (Gelbspan, 1997).

This Summit also produced Agenda 21, a strategy for how to (1) improve the quality of life on Earth; (2) efficiently use the Earth's natural resources; (3) protect the "global commons"; (4) manage human settlements; (5) manage chemicals and waste; and (6) provide for sustainable economic growth (Sitarz, 1994).

Transportation was not directly addressed in Agenda 21, but rather as a component of protecting the global commons. Several actions were suggested:

- The development and promotion of more cost-effective, efficient, less polluting and safer transport systems, particularly mass transit systems.
- The planning and development of transport facilities in developing countries.
- The provision of state-of-the-art technologies (in safety and low emissions) to developing countries.

- The educating of personnel to use these technologies.
- Increasing information on the relationship between transport and the environment.
- Developing transport policies that minimize adverse impacts on the atmosphere.
- Integrating transport strategies into comprehensive urban planning so as to minimize the environmental impacts of transport.

Agenda 21 sought to attack numerous global problems, and while transport was not immediately singled out as an area for emergency attention, it was definitely treated as an area where significant improvements could be made.

Negotiating sessions on the Climate Convention were held in New York, Berlin, Madrid, and Geneva in preparation for a major conference to be held in Kyoto, Japan, in December 1997. Most countries believed that the outcome of the Kyoto meeting could hardly be a schedule for reducing greenhouse gases since the countries were, for the most part, in disagreement as to how such an objective could be attained. Once they finally assembled, the U.S. delegates initially wanted no target for reductions in emissions; they then agreed to the idea of a target but were unwilling to set a specific numeric goal. They believed the target should be something less than the 10% below 1990 levels by 2005 and the 15% below these levels by 2020 that the United Kingdom and Germany proposed. Most other delegates believed that the developing countries should be allowed to generate more emissions in order for their economies to catch up with the developed world. From the outset, it seemed unlikely that any significant agreement would come out of Kyoto.

We have digressed too much from discussing of the global dimension by focusing on U.S. politics, but the United States remains a critical player in any international global warming agreement, and unless it is a full participant in the solution to this problem then the solution is likely to be unsuccessful. Although both are international in scope, the global warming problem differs from that dealt with by the Montreal Protocol problem in several ways. First, CFCs had a readily available substitute in hydrochlorofluorocarbons, whereas fossil fuels, the source of most carbon emissions, have no readily available substitute that is capable of replacing them cheaply at this time. Second, the science of the stratospheric ozone depletion problem was easier to convey to the public than the science of global warming. Third, the appearance of a hole over the southern polar region was clear evidence of a problem, whereas some scientists believe recent warming of the planet may still lie in the normal range of variation. Fourth, there remains some residual belief in the United States that the global warming problem is something we should try to adjust to rather than eliminate altogether (see Rosenberg et al., 1989).

Conclusions on the Scale of Effort

Depending on exactly what part of the transport sustainability problem is being addressed, then all units along the continuum in Figure 13.1 may potentially be players. For example, if local traffic congestion is the problem, then action by the municipality or county may be sufficient to handle this. Air quality problems may be handled in some cases at the state level, but national action may be necessary. Optimistically, if the sustainability component of major concern is global warming, then it must be treated at the multinational or international level initially. Once action is taken at that level, then the actions at lower levels of the scale continuum may be useful in attaining global goals for reduction of greenhouse gas emissions and so forth. Alternatively, initiatives at the national, state, or lower level, in the absence of international actions, are somewhat fruitless and will probably create more hardships than benefits for the units initiating them. In effect, local solutions are good for sustainability problems that are by nature local (e.g., congestion or urban air quality), but global solutions are required for global problems (e.g., climate change and ozone depletion). Notable exceptions to this generalization are the actions undertaken in California and the Netherlands, which have been influential on a global scale.

A BUSINESS SCALE CONTINUUM

At the risk of belaboring the scale vehicle, it is worth noting that there is also a business or private scale continuum that runs from the local shopkeeper to the multinational corporation. In general, the units of this continuum are controlled by business leaders and corporations, which oppose changes that could lead to transport sustainability. We have seen local business leaders oppose the loss of parking spaces in front of their shops that local governments want to use as bus stops to relieve traffic congestion. The American Petroleum Institute has repeatedly argued that developing alternative fuels might result in widespread unemployment, apparently believing that alternative fuel production, distribution, and sales requires no labor. At the same time, we have seen certain self-interested multinational corporations, especially petroleum companies, oppose the setting of carbon emission standards and in fact mounting major advertising campaigns to support their views.

Of course, there are some businesses and industries that support sustainable transport: the manufacturers of energy-efficient automobiles, fuel cells, electric automobiles, and the like come most readily to mind. However, these are relatively minor players in the business and industrial sectors. There are some energy companies as well that are investing substantial resources in alternative energy sources, but we are uncertain to what extent these are motivated by altruistism versus (more likely) self-preservation. We have not seen any of the largest petroleum companies take major steps toward alternative energy with the possible exception of BP ("beyond petroleum"). One can, however, point to some local undertakings of this type in the United States by energy-related companies. California Edison, for example, has made substantial investments in wind energy that could support electric car operations in the Golden State.

In 2000 the Ford Motor Company issued a report to its shareholders that included the following passage:

The fuel economy of SUVs is less than cars, particularly for larger SUVs, and the migration of car customers to SUVs has reduced the fuel economy improvements achieved by automakers, directly contributing to rising greenhouse gas levels and global climate change concerns; SUVs are permitted higher emissions than passenger cars because they are classified as trucks by U.S. regulations and these are subject to more lenient standards for emissions and fuel economy . . . ; SUVs can raise safety concerns for drivers and passengers in other vehicles because of the height, weight, and design differences between cars and SUVs, as well as the reduced visibility for cars in traffic with trucks of any sort; and SUV owners who use their vehicles for off-road recreation can damage the nature they and others seek to enjoy.

Ford promised a hybrid electric SUV by 2003 (which was available as the Ford Escape in 2005); a redesign of the Ford Excursion so that the risk of smaller cars sliding under it would be reduced; and, in the longer term, SUVs that meet the same emission standards that automobiles must meet. The passage above contains surprisingly candid statements from a company that during the 1970s professed that it didn't believe that emissions could be meaningfully reduced or fuel economy increased at all.

SCALE AND PUBLIC–PRIVATE VENTURES

There are few examples of public–private ventures in the transport sustainability area. These are not exactly found along a scale continuum running from the small to the very large, but there are enough of these efforts in the United States that are worth mentioning. The National Science Foundation has been willing to support local university research related to the creation of small business ventures. Several of these projects include elements that contribute to transport sustainability, for example, vehicle navigation or global positioning systems. This effort is minor in comparison to what is happening at the national level.

In September 1993 President Bill Clinton announced an initiative called the Partnership for a New Generation of Vehicles (PNGV) that was designed to accelerate the development of electric propulsion, ultra-efficient technologies, lightweight materials, and advanced manufacturing processes. It brought together the Big Three automakers (General Motors, Ford, and Chrysler) and the national laboratories (e.g., Oak Ridge, Argonne, Sandia) to accomplish these goals, but with no apparent increase in funding (Sperling, 1995). There is some question as to whether the Big Three were appropriate players in this undertaking since they had a vested interest in not cooperating. The program is described in detail in Chapter 15.

There is not a great deal of difference between the PNGV effort of the United States and the support given to automobile manufacturers in Europe (by the European Commission, with its EUCAR program) or in Japan for the development of such a vehicle. EUCAR's objectives are leadership in automotive technology, increased competitiveness with the United States and Japan, and environmental improvements. The European program also features explicit concerns about sustainability, an element missing in the PNGV program. Prototypes are mentioned, but production-ready models are not available at this time.

Japan's overriding concern appears to be vehicles designed to serve the California zero-emission vehicles market. If that is the case, then it has been rather successful in this effort. It had vehicles by Honda and Toyota that could meet that state's ultra-low-emission vehicle (ULEV) standard as early as 1998. By 2000 some 10 of the 13 most environmentally friendly vehicles being sold in the United States were produced by Honda, Nissan, Toyota, Suzuki, and Mitsubishi, so, Japan's implicit policy has proven to be a wise strategy (DeCicco & Kliesch, 2000).

CONCLUSIONS

We are of the opinion that actions to solve problems of transport nonsustainability must first be focused at the global scale, and there are examples of agreements working at this scale. At lesser scales success is problematic unless we are talking about a national or multinational effort to resolve the problem to which these nations are major contributors. Solutions of major problems at personal or local scales seem doomed to failure in the absence of a blueprint established at a much higher level.

Public–private ventures offer some potential for major solutions to the problems of sustainable transport. It is not immediately obvious that having the United States, Europe, and Japan all working on the same problem independently makes sense— there may be some merit in collaboration. The problems here are not national or multinational; neither are the solutions in most cases.

CHAPTER 14

The Special Role of Speed and Speed Limit Policies

Speed is the quintessential traffic safety issue, probably
due to the clearly perceived relationship between
vehicle velocity and human capabilities and limitations.
—FEDERAL HIGHWAY ADMINISTRATION (1998)

Motor vehicle speeds and speed limits are often disregarded when it comes to questions about transport sustainability. It was noted at the outset of this volume that transport sustainability has several dimensions. Among these are limited petroleum fuel resources, emissions that are harmful to human health and the environment, motor vehicle fatalities, and roadway congestion. To these could be added excessive demands on the use of land. Motor vehicle speed can create fundamental impacts on all five areas, although often this is not acknowledged since speed is an attribute of travel that many drivers seek. This chapter examines how speed impacts these areas and notes some of the current practices in North America and Europe related to speed.

As we have pointed out earlier, our current transport system, in particular our highway motor vehicle network, is nonsustainable since its major fuel is finite, and there are some indications it will not last through the current century. The use of this fuel also releases emissions into the atmosphere that are injurious to human health at the local level and detrimental to the atmosphere of the planet at the global level. Even if we change to an alternative fuel, we will continue to have problems related to fatalities and injuries in our transport system, the congestion of vehicles, and the excessive amount of land that becomes dedicated to this transport use.

Variations in the speed of motor vehicles can significantly decrease their efficiency in consuming fuel. As the incineration becomes less efficient, the pollutants emitted from the tail pipe increase. So, as we see in all other areas, as fuel consumption increases, so do the emissions that can harm human health and negatively impact the local and global environments.

It is possible for transport researchers to get into arguments regarding the role of speed in motor vehicle crashes and fatalities. In the United States many researchers argue that the common saying "Speed kills" is factually incorrect. While there is no clear linear relationship between speed limits and crash rates, we may be looking at noncomparable samples when we reach this conclusion. The matter will be examined later in this chapter.

At its extreme, congestion becomes gridlock, which represents the absence of speed or movement; therefore, we are tempted to attribute decreases in speed to congestion. This would be the correct inference in this situation. However, increases in speed can result in vehicles prematurely arriving at bottlenecks in excessive numbers, thus creating congestion at those locations. So, the problem may not be quite as simple as we think.

Linking speed to excessive land use is not as direct a connection as in the other four areas, but there is a linkage nevertheless. For example, U.S. highways that are designed for the highest operating speeds are parts of the interstate highway system. These highways consume massive amounts of land in that their specifications require a minimum of four lanes, a median, ample shoulders, and fencing. In this sense, speed comes with a very high land price and opportunity cost.

FUEL CONSUMPTION AND SPEED

We know that, as the speed of a motor vehicle increases, it tends to consume greater amounts of fuel, but the situation is not quite that clearcut. In reality, motor vehicles are designed to reach the optimal rate of fuel consumption at a specific operating speed. Therefore, if an automobile has been designed to operate most efficiently at 55 miles per hour and the vehicle is driven at speeds more than or *less* than this optimal level, then it will consume proportionately larger amounts of fuel.

This general pattern of fuel consumption is depicted in Figure 4.1 on page 41 (see also David, 1997). Slow speeds are generally less efficient, resulting in greater consumption of fuel in relation to speed. Increasing the speed brings the vehicle closer to its optimal design speed, which represents the lowest use of fuel per mile. Beyond this optimal point, proportionately greater amounts of fuel are again consumed. The figure is only typical since the actual relationship will vary by vehicle make, number of passengers, road surface, terrain, temperature, and a host of other variables.

Ironically, very little consideration is given to such factors in policymaking. For example, speed limits are set at different levels without any real concern for the attributes of the vehicle fleet that must comply with them. In the United States maximum speed limits of 55 miles per hour were enacted by Congress in 1974 in response to the Arab oil embargoes. This regimen was relaxed somewhat in 1987 to allow 65 miles per hour on rural sections of the interstate highway system. In 1995 the U.S. House of Representatives voted unanimously, with the Senate concurring 80–16, to repeal the national speed limit and allow states to determine the speed limits within their own boundaries. Table 14.1 lists the current resulting mix of maximum allowable speeds, ranging from 55 to 75 miles per hour; these speeds are probably not even close to optimal for more than one-quarter of the nation's auto fleet. Gasoline consumption increased by 2.02 billion gallons in 1996 as compared to 1995, or roughly 1.7% (FHWA, 1996, 1997), in response to relaxation of the nation's speed limits.

This discussion is not intended to suggest that increased fuel consumption is related solely or even primarily to higher speed limits around the United States. Certainly some of the increase was attributable to the surging popularity of minivans and sports utility vehicles during the 1990s and early 2000s. At the same time, part of the reason for these vehicles' increasing market share is their reasonable CAFE numbers, which endows them with both more power and naturally more speed. So, speed contributes to increased consumption indirectly here as well.

MOTOR VEHICLE EMISSIONS AND SPEED

Separating fuel consumption from emissions is nearly impossible: as the former increases, so does the latter. At the same time, the points raised about fuel consumption and changes in speed limits also apply here. Consuming fuel inefficiently results in incompletely combusted fuel components being emitted. These are released to the local atmosphere in the form of such emissions as carbon monoxide and hydrocarbons. Changes in speed limits that result in inefficient cruising speeds instead of optimal ones can only make this problem worse.

Table 14.2 shows the relationship between emissions production and various stages of the driving cycle. As can be seen, idling emits significant amounts of pollutants in the form of carbon monoxide and hydrocarbons. Decelerating is also a problem in that fuels in the process of being combusted are suddenly expended without creating the energy that they would have. The incompletely combusted fuels produce significant amounts of hydrocarbons and carbon monoxide.

These relationships were presented diagrammatically earlier in this volume (Figures 4.2–4.4, pages 42–43) in our discussion of air quality. The figures illustrate average estimates of emissions for three different pollutants in relation to average trip speed, as derived from current models (Mobil5a and EMFAC7F; see TRB, 1995). The fleet assumed is the 1990 U.S. fleet of light-duty gasoline vehicles. Carbon monoxide emissions (Figure 4.2, page 42) are at their highest at very low speeds and then drop as operating speeds approach 50–55 miles per hour. After that point, they begin to increase again. Volatile organic compounds (Figure 4.3, page 42) display a similar pattern, although at a much lower level. Nitrogen oxides (Figure 4.4, page 43) display a somewhat different pattern in relation to speed; They are produced at relatively low levels at low speeds, drop slightly, and then begin to climb as average speeds increase. Attempting to reduce all of these emissions can be difficult since they do not all behave in the same manner in relation to average speed. Hybrid vehicles that at lower speeds use their electric motor significantly reduce at

TABLE 14.1. Maximum Speed Limits on Interstates, by State (March 2009)

State	Car limits (rural)	Car limits (urban)	Truck limits
Alabama	70	65	70
Alaska	65	55	65
Arizona	75	65	75
Arkansas	70	55	65
California	70	65	55
Colorado	75	65	75
Connecticut	65	55	65
District of Columbia	n.a.	55	55
Delaware	65	55	65
Florida	70	65	70
Georgia	70	65	70
Hawaii	60	50	60
Idaho	75	75	65
Illinois	65	55	55
Indiana	70	55	65
Iowa	70	55	70
Kansas	70	70	70
Kentucky	65	65	65
Louisiana	70	70	70
Maine	65	65	65
Maryland	65	65	65
Massachusetts	65	65	65
Michigan	70	65	60
Minnesota	70	65	70
Mississippi	70	70	70
Missouri	70	60	70
Montana	75	65	65
Nebraska	75	65	75
Nevada	75	65	75
New Hampshire	65	65	65
New Jersey	65	55	65
New Mexico	75	75	75
New York	65	65	65
North Carolina	70	70	70
North Dakota	75	75	75
Ohio	65	65	55
Oklahoma	75	70	75
Oregon	65	55	55
Pennsylvania	65	55	65
Rhode Island	65	55	65
South Carolina	70	70	70
South Dakota	75	75	75
Tennessee	70	70	70
Texas	75 day; 65 night	70 day; 65 night	70 day; 65 night
Utah	75	65	75
Vermont	65	55	65
Virginia	65	65	65
Washington	70	60	60
West Virginia	70	55	70
Wisconsin	65	65	65
Wyoming	75	60	75

Source: Insurance Institute for Highway Safety, Highway Loss Data Institute (*www.iihs.org/laws/speedlimits.aspx*).

TABLE 14.2. Emissions Production during Various Stages of the Driving Cycle (Parts per Million in Exhaust from Gasoline Engines)

Pollutant	Idling	Accelerating	Cruising	Decelerating
Carbon monoxide	69,000	29,000	27,000	39,000
Hydrocarbons	5,300	1,600	1,000	10,000
Nitrogen oxides	30	1,020	650	20
Aldehydes	30	20	10	290

Sources: Organisation for Economic Co-operation and Development (1983) and Button (1993).

least some of the emissions noted as typical of slower speeds. Internal combustion engines generally perform best on emissions at cruising speeds rather than idling, accelerating, or decelerating.

Mullen et al. (1997) examined the impact that eliminating the national speed limit in 1995 had on the production of emissions. That action resulted primarily in states increasing their speed limits or holding to prior limits—that is, no state lowered its speed limits. They found nitrogen oxide emissions increased 6%, carbon monoxide emissions 7%, and volatile organic compounds 2% overall in the United States as a whole. In certain states nitrogen oxide emissions increased much more dramatically (e.g., 49% in Montana and 35% in Texas) due to substantial increases in those states' speed limits.

SPEED AND CRASHES

Vehicle speeds contribute to crashes and crash rates in several ways, though the data do not always support this idea. If we examine the number and rate (per 100 million vehicle miles traveled) for fatalities and injuries, we get the figures shown in Table 14.3. The table includes the number of crashes occurring in both rural and urban areas, based on the type of highway. This type of highway variable is not the same as speed, but one can generalize that the interstate highways are associated with the highest speeds and the local roads the lowest speeds. The table demonstrates that, as one moves up the scale in highway quality, in rural areas there is a decrease in the number of fatalities and injuries, with only minor exceptions. This observation would seem to suggest that as speed limits increase there is a decrease in highway fatality rates. However, as we move along the same scale in urban areas, we find the same thing occurring. These patterns would also appear to suggest that fatalities decrease as we move from slower to faster highways. However, we must not lose sight of the fact that there are significant differences in the fatality rates for all types of roads if one compares rural highways with urban highways, and the most fundamental of these is the difference in speed limits in urban versus rural areas. There may also be differences in policing and lighting, but the differences in speed seem dominant. Therefore, one can infer that higher speeds result in higher fatality rates for all types of roads.

TABLE 14.3. Fatal and Nonfatal Motor Vehicle Personal Injuries on Urban and Rural Highways (Rate per 100 Million Vehicle Miles), 1995

	Fatal		Nonfatal	
	Number	Rate	Number	Rate
		Rural		
Interstate	2,691	1.20	86,511	38.73
Other principal arterial	5,170	2.40	193,931	89.96
Minor arterial	4,730	3.09	194,690	127.23
Major collectors	5,681	3.05	259,541	139.38
Minor collectors	1,700	3.40	81,221	162.65
Local	4,015	3.82	231,255	219.92
		Urban		
Interstate	2,145	0.63	276,599	80.99
Other freeways and expressways	1,281	0.85	118,313	78.08
ther principal arterial	5,771	1.56	870,185	234.96
Minor arterial	3,716	1.27	535,171	182.48
Collectors	1,425	1.12	193,451	152.45
Local	3,473	1.69	572,196	277.89

Examining the data of Table 14.3, we find that rural interstate highways have a fatality rate of 1.20 fatalities per 100 million vehicle miles as compared with a fatality rate of 0.63 per 100 million vehicle miles for urban interstate highways. For all comparisons between the highway categories, there are higher motor vehicle crash rates per 100 million vehicle miles of travel in rural areas as compared with urban areas. Once again, the major differences in the roads are their location in urban versus rural areas and the differences in speed that these locations imply.

If we look at nonfatal crashes in Table 14.3, we get a somewhat different picture. In this case the number of nonfatal personal injuries is higher on urban area highways, which is most likely due to their higher traffic volumes. While the data are standardized by 100 million vehicle miles of travel, there apparently is a point where congestion in urban areas results in a higher probability of vehicles coming into contact with other vehicles or objects. Higher volumes result in a higher probability of crashes and nonfatal injuries, but not necessarily higher fatalities, in urban areas, particularly if the vehicles are moving at slower speeds.

To summarize, one can say that overall there is no clear relationship between nonfatal motor vehicle crash rates and highway speeds, although one could suggest an increase in crashes with decreasing speeds; the latter would be primarily "fender benders." On the other hand, there are clearly higher fatality rates per 100 million vehicle miles in rural areas as compared with urban areas for all classes of highways. Decreasing speeds in rural areas would likely decrease the rate of highway fatalities. Of course, other factors may also contribute to these figures; for example, falling asleep at the wheel probably causes numerous crashes during long drives in rural areas.

There is the inference above that higher speeds result in higher crash rates in rural areas. The reason for these higher rates has been understood for quite some time. Table 14.4 summarizes data from a study in the 1950s for seven U.S. states. This table gives the reported speed of vehicles and the number of fatal-crash drivers per 1,000 injury-crash drivers. It illustrates that, as the speed of vehicles increases from less than 20 miles per hour to over 50 miles per hour, motor vehicle crash fatality rates increase by a multiple of nearly eight (from 12 to 92). More recent research also documents the relationship between speed and motor vehicle crash severity (Aarts & van Schwagen, 2006; Bowie & Walz, 1994; Joksch, 1993).

This is not 1940, and technology has managed to reduce fatalities attributable to motor vehicle crashes significantly. Seat belt usage is one obvious change, but emergency medical technology has also made major leaps forward. Nevertheless, the human body is able to withstand only so much "blunt force trauma" from impacts, and this physiological fact virtually guarantees that, while the risk of fatal crashes at higher speeds may be reduced, it will not go away.

Vernon et al. (2004) examined the effects of repealing the national maximum speed limit (NMSL) law on traffic accidents in Utah. They found that the repeal had no discernible effect on the number of fatalities or injury crash rates on that state's urban or rural interstate highways. This result was to be expected, given that these highways are built for high speed. Repealing the NMSL, however, did appear to increase the *total number* of crashes on urban interstates and fatal crash rates on high-speed rural non-interstate highways.

There is one other aspect of speed as it relates to crashes that should be noted, namely, the impact of absolute speed deviation for vehicles involved in crashes from the average speed of other vehicles, or disparities in the relative speed of vehicles in the traffic stream leading to more crashes. These differences often occur because a vehicle must slow for a turn or to enter or exit a high-speed road. As Shinar (1998) has noted, "Data demonstrating the relevance of speed dispersion in the traffic stream and speed deviations of crash-involved vehicles are based on correlational effects and therefore cannot be used to indicate that if slow-moving drivers were to increase their speed, their crash probability would be reduced" (p. 271). Nevertheless, there is reason to believe that, at the extreme ends of the speed range, these deviations do play a role. Data also indicate a similar positive role for speed dispari-

TABLE 14.4. Speed and Motor Vehicle Crash Severity

Reported speed (miles per hour)	Number of fatal-crash drivers per 1,000 injury-crash drivers
20 or less	12
21–30	21
31–40	36
41–50	48
51 and over	92

Source: Matson, Smith, and Hurd (1955). Reprinted by permission of McGraw-Hill.

ties and crash probability on interstate highways, but additional data are needed in this area.

SPEED AND CONGESTION

Figure 7.1 in our chapter on congestion illustrates some of the fundamental relationships of traffic. The top graph (Figure 7.1a) shows that the relationship between traffic volume and vehicle density tends to be U-shaped. When speeds are increasing from the zero level, vehicle density begins to increase along with traffic volume as more and more vehicles enter the traffic stream. At some point, volume reaches a maximum level and then begins to decrease since the density of vehicles is increasing. The increasing density makes it impossible for the system to maintain its volume, and this begins to decrease. When density reaches a maximum, gridlock occurs and traffic volumes drop to zero.

The middle graph shows that as speed—that is, "mean free speed"—increases, so does the volume of traffic. At some point, volume is maximized and then begins to fall back. Note that as speeds increase beyond this point traffic volumes begin to decrease as drivers find it necessary to avoid other vehicles (because of excessive speed) on the roadway.

In the bottom graph we see the basic relationship between the average speed of vehicles and the density of vehicles on the highway. As can be seen in the diagram, as speed increases the density of vehicles tends to drop. Alternatively, density results in gridlock if speed drops to 0. The logic behind dropping speed limits to increase density is illustrated here. In the United Kingdom officials recognized this fundamental relationship between speed and vehicle density in the case of the motorway that encircles London. A pilot project was initiated on a section of the M25 London orbital motorway (also known as a beltway or ring road elsewhere in the world) in August 1995 to introduce variable speed limits. The situation that existed on this facility prior to the project was that vehicles traveling at very high speeds would frequently reach "seed points," locations where there was a natural tendency for traffic to slow, creating situations where traffic as a whole would slow significantly or even stop. The idea underlying the project was to reduce speed limits during periods of heavy traffic using a state-of-the-art signal system (known as the Motorway Incident Detection and Automatic Signaling, or MIDAS, system) with automatic camera enforcement of the new limits. The objectives of the project were to prevent congestion, reduce crashes, smooth traffic flow, decrease pollution and noise, increase driver comfort, and increase flow volumes (Harbord, 1997). Indications are that the project was quite successful: traffic did not become congested, the flow was smoother, and personal injury crashes declined 30% and damage-only crashes 25% during the first year. A survey of drivers found that 60% viewed the changes as an improvement. The system was viewed as so successful that it was installed on other sections of the British motorway network, some 910 kilometers by March 2006. In addition to its overall favorable impact on speed and congestion, by maintaining reasonable speeds (as opposed to high speeds or low congestion speeds) the system also results in decreased emissions. It is surprising that comparable systems have not yet been adopted on the same scale in North America.

DESIGN SPEEDS AND LAND USE

Although it may seem a bit of a stretch to bring land use into this discussion on speed, it is relevant. The smallest streets in our urban areas are usually relics of a bygone era—very narrow, often only slightly larger than a single car's width. In many cases, this is because they were originally designed for the horse and buggy and also for the slowest of speeds for a transport mode.

At the other extreme, we often have interstate highways in these same urban areas with four or six lanes in each direction, not including the exit and entrance ramp lanes. These highway segments are built to allow the road user to attain the very highest of *legal* speeds, although drivers frequently exceed these limits. The right-of-way width for such roadways may exceed 300 feet in the case of interstate highways, although many highways are considerably narrower than this.

Data on the amount of land actually dedicated to highways are not generally compiled and available. Greene and Wegener (1997, p. 183) estimated that the amount of land devoted to roads in the United States in 1991 was 53,400 square kilometers. Another 5,000–8,000 square kilometers are said to be devoted to parking (Delucchi, 1995). Clearly, a significant amount of land is used by highway transport. Moreover, the largest amounts are dedicated to roads that permit users to reach the highest speeds, which is our basic argument namely, that high-speed roadways require significant amounts of land dedicated to highway construction. Once the land is used for this purpose, it rarely returns to a different use, and this has relevance for other types of sustainability in urban areas (e.g., agricultural sustainability, recreational sustainability, etc.).

CONCLUSIONS

It should be apparent that speed is a fundamental element in any discussion of sustainable transport. This chapter has demonstrated its importance in terms of fuel consumption and the fact that higher average trip speeds will result in faster utilization of petroleum resources. Although the relationship between average trip speed and fuel economy is nearly linear and positive at speeds up to 40 miles per hour, the relationship becomes negative at speeds in excess of 40 miles per hour. While high average trip speeds increase emissions of certain pollutants, low average trip speeds generate higher relative emissions of carbon monoxide and volatile organic compounds. While hybrid electric vehicles reduce the lower-average-speed emissions, electric vehicles would eliminate all such emissions.

The speed of motor vehicles also importantly affects the number of fatalities and injuries suffered on the nation's roadways each year. The relationship is not as clearcut as one might suspect, and as a result policymakers feel relatively free to alter speed limits without any serious concern for the consequences. It appears unlikely that speed limits will be set at responsible levels since high speeds seem to be popular with the driving public.

Both theoretically and practically, speed and congestion are very much inter-related. While congestion leads to decreases in speed, it is also true that increases in speed can ultimately lead to persistent congestion. The solution lies in avoiding excessive speeds, thereby reducing gridlock—based on the U.K. experience with its state-of-the-art MIDAS system.

The positive relationship between the level of speed on a highway and the amount of land consumed by that highway was also noted. As we move toward higher and higher speeds, we have begun to consume extraordinary quantities of land. A pundit once suggested that New Jersey had the potential of becoming completely paved over with highways. Given the density of population, the public's desire for speed, and the land necessary for these high-speed roads, perhaps there is less humor in the statement than at first hearing.

Some solutions to the role of speed as it relates to the sustainability of trans-port have been suggested. These solutions may be planning-oriented, or they may rely on the engineering of new vehicles. Perhaps there is also a need for a mid-life education program similar to the type offered in American high schools that offer driver education courses. Do drivers forget the carnage that speed can produce? U.S. automobile advertising traditionally has often put the emphasis on speed and raw horsepower. In July 1997 the Advertising Standards Authority, an independent group created to ensure that the rules of the British Code of Advertising, Sales Promotion and Direct Marketing (2005) are adhered to, issued the following:

1. Marketing should not portray antisocial behaviour.
2. Speed and acceleration should not be the primary message of advertisements.
3. Speed in advertisements should not lead motorists to drive irresponsibly.
4. Vehicles should not be shown in dangerous situations that would lead to driving in an irresponsible manner. Capabilities of vehicles should be demonstrated on a circuit not used by the public.
5. Commercials should not give the impression of excessive speed. Vehicles should never appear to be exceeding U.K. speed limits.

It should be evident to the reader that American media are not subject to the withering reviews of a stateside counterpart to such an authority.

CHAPTER 15

National Policy Solutions

Policy-makers hoping to reduce congestion . . . must persuade
millions of Americans to alter some of their most cherished
social goals and comfortable personal conduct.
—ANTHONY DOWNS (1992)

The general problem of sustainable transport is open to a number of possible solutions, but broadly speaking it could be solved with public policy measures, technology, or a combination of the two. Public policy measures come in various forms and may be illustrated by a national policy on sustainability. Policy solutions may include methods of constraining demand for travel and transport through taxation, informational or educational programs, or subsidies for alternative modes, as well as other means. Europeans are more involved than Americans in solving the problem through policy solutions. Solving the problem technologically is typical of what could be called the U.S. approach to the problem. Included here would be the development of new alternative fuels, the invention of new types of batteries and fuel cells, improvements in catalytic converters, and other applications of technology. Neither approach will work alone, it being more likely that combining both policy and technology solutions will be necessary.

As suggested earlier (Chapter 13), approaches to sustainable transport may vary according to the scale of the area under analysis. Thus, individual actions may assist moves toward sustainable transport, but without some overriding national or international policy impetus such actions may not prove very effective. In this chapter we look at actions at the national, multinational, and global levels that offer promise in resolving the problem of transport sustainability.

Most actions to date can be categorized as being policy-oriented, technology-oriented, or a combination of the two. In this chapter we review national examples of each approach, with experiences gained in the United Kingdom, Israel, and the Netherlands illustrating the policy approach and experience in the United States serving to illustrate the technology approach (though lately the United States has moved to a more balanced position combining both technology *and* policy). Suggestions have also been made by both planners and commentators in this area (Blowers, 1993; Hughes, 1993), and these are addressed in passing, as well. We then move into the multinational arena and examine some actions that have been taken there (as, for example, in the European Union). Global activity has been sparse on the problem of sustainable transport. Nevertheless, we will examine some of the activities related to the Kyoto conference in the fall of 1997 and related movements. Perhaps one of the most promising global actions would be to create a carbon emissions trading system, and the merits of this proposal will be examined briefly.

U.K. SUSTAINABLE TRANSPORT POLICIES

The U.K. sustainable transport policy to be reviewed here is incorporated in a volume prepared by the government following the Rio Earth Summit (Department of Environment, 1994). That volume placed the policy within the context of a sustainable framework that seeks to strike a balance between a transport system that both serves development needs and protects the environment and the future quality of life; that meets the social and economic needs for access but also requires less travel; that reduces the negative impacts of transport on the environment while also sustaining the rate of traffic growth; and, that ensures that transport users cover the full costs of their transport decisions. The government also explicitly took note of trends suggesting that private automobile travel will double in the United Kingdom by 2025 and that strong economies generate higher levels of goods transport and travel as people choose to spend disposable income for that purpose.

Certain problems and opportunities coexist in this situation. Traffic growth will inevitably generate more emissions and demands for road construction. On the other hand, improvements in fuel efficiency and emissions standards and controls may not necessarily enable the United Kingdom to meet its environmental objectives. Before constraining transport, one must consciously acknowledge its importance to the economy. At the same time, much of the problem is attributable to individual decisions and behaviors, and government at the least should be able to influence these by introducing full costing in the transport sector.

The U.K. government initiated a fuel duty escalator (tax) that increased by 5% a year from 1992 to 1997 and by 6% a year from 1997 to 2000, its intention of being to have fuel costs more closely reflect the actual amount of damage fuel use entails. Such large increases were also expected to help the government meet its carbon dioxide emissions targets. The U.K. government also wanted to assist local areas in managing transport demand and using land use planning to reduce the need for travel and the pollution it generates. Local governments often follow up on this initiative. Nationally, the U.K. government also tried to establish better vehicle standards within the European Community as well as to improve ways of accurately assessing the impacts of transport programs. Overall, the objectives were to moderate the rate of traffic growth, to sharpen citizens' understanding of the costs and benefits associated with transport, to lessen the negative environmental impacts of vehicles, to increase public understanding of environmental impacts from all travel modes, and to explore the role the new technologies such as telecommunications might increasingly play in a long-term solution.

The U.K. transport policy overall illustrates the key features of the policy approach spotlighted at the outset of this chapter, namely, that it is emblematic of an educationally oriented policy that assumes that individuals well informed about the facts will ultimately do the right thing.

The United Kingdom has moved on since this early policy of the 1990s, and the goals and objectives have evolved as one would expect, in response to events and leadership changes. One of the most dramatic developments, of course, was the London congestion tax initiative. While the U.K. government appears unlikely to achieve all of its targeted carbon dioxide emission goals, its forceful efforts have brought it closer than numerous other nations to achieving them.

ISRAEL AND THE SUSTAINABILITY OF TRANSPORT

Feitelson (1996) notes that the goals of Israel's sustainable transport policy are to maximize mobility with minimal nuisances and thus contribute to intergenerational equity; to avoid barriers to growth through full costing, which should minimize environmental damage; and to eliminate, where possible, long-term nuisances caused by transport.

Objectives tied to these goals include:

1. Minimizing land use areas designated for transport facilities.
2. Providing accessibility to all, including the carless, to promote mobility while reducing dependence on automobile.
3. Minimizing the energy consumed by surface transport by both reducing the kilometers traveled and the energy consumed per kilometer.
4. Maintaining opportunities to be flexible in transport, thus preventing bottlenecks to growth.

Several specific actions were advocated to accomplish these goals and objectives. Among these were requiring the maintenance of motor vehicle environmental emissions systems; the scrapping of older vehicles; the use of environmentally friendly technology (e.g., encouraging electric car use); changing road surfaces to decrease nuisances; changing behaviors that favor use of the private automobile; increasing the cost of private car use and maintenance; decreasing the availability of parking; facilitating the operations of public transit; reducing the cost and increasing the comfort of public transit; and increasing public transit coverage in space and time. Mobility can be improved by managing when travel takes place, changing the modes available, changing employment locations, and educating the public. To some extent, physical planning will also come into play. In such cases development should be conditioned on the availability of public transportation at the site, incorporating transit into the physical planning (e.g., dedicated lanes and transit stations), and making public transit central to community planning.

This program is not purely a public policy approach. It puts added pressure on transport users, imposes additional regulatory constraints, and encourages technological innovations as key components of the solution. Overall, it appears to be a more pragmatic long-term approach to sustainable transport than that so far implemented in the United Kingdom.

THE NETHERLANDS' APPROACH TO SUSTAINABLE TRANSPORT

The central goal of transport policy in the Netherlands is to ensure accessibility of all to the transport system (Keijzers, 1996). However, the automobile has created unacceptable levels of congestion, thereby decreasing accessibility. The congestion can only be reduced through massive public investment in new facilities, entailing major impacts on the environment. Accessibility, however, could also be increased were it possible to reduce the growth in travel distances. To accomplish this aim, the following changes were recommended:

1. Improve motor vehicles: make them clean, economical, safe, quiet, and reduce their emissions—but limit infrastructure expansion.
2. Begin to restrain mobility and the average length of trips with a location policy for housing, work, and recreation, allow new development only where it is accessible by public transport; increase the price of *all* mobility; shift goods traffic to the most efficient modes; and make working hours more flexible.
3. Improve alternatives to the single-occupant automobile by improving cycling facilities and public transport as well as by encouraging car pooling; people should be persuaded to use cars less frequently, even if through involves negative incentives.
4. Improve roads selectively and only if alternative transport modes are inappropriate. Believing that accessibility to all parts of the country must be maintained at all costs, the Dutch government generally favors toll roads in congested areas except for necessary traffic or car pools.
5. Improve the areas of communications, collaboration, finance, investment, enforcement, and research as they relate to transport policy.

Some of these goals were to be accomplished by seemingly draconian measures. For example, all localities were assigned a specific accessibility profile, which determined how much parking would be provided there. This designation mandated the use of public transport in many cases. Authorities (who believed that public transit travel times to work for trips greater than 5 kilometers should not exceed automobile travel times by more than 50%) sought to make public transit more economical than automobile use, but this attempt largely failed.

The bicycle continues to play a key role in transport in the Netherlands, as it is viewed as the ideal transport mode for trips of up to 5–10 kilometers. Plans called for increasing the number of cycle routes. One gets the impression that the bicycle in the Netherlands has the status of the bald eagle in America, namely, as something that the nation will go out of its way to protect. Americans visiting Amsterdam are always impressed with the large number of bicycles in use. Yet, if one reflects on it, you realize that the bicycle is nearly an optimal mode of travel in that environment. The bicycle in the Netherlands is not an icon so much as an answer to the country's sustainable transport problem.

Of course, some Dutch citizens personally resist using bicycles themselves, typically citing the same reasons—the lack of sufficient bike routes or facilities everywhere, the risk of theft or crashes, bad weather, and a negative image—that Americans commonly cite for not using bikes.

U.S. POLICY

After the UN Conference on Environment and Development in Rio de Janeiro in 1992 (better known as the Rio Earth Summit), all major participating countries were asked to prepare strategies and action plans to demonstrate how they would implement the various agreements they had made. The United States was not very forthcoming initially. The first Bush administration fought the Global Warming Treaty (as well as the Biodiversity Treaty) during the Rio conference. Most of the positive activity that did take place in response to the Rio meeting didn't even begin until the middle of 1993. At that time President Clinton created by executive order (No. 12852, June 29, 1993) the President's Council on Sustainable Development (PCSD). The PCSD, however, did not get around to issuing its first document, a status report on its organizational activities, until the spring of 1995 (PCSD, 1995).

In September 1993 President Clinton announced the creation of an initiative called the Partnership for a New Generation of Vehicles as noted earlier, in Chapter 14. The program's major objectives were to accelerate the development of electric propulsion, efficient technologies, lightweight metals, and advanced manufacturing processes that could contribute to the development of a new motor vehicle. Dubbed "Supercar" by some, the vehicle was to be environmentally friendly, with triple the fuel economy (80 miles per gallon) of contemporary mid-size vehicles at comparable price, performance, and safety levels. Other objectives included improving U.S. competitiveness in the automobile industry and designing a vehicle that was commercially viable. As noted earlier, the PNGV initiative sought to combine the resources and resourcefulness of Detroit's Big Three automakers and the technical expertise of the major national laboratories active in the energy area to work toward the creation of such a vehicle. While no new funding was involved in this effort initially, later on allocated funds ranged from $200 million to 300-million annually for this purpose (Sissine, 1996).

The automobile manufacturers were free to cooperate with one another, but they ended up opting for independent efforts. At the 2000 North American International Auto Show in Detroit Ford introduced its Prodigy model and GM its Precept concept car that both achieved almost 80 miles per gallon on diesel fuel in vehicles that could seat a family of five. DaimlerChrysler also unveiled its concept car in early 2000, a Dodge ESX3, with a hybrid diesel and electric engine, fuel economy of about 80 miles per gallon on diesel fuel (vs. 72 on gasoline), and able to seat five occupants. These were solely prototypes, with commercial production, at best, only a distant possibility.

In October 1993 the Clinton White House presented its Climate Change Action Plan (Clinton & Gore, 1993), which proposed reducing greenhouse gas emissions to 1990 levels by 2000 (as earlier touched on in Chapter 13). While a general reduction of 108.6 millions metric tons of carbon equivalent (mmtce) in greenhouse gas emissions was targeted overall, the transportation sector was asked to produce only 9% of that amount (some 8.1 mmtce). To accomplish this reduction four federal programs were to be put into place (Black, 1996).

First, employees of large firms were to be offered the opportunity to recoup the value of their worktime parking place as additional income in return for arranging their own transport to work via vans, buses, or carpools. This program would require changes in the federal tax code—otherwise the Internal Revenue Service would tax the money given to employees. Second, states would be encouraged to develop transportation system efficiency strategies that could include market techniques to encourage people to drive less, additional parking charges, emissions-based fees, and transit subsidies. A third was to promote greater use of telecommuting in order to decrease travel. And lastly the Department of Transportation was to establish a system for labeling the fuel economy of tires. Unfortunately, the DOT was unable to arrange the needed tax changes until much later than originally anticipated. While some employees did opt parking-space cash, it quickly created enough problems and it was dropped as a federal program by 1996 (although it was emulated by a few states for a period of time). Since these were predominantly voluntary programs, assessing their effectiveness in reducing emissions is very difficult. Nevertheless, these programs were steps in the right direction. Unfortunately, a 1995 vote by Congress that permitted states to set new speed (and higher) limits probably more than offset any positive impact these programs produced.

A third advisory group, the Presidential Advisory Committee to Assist in the Development of Measures to Significantly Reduce Greenhouse Gas Emissions from Personal Motor Vehicles (more generally known as the Car Talks) was formed in September 1994. The group consisted of environmentalists, consumer advocates, and representatives of the American Automobile Association, the Big Three automakers, and oil companies, among others. This group was unable to reach any meaningful consensus, and it was disbanded later in the decade.

The President's Council on Sustainable Development issued its second report, titled *Sustainable America*, in March 1996 (PCSD, 1996) in response to the Rio Earth Summit's request for strategies and action plans. This report identified four sets of steps that sought to put prescriptions for transportation more in line with sustainable development notions. They were:

1. Improve community design to contain urban sprawl better, expand transit options, and make efficient use of land within a community. Locate homes for people of all incomes, places of work, schools, businesses, shops, and transit in close proximity and in harmony with civic spaces.
2. Shift tax policies and reform subsidies to significantly improve economic and environmental performance and equity in the transportation sector.
3. Make greater use of market incentives, in addition to changes in tax and subsidy policies, to achieve environmental objectives.
4. Accelerate technology developments and encourage public–private collaboration to move industrial sectors closer to economic, environmental, and equity goals.

To evaluate progress in the transportation sector, the report suggests the use of indicators that would assess: (1) decreases in congestion in urban areas; (2) reductions in dependency on oil imports as a way of increasing economic and national security; (3) decreases in rates of freight and personal transportation emissions of greenhouse gases and other pollutants, including carbon monoxide, lead, nitrogen oxides, small particulate matter, sulfur dioxide, and volatile organic compounds to achieve transportation efficiency; and (4) move toward stabilizing the number of vehicle miles traveled per person while increasing the share of trips made using alternative transport modes as a way of assessing improvements in travel patterns.

There is certainly little to take issue with in these goals and performance indicators. The interrelationships between the goals or steps to be taken and the indicators are not very clear, but one can imagine certain linkages, even though they may be more apparent than real. The document does not set targets for its indicators but suggests that these might be forthcoming in another report.

In the fall of 1997 President Clinton proposed a program that offered a relatively painless solution for the United States to reduce its carbon dioxide emissions. It included a $5-billion program of tax cuts for industries that invested in energy-saving technology and for government research. Also included was an emissions trading program. These programs were also largely voluntary.

At the Kyoto meetings in December 1997 the Clinton administration agreed to cut emissions of carbon dioxide to 7% below the 1990 levels by 2008–2012. At the same time, the Kyoto Protocol had to be ratified by the U.S. Senate to become operative for the United States, and this obviously did not occur. In July 1997 the Senate passed the Byrd–Hagel Resolution by a unanimous vote of 95–0 urging no ratification of the Kyoto Protocol so long as developing nations, particularly China and India, were excluded from the greenhouse gas reduction mandates.

The administration of George W. Bush, as earlier noted, was noteworthy only for its reluctance to face up to the issue of transport sustainability. In its first term the administration saw only a need to study the question of global warming further and preferred to ignore the Kyoto Protocol altogether. It very weakly funded some hydrogen car initiatives, but only after the 2006 election and the loss of Republican majorities did the Bush administration begin to pay any attention to the question of climate change. By that time the war in Iraq had so drained government resources that many domestic programs were unduly hampered.

In December 2007 the U.S. Congress sent a new CAFE standard to President Bush requiring manufacturers to produce vehicles by 2020 that will average 35 miles per gallon. The National Highway Traffic Safety Administration has established an interim target for 2015 that would require automobiles to average 35.7 miles per gallon and trucks 28.6 miles per gallon. These are certainly steps in the right direction, albeit tardy ones.

Town and Country Planning Association

Blowers (1993) has summarized proposals by the Town and Country Planning Association in the United Kingdom for creating a sustainable transport environment. Solutions fall into four broad classes that include:

1. Regulatory mechanisms to control emissions.
2. Tax increases that would favor energy-efficient transport modes.
3. Support for new technologies and alternative modes.
4. Planning approaches that would lessen the need for automobile travel.

On their face, these are good proposals for moving toward sustainable transport, but they leave a little too much to the imagination; they are too broad and not specific enough for anyone to know what should be implemented or what form the proposals should take.

Hughes's 12-Point Plan: A Critique

In his interesting treatment of "personal travel and the greenhouse effect," Hughes (1993) offered a 12-point plan for sustainable emissions from personal travel (see Table 15.1). It should be noted that Hughes was concerned primarily with the United

TABLE 15.1. Hughes's 12-Point Plan for Sustainable Emissions from Personal Travel

1. Motor vehicle fuel economy labeling
2. Fuel economy feebates and rebates
3. Programs for the development of alternative fuels
4. Reduced speed limits
5. Employee travel schemes
6. Environmental impact assessments of transport projects
7. Increased spending on mass transit
8. Redistribution of transport taxes to more energy-efficient modes
9. Accessibility taxes
10. Area licensing and road user fees
11. Land use planning
12. Carbon taxes to lessen motor vehicle use

Source: Hughes (1993). Copyright 1993 by Earthscan Ltd. *www.earthscan.co.uk*. Reprinted by permission.

Kingdom, and he may have been unaware that several of these actions had already been introduced in the United States. The points were critiqued elsewhere, and the discussion that follows is drawn from that source (Black, 1996).

The United States has attempted to solve sustainability-related problems using several of the policy solutions listed in Table 15.1. Others have not been tried and will not be tried in the near term, because they involve the use of taxes, or more specifically tax increases, additional regulatory mechanisms, or subsidization. Congress was opposed to all of these through the first half of the George W. Bush administration. Let us examine the U.S. experience and policy in each of the solution areas.

Motor Vehicle Fuel Economy Labeling

Fuel economy labeling has been practiced in the United States for several years. All new vehicles sold have estimated city and highway miles per gallon posted prominently on the sales sticker, and comparison data for other vehicles in that class (compacts, vans, etc.) are readily available. In addition, the U.S. Department of Energy and the Environmental Protection Agency (1993) began publishing a Gas Mileage Guide that gives fuel economy estimates and annual fuel cost estimates for all vehicles used for personal transportation. This guide first appeared in 1975 and is now available over the Internet.

In spite of this labeling, the United States saw a move away from the most energy-efficient vehicles as the market share of light trucks continued to grow. Light trucks were 19% of light-duty vehicle sales in 1975, rising to 30% by 1988 (Schipper et al., 1993). The success that has been experienced in terms of fuel efficiency appears to be attributable almost entirely to the CAFE standards enacted as a result of the 1976 Energy Act (Greene, 1990, 1998). Unfortunately, differential standards were set for automobiles (27.5 miles per gallon) and light trucks (the variable standard is currently 20.7 miles per gallon) that result in the latter having more power and being more attractive to consumers for that reason. In 1983 minivan sales represented 36,000 new vehicles. The market share increased to 1.3 million by 1994, and the number did not drop below 1.2 million until gasoline prices began increasing significantly halfway through the following decade.

The appearance of sports utility vehicles during the 1990s only made this situation worse. These vehicles proved to be very popular, in spite of very poor fuel economy, and motor vehicle manufacturers significantly increased their production. The SUV market share exceeded 50% by the late 1990s, and, as with light trucks, only significant increases in the price of gasoline during the 2006–2008 period caused their growth and popularity to slow and ultimately plummet by mid-2008. In terms of fuel economy, SUVs were required to meet the truck standard of 20.7 miles per gallon on average, and one could therefore perhaps rightly assert that the CAFE standards (as defined) resulted in the appearance of this market segment.

Even full awareness of the wide variations in fuel economy among vehicles does not necessarily influence consumers' purchases decisions. Those who do take these factors into consideration might not if they knew the idealized conditions under which fuel economy values are determined. The U.S. Environmental Protection Agency is in the process (as of 2007) of changing the manner in which fuel economy values are derived; they are trying to make these a better reflection of real driving conditions. If vehicle purchases are influenced by the desire to minimize emissions of various pollutants, then consumers would also be disappointed in the reliability of the emissions estimates (German, 1997; Ross & Wenzel, 1997).

Prior to the 2007 change in the CAFE standards, there was great reluctance in certain quarters to consider changing the standards. Some critics focused on the negative economic impacts of such changes (Bezdek & Wendling, 2005), while others argued that additional fatalities would result from the use of lighter materials in vehicle production. As noted earlier, the first changes will not be required until 2015, so it will be some time before these concerns are tested by real-world experience.

Fuel Economy Feebates and Rebates

Feebates may take the form of fees or taxes added to the purchase price of new vehicles that have low fuel efficiency; or, alternatively, rebates or reductions in the purchase price of new vehicles that have high fuel efficiency may be used to encourage fuel economy. In general, the sum of the fees collected would equal the sum of the rebates paid out; the two would operate together (Train et al., 1995, 1997). There is no explicit feebate (fee/rebate) program for vehicles in the United States, although California came close to enacting such a program in 1990. On the other hand, the United States has had fee and partial rebate programs that operate independently of one another (Green, Patterson, Singh, & Li, 2005).

The gas guzzler tax in the United States might properly be regarded as a feebate program, in that it essentially adds a tax to the price of the vehicle based on its fuel economy. This tax is forwarded by the manufacturer to the Internal Revenue Service. The tax is included on the vehicle price sticker of new vehicles (Miles-McLean et al., 1993), and it is paid by the consumer when the car is purchased. The gas guzzler tax applies only to cars, not trucks, and therefore is not applicable to either pickup trucks or SUVs. Figure 15.1 shows the tax levels for various levels of vehicle fuel consumption.

In June 2009 the Obama administration, in its first legislative foray in behalf of sustainable transport, enacted a "cash for clunkers" program that awards $3,500–$4,500 vouchers for anyone trading in a vehicle getting 18 or less miles per gallon for one getting at least 22 miles per gallon (which qualifies for the $3,500 voucher); to qualify for the full $4,500 the difference in fuel economy must be greater than 10 miles per gallons. Cars sold between July and November 2009 qualified for the program.

One could also say that the United States has had a rebate program. This "rebate" came in the form of a federal tax credit for those buying hybrid vehicles. The federal program ended in the fall of 2006, and it reportedly had only a minor impact on the sale of hybrids (though a lack of data and subsequent price increases for gasoline may have masked the true impact).

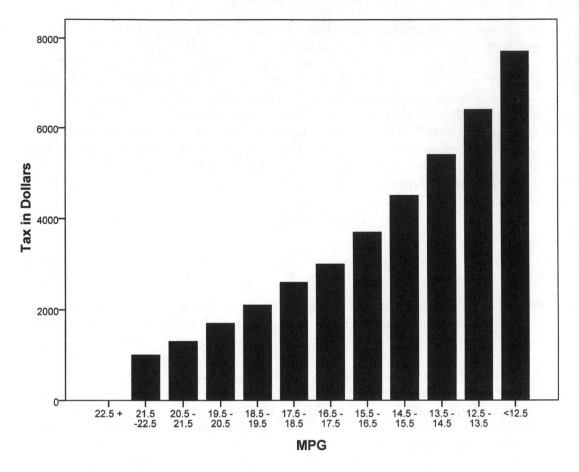

FIGURE 15.1. Gas guzzler tax as it relates to fuel economy. Data source: U.S. Department of Energy (2008a).

Dumas et al. (2007) have outlined and evaluated the manner in which a feebate program would work that involved the United States and Canada. They have also assessed the impact that it would have on motor vehicle sales in the two countries.

Some commentators believe that the savings realized in operating costs should be enough of a financial incentive to encourage consumers to acquire more energy-efficient vehicles. Such vehicles as the Honda Civic and the Toyota Camry use only about one-half to two-thirds of the fuel that larger passenger cars like Buicks or Chevrolets use. However, given the higher cost of electric vehicles, at least initially it may be necessary to offer a rebate program. Such a program is in place in France, where the national government and the state-owned electric utility make up most of the current average cost difference between gasoline and electric versions of the same Peugeot or Renault, placing these vehicles in a much better competitive position in the automobile market. In 1999, this difference, or subsidy, was approximately $3,000 (Funr & Rabl, 1999). As of 2009, this subsidy is approximately $5,500 (Speer, L. J., 2009).

Programs for the Development of Alternative Fuels

The major alternative fuels promoted by the federal government in the United States are ethanol and hydrogen. At the same time a considerable amount of research has been undertaken by entrepreneurs and petroleum companies in the area of ethanol technology. In addition, the U.S. Department of Energy (2007) is investing up to $385 million for six cellulosic biorefineries that should be capable of producing more than 130 million gallons of ethanol when fully operational.

President Bush put a program in place for research on hydrogen. Funding was set at $1.2 billion in 2005. The Obama Administration has halted the program since the general belief is that hydrogen-fueled vehicles are 20 to 30 years away, and other fuels may be ready sooner (Roland, 2009). The automotive industry continues its research on fuel cells.

Reduced Speed Limits

For more than a decade after 1974, the United States instituted a national speed limit of 55 miles per hour. This was changed in 1987 to 65 miles per hour for nonurban sections of the interstate highway system even though the higher speed limit seemed likely to result in the use of 15% more fuel per mile. In November 1995 a new highway bill was signed into law. This statute relinquished the speed-setting authority back to the states in the belief that they were in a better position to decide what the speed should be on their highways. Twelve states (Arizona, Colorado, Idaho, Nebraska, New Mexico, North Dakota, Nevada, Oklahoma, South Dakota, Utah, Texas, and Wyoming) almost immediately raised their speed limits to 75 miles per hour on rural highways. Initially, Montana decided to have no speed limit during daylight hours, but it subsequently changed its speed limit to 75 miles per hour (see Table 14.1).

As was noted earlier, Congress's action resulted in increased emissions and fuel use—and, most likely as well, additional fatalities and injuries from crashes. The data are not totally conclusive on these points, but the decreases expected from improved vehicle technology have not fully materialized. One wonders what the U.S. Congress was thinking!

Employee Travel Schemes

Employers with more than 100 employees located in ozone nonattainment areas, as defined by EPA, were required to develop employee travel plans through a provision of the 1990 amendments to the Clean Air Act. Those plans were intended to provide a mechanism for companies to increase auto occupancy during their employees' work commute by 25%. Some states and urban areas additionally developed their own programs, but these were generally confusing and difficult to implement and monitor. As a result, the EPA backed away from requiring companies to create such programs, and in 1996 the requirement was repealed. States and urban areas can now take other actions (e.g., telecommuting) to satisfy this requirement.

Environmental Impact Assessments of Transport Projects

In the United States all federal transport projects as well as projects regulated by the federal government or receiving federal funds must undergo an environmental impact assessment or analysis since the 1969 passage of the National Environmental Policy Act. If significant negative impacts are identified, then the EPA will try to pressure the responsible parties to mitigate such impacts. The EPA does not have the power to stop such a project—or at least they have not done so to date—and the presence of this requirement does not result in the cancellation of highway projects and the initiation of new transit operations. It usually just means that agencies must defend their plans in more detail.

Increased Spending on Mass Transit

The provision of federal funds for public transit dates back to the middle 1960s in the United States. Similarly, the provision of federal funds for Amtrak dates from 1970, when that rail passenger corporation was created. No one really expected these transport modes to necessarily be profitable after several years of funding but rather thought it important for such modal alternatives to be available to the public. This view of Amtrak, however, was not shared by the George W. Bush administration, which sought to have the railroad eliminated as a national system. It does seem appropriate that a sustainable transport system should have an alternative mode available to both automobile and air travel.

    If any municipality is determined to move away from dependence on the automobile, then it must have a mass transit alternative available that works and makes sense.

Redistribution of Transport Taxes to More Energy-Efficient Modes

Discussions of redistributing transport taxes—specifically, the federal motor vehicle fuel tax—have occurred several times over the past 30 years. These revenues have been available for public transit projects since 1982, but currently about 80%of these taxes are spent on highway projects because of the differences in the capital costs of highways and transit. Requiring that a larger share be spent on transit is not very likely since the fuel tax does not provide sufficient funds to maintain the highway system. In 2009 President Obama had to sign a bill into law that would transfer $7 billion into the Highway Trust Fund to keep it solvent through the end of the fiscal year. These funds are available for both highway and transit projects. There are numerous other sources available for mass transit, as noted by Ubbels et al. (2004). This is usually not the case for highway construction or maintenance.

Accessibility Taxes

The accessibility tax—that is, the idea of taxing entities that are relatively inaccessible but that nonetheless generate travel—is one tax that has not been used in the

United States. Instead, the United States generally uses zoning regulations to control the development of inaccessible land parcels. This system is not free from appeals or variances, so development sometimes occurs, but such mechanisms would also have to be available for accessibility taxes, were they to withstand a legal challenge to their constitutionality.

Area Licensing and Road User Fees

The basic purpose of area licensing or road fees is to restrict traffic from certain areas or to decrease volumes on selected roads. Area licensing, restrictions on vehicle use based on the location of one's residence, has not been used in the United States. Even apart from the basic unpopularity of such a procedure, it would require a rather high level of transit supply that is too often missing from U.S. cities. On the other hand, however, it has been applied successfully in London (which we discussed earlier, in Chapter 10). Suffice it to say that the British experience has been viewed as so successful that this mechanism to restrict traffic is being considered by several U.S. cities.

Road fees, more specifically congestion taxes, have been examined in the United States since the early 1990s (see TRB, 1994a, 1994b). The basic idea is that individual drivers would be charged fees if they used their motor vehicles during the periods of greatest demand. Significant amounts of research and development funds have been dedicated to procedures for scanning car license plates, and this practice has been usefully implemented in numerous metropolitan areas in the United States.

One objection that arises is that this is an unfair method of taxing since the individuals that must travel during periods of peak travel demand are often those with the lowest incomes. As a result, one would expect some type of credit system to be initiated for lower-income drivers; unfortunately this has not happened. Instead, individuals often have slower lanes made available for their use. Another problem with congestion taxing is that it is only successful in corridors with limited highway alternatives—otherwise, it may result in traffic being diverted through residential areas. So, although evaluations of congestion pricing continue, its widespread use in the United States remains doubtful.

On the other hand, placing tolls on currently free roads is likely to become a very common revenue source in the years to come. Recent federal highway legislation permits states to begin imposing tolls on sections of the interstate highway system.

Land Use Planning

One of the benefits of the OPEC embargo of the 1970s was that researchers began looking into the influence of urban spatial structure (i.e., the way cities are laid out geographically) on energy use. Such studies were often done in the abstract, but they nevertheless demonstrated significant potential savings. The problem with the use of these ideas in developed urban areas is that there is little that can be done to change the way land is currently used. If new development is taking place, then land use planning may go a long way in reducing energy use and negative air quality impacts. However, the principal benefits to be achieved by land use planning will probably be in the developing world, where major urban growth and "rapid motorization" are now occurring.

Another land-related problem that is not very significant in the United States, although it is elsewhere, is the use of land for motor vehicles. Whether we are talking about land for residential garages, urban parking facilities, or street parking, it is apparent that many parts of Europe simply cannot find sufficient land for this purpose if automobile ownership continues to grow. Where the problem is worst, we will begin to see peripheral parking facilities with shuttle buses linking these areas to residential, commercial, or industrial areas.

Carbon Taxes to Lessen Motor Vehicle Use

Carbon taxes have been proposed as a means of decreasing carbon emissions that contribute to global warming. The basic idea is that high carbon producers would pay a tax and low carbon producers might actually earn a credit. This translates into developed nations paying a tax and underdeveloped nations earning a credit. The tax may not involve monetary payments, but it could help technology to increasingly reach less developed areas. Exactly how these taxes or credits would be assessed or assigned is a subject of current interest. Although population level as a possibility comes to mind immediately, one would not necessarily want to see the developing world's population growing faster than it already does in response to the benefits of carbon credits. Perhaps a set fee based on a country's population level prior to initiation of the tax system would be best.

Without some type of annual reduction in the carbon level permitted in this system, carbon taxing would only result in maintaining the status quo. Such a reduction is seen by some as having a potentially negative impact on economic growth, and for that reason it has been opposed by some countries, including the United States at various times. The new Obama administration appears to be much more receptive to such ideas.

There are some areas of the United States that have established pollutant emissions trading systems, something conceptually akin to carbon taxes. The examples in the United States mostly involve electric utility companies and have demonstrated that such mechanisms work, that is, they maintain the status quo.

Closure on Hughes's Points

It would appear that most of the points suggested by Hughes—at least to the extent that they have been tried in the United States—are not very successful in achieving sustainable transport, representing only small steps toward that goal. These would include motor vehicle fuel economy labeling, programs for the development of alternative fuels, employee travel schemes, environmental impact assessment of transport projects, increased spending on mass transit, redistribution of travel taxes to more energy-efficient modes, and land use planning. Some of the other points have not yet been tried in the United States, but they don't seem to offer much hope for success either. These include fuel economy feebates and rebates, accessibility taxes, and area licensing and road user fees, although we do have some variations of these. Reduced speed limits for motor vehicles might offer some potential, were they better understood. Carbon taxes to lessen motor vehicle use might also offer some potential, but a suitable approach to this idea has not yet been implemented. Albeit they are incomplete solutions, all of these should be tried in some form if we going to move toward a more sustainable transport system.

THE EUROPEAN UNION

Known as the European Community until 1994, the European Union consists of 27 countries: Austria, Belgium, Bulgaria, Cyprus, the Czech Republic, Denmark, Estonia, Finland, France, Germany, Greece, Hungary, Ireland, Italy, Latvia, Lithuania, Luxembourg, Malta, the Netherlands, Poland, Portugal, Romania, Slovakia, Slovenia, Spain, Sweden, and the United Kingdom. Originally, 12 countries that convened in Maastricht, Netherlands, in 1991 and agreed to certain treaties on monetary union and political union. The single economic union that flowed from this is intended to create an economic power that is the rival of the United States and Japan combined. Since it is growth-oriented, it is bound to create negative environmental impacts, and many of these have a transport origin (see Whitelegg, 1993). The EU, rather than allowing transport to become an environmental drain, has actively sought to create transport policy that is comparatively friendly to the environment (Commission of the European Community, 1993a, 1993b).

A parallel organization that operates in a collaborative manner with the EU is the European Conference of Ministers of Transport, which was responsible for some of the first transport policy related to climate change to come out of Europe in response to the 1992 Rio Earth Summit. The ECMT noted that, given existing trends, it was likely that carbon dioxide would increase nearly 25% between 1990 and 2010—but also expressed the view that a 25% reduction during that same time interval would not be impossible (see ECMT, 1993; Dickerson, 1995)! That level of reduction would essentially take Europe back to 1990 levels. The notable thing about this was that no other multinational group had begun talking about such targets at the time, although the Kyoto conference in 1997 was to go much further.

THE KYOTO CONFERENCE: A GLOBAL APPROACH

During December 1997 the representatives of more than 159 countries met in Kyoto, Japan, to try to reach agreement on how to curtail production of greenhouse gases that are pushing the planet into an era of global warming. Through negotiations the gathered nations reached agreement on certain provisions generally referred to as the Kyoto Protocol or Treaty. The agreement requires that the developed nations reduce emissions of carbon dioxide and five other "greenhouse gases" (methane, nitrous oxide, hydrofluorocarbons, perfluorocarbons, and sulfur hexafluoride) an average of 5.2% below 1990 levels by 2012. The specific targets vary by individual country: the U.S. reduction was to be 7%, Japan's 6%, and the 15 member countries of the European Union at the time were to reduce their emissions to 8% below 1990 levels (see Table 15.2). Developing countries were not required to make any cuts unless they chose to do so. The Protocol also permitted countries, once they met their reduction targets, to sell excess reductions to other countries that falling short of their targets. Heavily forested countries were to receive certain credits since trees absorb carbon dioxide.

Precisely how the emissions trading system would work and how penalties would be assessed in cases of noncompliance were not resolved, nor have they been since (these matters were deferred to a later meeting in Argentina in November 1998 but not resolved at that time).

CONCLUSIONS

The various sustainable transport policies of the countries discussed in this chapter all have certain attractive aspects in common. On the policy side, the softest approach emanates from the UK, where government involvement in even local aspects of the problem remains interesting but so far inconclusive as to its ultimate effectiveness. The Netherlands and Israel tried policy approaches that bordered on harshness, but they had some success in achieving reductions. However, at least in the case of the Netherlands, their ideas on increasing transport costs were resisted by the local populace.

The United States retains its steadfast belief in technology as the ultimate solution to the problem. This is not to say that the United States has totally neglected policy approaches (not so, as illustrated here); it is just that no one expects much success from these. There is far more faith in technologies of new fuels, new cars, new batteries, and the like. For policy approaches to be truly effectual, they must exert forceful control over human behavior or be accompanied by stringent enforcement mechanism, neither of which seem likely to see widespread adoption in the United States over the near term.

The European Union and the ECMT have from time to time made commitments about reductions in emissions, but these have been largely superceded by the Kyoto Protocol. Unlike the Montreal Protocol on chlorofluorocarbons, the Kyoto agreement is much more difficult to implement. At the Rio Earth Summit in 1992 the countries of the world pledged to reduce emissions to 1990 levels by 2000, but this goal was not met. The participants at Kyoto gave themselves more time, but the targets they have set are even more difficult to achieve.

As of June 1998 (3 months after it was opened for signatures) only a few countries had signed the protocol—the United States, Australia, Japan, and the countries of the European Union being noticeable absent. The EU nations and Japan have since ratified the agreement, and the protocol went into effect on February 15, 2005. Its ratification required at least 55 countries representing at least 55% of the emis-

TABLE 15.2. Kyoto Targets for Emissions Reductions (vs. 1990 Levels)

Country	Target (%)
Australia	+8
Austria	−8
Belgium	−8
Bulgaria	−8
Canada	−6
Croatia	−5
Czech Republic	−8
Denmark	−8
Estonia	−8
European Community	−8
Finland	−8
France	−8
Germany	−8
Greece	−8
Hungary	−6
Iceland	+10
Ireland	−8
Italy	−8
Japan	−6
Latvia	−8
Liechtenstein	−8
Lithuania	−8
Luxembourg	−8
Monaco	−8
Netherlands	−8
New Zealand	0
Norway	+1
Poland	−6
Portugal	−8
Romania	−8
Russian Federation	0
Slovakia	−8
Slovenia	−8
Spain	−8
Sweden	−8
Switzerland	−8
Ukraine	0
United Kingdom and Northern Ireland	−8
United States of America	−7

Source: United Nations Framework Convention on Climate Change (1999).

sions. As noted earlier in this volume, there seems to be serious question in certain quarters as to whether the U.S. Senate will ever ratify the Kyoto Protocol. However, going forward, the Obama administration may well set the United States on a path toward ratifying eventually the protocol.

The global approach appears to be the only approach that can be taken to the twin problems of climate change and transport sustainability that has a better than even chance of being successful. Kyoto's goals though elusive, may well be our best hope and therefore worth working for. Even though the goals targeted may not succeed in reducing the threat of climate change near term, the Montreal Protocol's initial targets were also seen as too weak and later strengthened (which may happen in the case of Kyoto).

Of course, this book focuses not only on these problems but also on diminishing fuel reserves as well as such related problems as excessive traffic congestion and fatalities and injuries attributable to a nonsustainable transport system. Clearly there is a dire need for technological breakthroughs because without them we may well regress into a less mobile future.

CHAPTER 16

Sustainable Travel Demand Management

> Probably the most important consideration in implementing
> TDM actions is related to the fact that they focus on changing
> individual travel behavior. In the typical transportation context
> of today's urban areas (i.e., predominant use of the automobile
> for personal transportation), this is perhaps the most telling
> challenge to successful TDM implementation.
>   —MICHAEL MEYER (1999)

A brief history of travel demand management (TDM) is available in Meyer (1999). Both Ferguson (2000) and Meyer summarize the numerous techniques that have been developed and in some cases implemented to manage travel demand. Some of these techniques are discussed elsewhere in this book, but we would be remiss if we did not devote more attention to them because they can often be implemented easily and they may be very effective. We have focused on pricing as it relates to congestion in Chapter 10, and we will examine telecommuting in Chapter 18, so we do not examine them here but instead discuss some other aspects of pricing that are not related to congestion directly. These various methods and ideas were not developed with the idea of making the transport system more sustainable, but that is in essence what they attempt to do, and as a result they are viewed here as sustainable travel demand management techniques.

The techniques discussed are not necessarily directed toward just one of the five major problems noted at the beginning of this volume, but they may offer some assistance in solving multiple problems simultaneously. For example, anything that decreases or discourages one's inclination to drive also decreases fuel consumption, total emissions of carbon dioxide as well as the other criteria pollutants, the risk of an accident, and potential traffic congestion, since all of these increase with driving. We will not examine the various techniques in any particular order.

TRAFFIC CALMING

As the name implies, traffic calming is intended to slow the movement of traffic. It is applied most frequently in residential areas in an attempt to dissuade drivers from passing through the neighborhood or in areas of high pedestrian activity: schools, campuses, shopping centers, malls, or downtown areas. The obvious goal is to increase the safety of residents, pedestrians, or shoppers.

Common techniques to accomplish calming are the placing of (asphalt) bumps in the street that are sufficient to cause the driver to slow down in order to avoid damage to his or her vehicle. A common practice in a downtown area would be to place large concrete pots in the roadway that require the driver to carefully navigate around these at a slow speed. On the other hand, residential areas may use one-way streets or street closures to accomplish calming.

As one might expect, these physical devices are usually welcome in the residential areas where they are placed, but it is nevertheless wise to get the support of residents in advance (Taylor & Tight, 1997). They are not particularly liked by drivers, but this is not surprising. In the downtown area merchants are sometimes opposed to the pots, as they may diminish ready parking access to the businesses.

Elvik (2001) has undertaken a meta-analysis of 33 studies to evaluate the safety effects of traffic calming. He found that on average these various devices result in a reduction of personal injury accidents of about 25% in residential areas and 10% on main roads. The study of a main road through Storuman, Sweden, by Leden et al. (2006) noted significant improvements in safety from traffic calming devices and code modifications on the road, thereby reducing the need for a bypass around the community.

VEHICLE REPLACEMENT OR RETIREMENT

Several years ago a major source of emissions in California was thought to be older vehicles still on the highway, those manufactured prior to emissions controls being required. Authorities thus decided that emissions could be significantly reduced by removing these vehicles from the highway. California there upon set up a program to purchase any operating vehicle manufactured before 1971 for $750. In general, the program was a great success, with reduced emissions fully realized. Allegedly there were some administrative problems, but the idea definitely seems worthwhile for areas where older vehicles still operate in large numbers.

The car retirement program continues in California. In order to qualify for the retirement program you must be the registered owner of the vehicle, and you must have paid the appropriate registration fees. In addition there are numerous specific requirements for the vehicle (see Table 16.1). The program is rigid to some extent but not unreasonably so; earlier versions of the program were subject to some problems, and these requirements are obviously an attempt to prevent a reoccurrence of those events.

Dill (2004) has suggested that the estimated emissions reduction benefits of the program may be overstated because the vehicles scrapped may not be driven as

TABLE 16.1. California Car Retirement Program Requirements

1. The vehicle must have failed the biennial Smog Check inspection.
2. The vehicle must not have an emissions control system that was tampered with.
3. The vehicle must not be in the process of being sold.
4. The vehicle must not be registered to a business, fleet, or nonprofit organization.
5. The vehicle must have failed its Smog Test within 120 days of its current registration.
6. The vehicle must have been registered in California for 2 years prior to its current registration.
7. The vehicle must be currently registered.
8. The vehicle must be a passenger vehicle or light-duty truck.
9. The vehicle must have a qualifying Smog Check failure.
10. The vehicle must also have: all doors present; hood lid present; dashboard present; windshield present; at least one side window glass present; a driver's seat present; at least one bumper present; exhaust system present; all side and/or quarter panels present; at least one headlight, one taillight, and one brake present.
11. The vehicle must be driven to the dismantler under its own power.
12. The vehicle must start readily.
13. The vehicle's operation must not be inhibited by any body, steering, or suspension damage.
14. The vehicle must be able to move forward a distance of 10 yards under its own power.
15. The vehicle's interior pedals (gas, brake, clutch) must be operational.

Source: California Department of Consumer Affairs (undated).

much as assumed; they might not last as long as expected; emissions may have been overestimated; and the vehicles purchased to replace those scrapped may be older than the fleet average. Van Wee et al. (2000) suggest that putting catalytic converters on older vehicles may be more effective in reducing emissions.

FEEBATES

Feebates, which are fees or taxes added to the purchase price of new vehicles that have low fuel efficiency or rebates or reductions in the purchase price of new vehicles that have high fuel efficiency, were already discussed at length in Chapter 15.

There is a tax on gas guzzlers in the United States, but this tax applies only to about 2% of the vehicles sold. A major reason for this low percentage is that light trucks and SUVs were considered work vehicles and excluded from the tax. This tax is paid to the federal government by the manufacturer, not the consumer, although the tax is listed on the price sticker of new vehicles (Miles-McLean et al., 1993) and is ultimately paid by the consumer as part of the cost of the vehicle.

CARPOOLING

Carpooling is one of the oldest techniques for reducing traffic on a highway, and therefore it is sometimes discussed as a method of reducing congestion. It reached a peak during the late 1970s and early 1980s in response to the gasoline shortages then prevalent. It began to decrease after that point in time. Garrison and Ward (2000) have identified the conditions that make it possible for two individuals to readily carpool. These individuals must:

(1) live reasonably close to a common route to work;
(2) work at the same place, or at least places close together;
(3) work nearly the same hours;
(4) have jobs that rarely demand variation in their start and stop times; and
(5) commute far enough that it's worth the extra hassle and time of picking up the passenger(s) and delivering them back home. (p. 49)

One wonders how car pools involving more than two people were ever created at all!

While it was remarkable that there was as much carpooling as there was during the 1970s and 1980s, it is not surprising that it began to diminish. Over the intervening quarter-century the chief participants have changed jobs, retired, or died. Given the turnover in employment, especially in recent years, it is unlikely that workers generally know one another as well today as they did earlier, something that would tend to discourage the formation of such groups. In addition, there is less governmental emphasis placed on the formation of carpools today.

Nevertheless, individuals have set up websites that enable potential carpool participants to identify others with similar needs and attributes. Anecdotal evidence would suggest that the significant gasoline price increases of 2007–2008 led to an increase in carpooling.

CAR SHARING

Car sharing is a relatively new service that provides members with access to a vehicle on an hourly basis. Members can reserve a car online or by phone, walk to the nearest parking space, open the doors with an electronic key, and drive off. They are billed monthly for the time the vehicle is used and the miles the member drives (Millard-Ball et al., 2005).

This is not yet a major program in either the United States or Canada, with an estimated 100,000 or fewer participants in the program in both countries. It is most attractive in areas that are densely populated, where residents typically don't own or frequently use a car. It is believed that the program decreases vehicle ownership and vehicle travel, but the latter point may be open to argument. Those who participate in the program will drive less than those who own a vehicle, but those who do not have a vehicle will end up driving more than they would otherwise. As a result, one could argue whether the reduction in driving exceeds the induced travel, a point not yet sufficiently researched. Nevertheless, it is believed that car sharing programs lower emissions (due to less driving), increase transit trips (when a car is not necessary for the trip), result in consumer cost savings (since purchasing a car is not necessary), and generate a higher level of mobility (for those who only had mass transit available before). Fellows and Pitfield (2000) suggest that car sharing programs can produce high net benefits to society that are comparable to highway projects.

CASH-OUT PROGRAMS

One of the provisions of the Climate Change Action Plan announced by the Clinton administration in October 1993 was a program in which employees would be able to opt for the value of a parking place as additional income and arrange for their own transport (via vans, buses, or carpools) to work (Clinton & Gore, 1993). The proposed federal program was not that different from a California program enacted by that state's legislature in 1992, which required any employer who subsidized commuter parking to offer its employees what was referred to as a cash-out program.

Shoup (1997) examined the cash-out programs of eight employers in California and found the following:

1. The number of workers driving to work alone dropped by 17%.
2. The number of carpoolers increased by 64%.
3. Transit riders increased by 50%.
4. Those walking or biking increased by 39%.
5. Carbon dioxide emissions dropped by 367 grams per employee per year.
6. Employers' commuting subsidies increased $2 per employee per month (because the cost for parking did not decrease as much as expected).
7. Vehicle miles of travel for the firms examined dropped 12%.
8. Federal and state income taxes increased $65 per employee per year because more employees opted for cash.

From all of the above indications, cash-out programs appear to work.

PARKING RESTRAINT AND TAXES

Parking is important in any urban area for several reasons. First, parking and more specifically its price will alter the cost of travel, and this will affect the transport modes chosen by urban residents. If parking costs are too great, commuters and others may well select a different mode of travel, usually public transit in one of its various forms. Second, the convenience of parking can influence the destinations selected for various types of trips. For many years, the obvious example was the downtown district trying desperately to compete with the fringe shopping mall, the former featuring parking meters and the latter free parking. Needless to say, the downtown shopping area lost out in most cases until it decided that free parking and consumers were more important than parking revenues. Third, parking may well be an important revenue source, as it was for many years in most urban areas and continues to be for those urban areas that have come to rely on municipal garages and other parking structures in the central city area.

Parking restraint is usually undertaken for several different reasons. It may be that some activity generates so much traffic that it spills over into an adjacent community, and some type of parking restraint is necessary to allow parking to be available to urban residents in the spillover area. This is a case where permits are usually necessary to park in the area on certain days or at certain times of the day. A second reason for parking restraint may be that vehicles in a particular area generate or contribute to air quality problems. In this case vehicles are simply not allowed in the area under any circumstances. A third case might be an attempt on the part of planners to keep vehicles out of an area for traffic safety reasons, say, where there are large concentrations of pedestrians. All three cases seek to keep vehicles out of certain areas through very explicit regulatory actions.

Parking taxes are usually charged for the purpose of increasing the price of parking and, among other things, encouraging individuals to use alternative (less expensive) transport modes. In those cases where employers charge employees for parking on their property, one could regard this as a tax for parking since it is a very uncommon situation. However, this is a very common situation on university campuses. Apart from their obvious revenue implications, the goal of these charges (or taxes) is to discourage individuals from using automobiles and encourage them to use public transit, ride bikes, or walk. If public transit is the preferred transit mode in diverting such additional traffic, then the area charging the fee or tax should have a reasonably good transit system to replace the automobile. All too often this is not the case.

There is surprisingly little literature on the various uses of parking restraint and parking taxes. Instead, a large body of literature is devoted to parking requirements as part of the planning and development process in urban areas (Ferguson, 2004) and examining the extent to which various parking restraint systems hurt central cities (Still & Simmonds, 2000); only Feitelson and Rotem (2004) have rigorously examined the concept of taxing for parking.

TRANSIT VOUCHERS

The idea of transit vouchers was first proposed in part by Root (2001); these would be tax-free vouchers for employees to encourage them to use public transport. The basic idea is that employers would issue the vouchers and claim the cost of these as a tax deduction from the government. The local transit provider would also benefit from the program, as it would increase revenues for such transit operators. Although Root found acceptance for the idea in rural areas where commutes are longer, the viability of such a program beyond rural areas has not been assessed.

ELIMINATING COMPANY CARS

Even broaching the topic of company-leased cars might seem a "stretch" in filling the subject matter of this chapter. On the other hand, we know so little about where and when company cars are provided and how much they are used. For example, probably few of us know the employees of one's organization that are provided with a "company" car, and most of us probably don't care about such frills. At the same time, such privileges usually come with free parking and a credit card that covers fuel costs. In effect, there is little that we can do to those who operate a company car to discourage their overuse of such a vehicle.

This may seem trivial unless we suddenly discover that there are far more company cars out there than we realized. The author is not privy to the extent of this problem in the United States and Canada, but he is aware of the situation in the Netherlands. In that particular case, company cars account for 42% of total annual car sales of new cars (Rietveld & van Ommeren, 2002). This becomes a serious problem when numbers reach these levels, but the problem has not been researched sufficiently in North America to recognize whether it is a problem here or not.

CONCLUSIONS

This chapter has not covered all of the sustainable travel demand management techniques for urban areas. Some of these are of such importance that they are discussed in separate chapters devoted to them exclusively. This is clearly the case with various pricing ideas (discussed in Chapter 10) and CAFE standards (discussed in Chapter 15).

For the discussion in this chapter we have viewed and reviewed techniques that are not as common as pricing and fuel economy. Within that context we see almost all of the topics of this chapter worthy of consideration, including car sharing, carpooling, eliminating company cars, transit vouchers, parking restraints and taxing, feebates and rebates, and cash-out programs as reasonable mechanisms to pursue to increase the sustainability of travel within urban areas. Of less certainty are the benefits of vehicle recycling, retirement, or replacement programs, given that the vehicles in many cases are not that old and may not be replaced by the best vehicles on the highway (as assumed).

A particularly useful source of information on sustainability as it relates to travel demand management is available as an online encyclopedia (Victoria Transport Policy Institute, 2009). This source is continually updated.

EDUCATION

CHAPTER 17

Educating for Change

> In place of product innovation, the automobile industry went on a two-decade marketing binge which generally offered up the same old product under the guise of something new and useful. There really was nothing essentially new.
> —J. PATRICK WRIGHT (1979)

Wright's statement above sheds insight on how advertising transformed a nation of walkers and transit riders into a nation of automobile users. Mass marketing was capable of not only doing this but also convincing consumers that they just had to have the newest model released by Detroit even though the vehicle was no different than last year's except for some minor modifications in the body to make it look different, if only slightly so. Marketing as a form of education can obviously be very powerful in bringing about change, but let us not give the credit completely to advertising. There was more to it than that.

THE WAY WE WERE

In the 1920s and 1930s the appearance of a new automobile was a major media event covered by the newspapers and magazines of the day. Even in small-town America when a new Cadillac was purchased it was cause for a major article in the local newspaper—even if the new owner was also the owner of the Cadillac dealership! It was free advertising for the local dealer, and people would flock to the showroom just to see what the vehicle looked like even though few could afford to buy one during the depression.

The sales pitch continued in the post-World War II years and was far more successful. People had money, and automobile purchases began to climb significantly. Congestion became a problem that was attacked almost immediately with the passage of the interstate highway act in 1956, although it was nearly 16 years before that system was close to completion.

Automobile marketing shifted into high gear by this time: we were told to "See the USA in your Chevrolet" by major entertainers of the day. In smaller cities and towns the release of the new models in September or October for the coming year was a social event on the level of a July 4th parade. The following was typical of the newspaper advertisements of the day:

> SEE THE 1956 CHEVROLET at Hughes Motor Co., 153 W. Broadway now! Longer, lower, more powerful, more beautiful than ever! Be sure to register for valuable door prizes. Favors for the ladies—balloons for the kiddies.

As a child growing up in the 1950s, this was a big day. There were certainly balloons, but there was also plenty of candy, and if you got there early enough you might receive a toy that was a scale model of the vehicle being featured! This was happening all across America at the time.

Of course, television was also making its way into every living room, and the industry did not waste any time in becoming a major sponsor and advertiser for this medium. Now the vehicles could be seen in the comfort of your home, over and over again! It wasn't just the automobile industry that moved much of its advertising to television, it was also the related industries—particularly the oil companies.

If owning an automobile was a necessity for those who could afford it, owning a new one every 2 years became something of a status symbol that could only be explained by a sociologist specializing in consumer behavior. Clearly there could be little wear and tear on a vehicle of the day in only 2 years, so the purchase was not dictated by necessity.

Wright (1979) refers to the industry efforts as marketing, but it was really a type of education—not particularly good education, but education nevertheless. Bear in mind that the time period being discussed by Wright was the 1960s and 1970s. Americans were also being told about the major problems of air pollution, much of it attributable to automobile emissions, and the late 1960s and early 1970s brought the first major environmental laws: the National Environmental Policy Act (1970) and the Clean Air Act (1963 and 1970). In addition, traffic fatalities were on their way to an all-time high for the United States that was reached in 1972. Yet, here was the automobile industry countering all of this bad news with an advertising campaign that still made owning an automobile—a large one, at that—make sense to the public. The only thing that brought this mania to a halt was the oil embargo of 1973. The auto-consuming mania might have resumed afterward were it not that a number of foreign automobile companies began to sell cars in the United States that used less fuel and polluted the environment less flagrantly.

Today there is a growing interest in doing something about the obsession that some people have with automobiles. For many, the glowing teenage years are timelessly intertwined with two significant rites of passage. The first is obtaining a driver's permit at 16 (or thereabouts, the age varies by state). This permit gives the young person the right to drive so long as he or she is accompanied by someone else with a driver's license, the obvious purpose being to enable young people to learn to drive. The second rite of passage is taking the drivers' test—first the written exam and then finally the road exam. Assuming one passes these tests, he or she is then adjudged ready to join others on the open highway entirely free of one's parents.

Why the obsession with driving? First, not everyone is so obsessed, although we frequently ignore those who are not. People in the Midwest are always surprised when they encounter someone in their 30s or 40s from New York City who does not know how to drive a car. That city has a reasonably good public transportation system, a genuine shortage of parking places, virtually no private residential garages, and little need to know how to drive. There may be some lessons to be learned here.

A NEW DIRECTION

Looking back to simpler times (as we just did) may be suggestive of a new direction that we can take to make transport more sustainable in the United States. It is not a quick fix to our many sustainable transport problems, but it does seem to be a move in the right direction.

There are a couple of preliminary matters we should dispense of before proceeding. The first is that we must acknowledge that the automobile is and will continue to be the dominant transport mode in the United States. Some people would like to see mass transit become far more readily available in the United States, but doubling our investment in public transit—even if it doubled transit ridership—would still leave more than 90% of the trips by automobiles. It is pointless to assume that we could make a radical switch to another transport mode when we have neither the funds nor the will to make this change real—a position that is both well founded and held by others (Webber, 2006; Garrison & Ward, 2000).

The Role of Education

What is being advocated here is a change in the way we look at transportation, one that will necessitate some major changes in the content of education in this country. Of course, education can not handle all of the problems, but there are some problems that could benefit from an attempt to change the mindset in this country regarding transportation. Some of the education would indeed be in our school systems, but other parts would be in advertising—or marketing, if you will.

The Environmental Impact of Automobiles

At least *some* of our schools are teaching students about the environment. It would be a minor stretch for teachers to develop teaching units on the problems, not of the automobile, but of excessive use of the automobile. Included would be the problems of using up fuel that is nonrenewable, the pollution that is generated by driving for short trips rather than walking or bicycling, and the adverse consequences of such pollution for both our health and our planet's climate. These are illustrative of the kinds of teaching units that could be created and adopted across the various grades as appropriate.

It is clear that in the past there has been no concerted attempt to point out the problems created by the automobile for the environment. As a result most young people were relatively unaware of these and had very positive attitudes toward the car. However, such attitudes may be changing, according to Sandqvist (1999), who examined attitudes among young adults toward automobile ownership in Sweden and found that fewer of the current generation have an interest in automobiles. She notes that "the young adults (who have usually grown up with a family car), seem less appealed by the idea of having their own car, more concerned with the environmental drawbacks of cars and less eager to obtain a driver's license, even though the infrastructure now makes a car less dispensable in everyday life." This attitude does not appear to have come about through organized education, although the cause of the shift is unclear. It is also unclear how widespread the new attitude is in other parts of Europe or North America.

There is a clear need for a structured program that could be used by teachers in their classes at the elementary or secondary level. O'Brien (1999) notes the existence of such a program, titled "Learning for a Sustainable Future," that has developed a sustainable transport element. Available via the Internet, the program includes assistance with curriculum development and materials to support teachers in this area of education.

Driver Education

It is surprising that many schools across the United States do not offer courses in driver education to their students. It is also surprising that some of the schools that do offer driver education make the students pay hundreds of dollars for the class. What in the world are educators thinking? As we have noted elsewhere, motor vehicle crashes are the major cause of death of young people of driving age in the United States, and we are only going to allow the wealthy to have the benefit of this training?

These classes, in addition to teaching how to drive properly, should teach aspects of physics and the difficulty of controlling vehicles at high speeds. These courses should be intensive and cover all dimensions of driving. Rarely do they do this. Usually they are taught after the normal school day by a teacher who needs extra income.

Back to School

It should be apparent to anyone who does drive that many of the other drivers that you share the road with do not quite know what is going on nowadays in the world of motor vehicles and highway safety. We would probably be wise to have drivers take a refresher courses in driving from time to time. In many cases if you passed that written exam back when you were 17, you can reach 70 without ever having to pass any other test except possibly a vision test.

Perhaps more than a 1-hour class would be needed, but there are definitely some changes that have occurred in the past thirty years that drivers should be aware of. For example, most drivers have no idea that turning right on red (after a full stop) is now permissible at all intersections as the result of a federal law, unless a sign expressly forbids it; most drivers, similarly, are completely unaware of the left-on-red rules and when they apply. We have all followed a driver moving very slowly toward an intersection waiting for the light to change, when in reality demand-responsive intersections will not change until you arrive at the intersection. Center lanes that are set aside solely for turns baffle far too many drivers who treat them as a median that you can drive across. Finally, how to correctly merge your car onto a major highway is apparently not taught very well since most driver education classes and nervous parents prefer to teach driving only on local streets. We could go on, but you get the idea. It wouldn't hurt to have a class or, failing that, a little booklet that explains the "new things" that were not in the old booklet.

The Merits of Bicycle Riding

Every attempt should be made to encourage people to walk or ride a bicycle more often. The author once thought that biking was just too selective in terms of which members of the population would engage in it, but that was prior to his first trip to Amsterdam. Anyone who has been there is aware that everyone from the very young to the very old use bikes. This is not to advocate a massive shift to this transport mode for the U.S. population as a whole but rather to make it practicable, acceptable, and safe to continue using a bike beyond one's teenage years—not just for exercise or recreation but as a practical transport mode.

Of course, the primary concern is the safety aspect since bikes do have one of the worst safety records on a per mile of travel basis. Bicycling can definitely be made substantially safer than it is in virtually every city in this country. At the same time, there are some cities where bikes are not very feasible, except for short trips, namely, in the more dispersed cities of the West or Southwest, for example, Los Angeles and Houston.

The Merits of Transit and Subsidies

For longer trips in many communities there is usually a public transit system. Some individuals use bus transit, but a sizable number of people will have nothing to do with it, perhaps viewing it as a mode for the carless, the aged, the poor, and the handicapped. The specific origins of this negative attitude toward bus service are not clear. In any case, attempts to alter this perspective—which, interestingly, does not carry over to light rail or subway systems—should be made.

Related to this perception is the generally negative attitude that many have toward subsidizing public transit of any kind. Many individuals in this country have no desire to drive an automobile. If they do not and if there is no transit readily available to them, then they will be victims of social exclusion from much of what is possible in life. Public transit, at a minimum, is a social service that every community should provide to its citizens, that will need to be subsidized in nearly every case, and that the community's leaders and voters should be willing to embrace. Unfortunately, too many adults have grown up not sharing this sense of altruism toward the community at large.

Educating through Brochures

Beyond using the classroom to educate about sustainable transport, one can conceive using flyers or brochures that describe some specific remedial program or that educate the public about a problem. Four representative brochures are worth discussing here. The first, from Hampshire County in the United Kingdom, discusses a program called Headstart, a transport awareness campaign that seeks to make people aware of the negative consequences of increasing automobile use. While it does not ask people to give up the use of their vehicles, it urges them to use them more thoughtfully. Thus, the cover of the brochure poses the question, "Will you be using your head?" and the text goes on to advocate walking, cycling, ride sharing, and public transit in place of automobile travel.

The second brochure comes from Nottingham, also in the United Kingdom. Titled "Green Commuter Plans: An Employer's Guide," it outlines the steps an employer should go through in setting up a "green commuter plan," which involves getting the lone driver-worker out of his or her car and into a carpool, electric vehicle, bus, or subway car, or into cycling or walking. The justification cited for this change is the increasing "dangers of a fume-filled and traffic-congested city caused by the uncontrolled use of the car."

Traffic crash statistics are the focus of a brochure from the Environment and Technical Services Department of the Durham County Council in the United Kingdom. Their brochure identifies the crash (accident) reduction target for Durham County and then proceeds to note where the county stands based on 1996 statistics. Although the document is well done and presents statistics that should be known to the public, it is doubtful whether dry statistics are apt to catch the reader's attention. Certainly statistics are not as graphic as the crash photographs displayed in the daily newspaper or the grisly film segment covering a local motor vehicle crash shown on the evening television news. Of course, Durham is not intending to solve the national problem—just their piece of that national problem of too many fatalities and injuries. Nevertheless, if there is even a slight chance that your brochure will reduce overall fatalities, it is probably worth trying.

The final brochure from the United Kingdom, also addressing the topic of motor vehicle crashes, poses the question on its cover "WHAT WOULD YOU KILL FOR?" The text next proceeds to ask why people drive too fast and then cites the obvious potential consequences. To catch a train? To get to work 5 minutes early? The Department of Transport in the United Kingdom, the sponsor of this brochure, notes that 77,000 injuries and 1,000 fatalities a year result directly from excessive speed. Of course, a brochure is only a partial remedy to the problem, but the reduction of even one fatality a year would make this a worthwhile approach.

These brochures are obviously low-tech and relatively inexpensive. They seek to educate people about the problems that increased automobile use brings in its wake, which may seem naive to some, but the reality is that many individuals do not think about these problems, or if they do they seem to think there is nothing they can do about them. The reality is that individuals can do something about these problems although their impact may be marginal. In point of fact, most of Western society has been "educated" to believe that acquiring an automobile has no hidden societal costs—when, in fact, it does! Although brochures seek to reeducate individuals, some believe we should attack the original education problem posed earlier in this chapter about reeducating the masses.

THE USE OF TELEVISION

In the United States we tend to use fewer brochures and more television time to get our message out to the public. This is because U.S. television stations are required by the FCC to devote a certain amount of their airtime to "public service announcements." In the area of motor vehicle crashes, the U.S. Department of Transportation has made available "infomercials" on crashes, with crash dummies doing the narration in many cases, the implication being that dummies (much more so than humans!) can walk away from severe crashes. These were followed by 30-second "spots" that were very realistic and more hard-hitting. One of these shows an ultrasound of an unborn fetus with its heartbeat clearly audible; the screen then dissolves to a little girl's name and the statement "Killed on her way to being born." Such spots are certainly a more effective use of television in this area than has been seen heretofore.

At the same time, the public is constantly exposed to TV dramas that involve high-speed chases or speed for its own sake, resulting in crashes but surprisingly few fatalities. The implications are that people can walk away from motor vehicle crashes with minor injuries, if any at all. We have little appreciation of what the long-term effects of such depictions might be on the thinking of young children. From time to time there are organized campaigns to limit the amount of violence that children can view on television, usually through the entertainment industry's attempting to monitor itself.

CONCLUSIONS

Changing prevailing attitudes toward the automobile through education, brochures, and television have been the subject of this chapter. Some of these mechanisms seem effective, but thoroughgoing assessments are hard to come by. These efforts certainly do not do any harm, and they may be sufficient to change perspectives on the use—or rather overuse—of the car.

Assuming transport sustainability is a global problem, we should not assume that any local area can solve it alone. Nevertheless, through the actions discussed here local areas may improve their own sustainability by reducing traffic deaths and injuries, congestion, and local pollution. Some believe that this problem can be solved through the united actions of many communities, but that assessment seems foolhardy to this observer. These communication tools will have a global impact when the nations of the world undertake a comprehensive top-down approach to the problem, thereby stimulating local areas to implement their own bottom-up solutions in response to concerted worldwide action.

TECHNOLOGY

CHAPTER 18

Telecommuting, Information and Communication Technologies, and E-Commerce

> Here we are in the middle of the information age and we're still moving around a lot. What's going on?
>
> —JOHN NILES (2002)

Journeys to and from work pose particular problems in providing sustainable transport. Heightened peak-hour flows create extraordinary demands on roadways and public transit facilities that may well exceed their normal capacities. Employers have begun to adopt a variety of measures to reduce and control the demand for transport to their work sites, galvanized by external forces and opportunities as well as their own motivations. Three aspects of work travel policies will be assessed here. First, we examine the potential of substituting telecommunications directly for travel. There is little agreement about the total number of telecommuters in the United States (Mokhtarian et al., 2005), some suggesting as few as 10 million and others estimating as many as 30 million. Second, there are serious questions whether telecommuting will really help make transport more sustainable. Third, there are intriguing questions about the secondary effects of telecommuting on society as a whole.

Similarly, there is a great deal of interest in the concept that information and communication technologies (ICT) offer the potential of drastically reducing the amount of transportation taking place, a notion that we examine in some detail.

Finally, we look at e-commerce, a growing sector of the economy that some researchers believe will significantly alter the way in which businesses deal with consumers and other businesses. We concur that the changes are significant, but as our concern here is with travel, it is less clear that e-commerce will have truly profound impacts in that sector.

TELECOMMUTING AND SUSTAINABLE TRANSPORT

"Telecommuting" is chiefly an American-coined term meaning the substitution of remotely based telecommunications for travel to a workplace. The British prefer the word "teleworking," which suggests that employees are working remotely by means of some telecommunications link. The telecommunications linkage may be through some type of fiber optic cable and modem that connects the remote site with the workplace. For at least the past decade, these terms have been used with less rigor than should be the case, especially so as they relate to this topic.

If you have to write a report and stay at home to do it on your personal computer rather than at your office, are you a telecommuter? By most definitions you would qualify as a telecommuter, but this is really not the classic definition of the term. In 1993 the U.S. Department of Transportation estimated in a report that there would be 20 million telecommuters in the United States by 2000 (USDOT, 1993), an estimate viewed with skepticism at the time, but this was because readers had the impression that telecommuters were workers who would telecommute all the time. In reality, a worker was a telecommuter if he or she worked at a remote site electronically connected to a workplace for *1 day a week or more*. The fact is that there are very few jobs that can be performed 5 days a week remotely.

It is reasonable to ask what the role of telecommuting is with regard to sustainable transport. A review of the major failings of transport sustainability today (see Chapter 1) reveals that we are running out of fuel, polluting the local environment and global atmosphere, that the transport system is congested, and that its use results in far too many fatalities and injuries. Telecommuting has the potential of decreasing fuel use, pollution, congestion, and fatalities if it is adopted on a large enough scale. Whether the potential will be realized is currently unknown since the statement makes the assumption that there will be a reduction in travel if enough workers telecommute, and we are uncertain whether this will actually occur.

Questions about Telecommuting

Whether travel will actually decrease is only one of the research questions that is currently unresolved regarding telecommuting. Mokhtarian (1997) has reviewed the numerous unknowns in this area and concluded that with telecommuting:

1. The number of work trips should decrease.
2. Noncommuting trips may increase.
3. Trips may shift to off-peak periods or to different days of the week.
4. Work trips may be made to a local telecommuting center.
5. Nonwork trips may be shorter in length.
6. Carpools and vanpools could lose members and cease operations.
7. Transit operators may lose passengers and their revenues.
8. Short trips may be made by walking or biking.
9. Current trip-chaining behavior (handling several trip demands in a single trip) may be replaced by more single-purpose trips.

10. Trip-making roles may change within the household.
11. The need may lessen for households to have an additional car.
12. Households may find it advantageous to relocate to more distant, but lower cost locations since total travel time and expense may still be less than it had been.

This may seem like an excessive number research issues not fully resolved yet, and it is. The primary reason why these points have not been definitively established is the lack of large-scale research data to evaluate them. Most of these issues have been examined in small case studies, but the conclusions that have emerged may be primarily influenced by geographic differences in behavior attributable to destination density and current travel behavior—but this is also just a hypothesis. Let's examine these 12 points in more detail and specify what is known about each.

Work Trips Decrease

If workers are telecommuting, there is every reason to believe that for a given household total work trips will decrease. However, if two members of the household share a vehicle as part of the work trip, then more commuting could result, as the family member telecommuting has more freedom to go to the office when he or she finds it most convenient.

Noncommuting Trips May Increase

Trips previously made as part of the work trip now require additional trips that were embedded in that previous work trip. It is also possible that the prior trips may be still undertaken by another household member (if there is one) who continues to commute.

Period of Trip Making May Shift

It is hoped that necessary trips made by telecommuters will be made off-peak and thus decrease problems related to congestion at peak hours or on peak days.

Work Trips May Be Made to a Telecenter

For various reasons an employer may not want to have employees working at home, but the employees may find working at a different remote site more attractive. These sites often involve several employees, perhaps of different employers, working in a single facility that has come to be called a telecenter or televillage. There are numerous reasons why these may be more attractive to employers than a home location. In some cases employers have to ensure that they are providing a safe work place for their employees. Most companies would not want to have to do this for their employees' homes. As a result, a telecenter begins to look more attractive. However, if the center is not located near those telecommuters that wish to use it, the result may be a greater amount of travel than was involved in the employee's previous commute to the workplace.

Nonwork Trips May Increase Total Travel

When workers are having a telecommuting day, they may drop off their spouse at the office so they will have a car available, drop off or pick up the youngsters at school, stop and get the dry cleaning, or pick up a few things at the grocery store. It is possible that having extra free time could, in effect, lead to less judicious use of it and in so doing exacerbate the sustainability problem. The ideas of Hagerstrand (1970) regarding space–time prisms have convinced some observers (e.g., Black, 2000) that this will occur.

Carpools and Vanpools Could Lose Riders

Telecommuting will reduce work trips, and this may threaten the viability of semi-formal transportation arrangements such as carpools and vanpools since they rely on a set number of participants. Data suggest that these arrangements were already losing ridership during the 1990s for reasons documented by Ferguson (1995). It is doubtful that this was more attributable to telecommuting than, say, employee turn-over or the downsizing of firms. The impact of fuel price increases on carpooling has not been assessed to date.

Transit Ridership Decreases

The potential loss in transit ridership related to telecommuting would simply reflect people making fewer work trips by transit. Of course, work trips by transit are not that great nationally outside of major metropolitan areas, so it is doubtful that this loss would represent much of an impact.

Bicycling and Walking for Short Trips Increased

If telecommuters remain at home and short trips can satisfy some travel demands, it is likely that these may be made by walking or bicycling. Of the two, bicycling is the mode most likely to see an increase in the United States, as walking is not usually practicable, given the distances involved. Both activities could increase in Europe.

Trip Chaining Is Replaced by Short Single-Purpose Trips

A decrease in work trips would eliminate an important organizational mechanism for trip chains, in which several other trips are combined into the work trip. The belief is that this may lead to more single-purpose trips; however, it is perhaps equally possible that these shorter trips would also be assembled into a chain.

Trip-Making Roles within the Household May Change

Whether household role changes occur will depend on a host of factors that identify whether it is more efficient for the commuter or telecommuter to pick up these tasks. It seems reasonable that efficiency will govern this process, although there is a tendency for most Americans to assign marginal tasks to the woman (Longerbone, 2000).

Need for Additional Vehicles Is Reduced

It is conceivable that telecommuting could reduce the need for an additional car. The assumption is that the telecommuter could ride along with the commuter member of the household on those days where commuting became necessary for the former. Given the rather loose definition of telecommuting, we must remember that someone telecommuting just 1 day a week would be a telecommuter. If this definition applies to most in this category, it is unlikely that any 4-day commuter would give up an automobile or cease to buy one because of his or her 1 day a week of telecommuting.

Telecommuters May Relocate Their Residences

The individual who is able to telecommute 4 days a week may see certain merits in relocating his or her residence to a more distant location where land costs are lower, the environment more pleasant, crime less, and so forth. For the present time, these telecommuting programs are largely experimental, and whether they will actually affect residential decisions in this way remains to be seen. While land use theory might suggest relocation, surveys of critical factors in housing decisions have not placed the "length of commute" as a critical factor in such decisions for more than 20 years.

The Telecommuting Market

Before we get too excited about telecommuting, it is important to realize that one cannot telecommute to the vast majority of jobs. Those working in the lumber, mining, fishing, manufacturing, and transportation industries may find it difficult if not impossible to telecommute. But the critical point is not the specific industry so much as it is the type of job being done. It appears that those in clerical and secretarial jobs are attractive targets for telecommuting. Similarly, those involved in marketing, computing, and numerous service and retail activities need not be in a central office and could quite easily telecommute. So, the market for telecommuting is substantial. The U.S. labor force in 2006 consisted of 133 million workers over the age of 16. If we accept the 20 million telecommuters estimate given earlier and the current definition of 1 day a week as a telecommuter, then on any given workday there would be 4 million fewer telecommuters on the highways. This would represent approximately 3% of the workers or 3% of the work trips. Assuming this reduction of work trips were distributed across all of the highways in any given city, it is not likely to be very significant in reducing congestion, decreasing fuel use, or lessening pollution or vehicle crashes. If we factor in the observation that many workers have been doing this for decades, the reduction in traffic is even less impressive.

Employer Perspectives on Telecommuting

It should be apparent that telecommuting may offer some advantages in helping to make transport more sustainable. However, it requires industries to change the ways in which they have operated in the past, and this is never easy for either large corporations or small businesses. Nevertheless, a great many corporations have shown a willingness to experiment with telecommuting, and perhaps some examination of this inclination might prove instructive.

The major factor leading U.S. corporations to consider telecommuting was passage by Congress of the Clean Air Act Amendments of 1990 and the Intermodal Surface Transportation Efficiency Act (Howitt & Altshuler, 1999). The former legislation put in place the requirement that any firm with more than 100 employees had to increase the average occupancy of vehicles commuting to their worksites during the morning peak period to a level 25% above the area-wide baseline average. The solution seemed simple enough: have the employees use transit, carpools, vanpools, or have the workers telecommute. But, presumably, if transit were attractive (or available), it would already be used. The same could probably also be said of carpools. Vanpools almost always required that the firm become heavily involved in transportation planning, perhaps through purchasing the vehicles and/or maintaining them. This was something that most firms shied away from. And for many firms, telecommuting had to be an obviously attractive option before they were willing to undertake it, but they did not rush to this conclusion. In short, this federal legislation has since been repealed.

Admittedly, there are potential cost advantages to any firm that increases the number of its employees who telecommute. Growing firms located in expensive central cities may well find it more desirable to have some employees telecommute than to secure additional office workspace for them in such areas. Office space is not the only thing at a premium in urban areas; parking has also become scarce and very expensive. Having employees telecommute from a home site or to a telecenter has to look more attractive to employers in that light.

In the United States, labor laws require that companies provide their employees with a safe working environment, an assurance few if any employers would make for home environments. An initial opinion by the Occupational Safety and Health Administration on the assurance question suggested that employers might be responsible for the working conditions of telecommuters in the home. However, the agency quickly backed away from this position. Telecenters and televillages are much more attractive options for employers in that these facilities are generally safe, secure, and well maintained, containing state-of-the-art computer work stations that corporations rent from their owner or operator. Although this is the original idea for this concept, it seems reasonable to assume that it might make more sense for the firm to build such facilities where it finds them advantageous. In other words, the operators of such facilities will have to set the usage fees low enough that the firm will not be better off building its own facility, installing equipment, and using what would have been the usage fees to retire the debt incurred. It remains to be seen whether this development will occur, but it does seem likely.

One final incentive for employers wanting to see increases in telecommuting is that some of their employees may be more productive if allowed to work alone and undisturbed. It is believed that some people just work better this way. In this case, we are talking about the employee that probably works in his or her home.

Employee Perspectives on Telecommuting

Some employees find the idea of telecommuting attractive. It seems to imply freedom to many workers who imagine being able to work without a manager constantly looking over their shoulder. Others find the idea of no interruptions from coworkers attractive. But the reality may be different from the idealized concept.

A considerable amount of our social interaction occurs in the workplace. Many people meet their future husband or wife in the workplace. If this is not the case, then at least a considerable number of your friends are also your coworkers. The individual that telecomutes is isolating him- or herself from such relationships, interactions, or friendships. Telecenters may offset this somewhat but not completely.

There is an expression, "Out of sight, out of mind." In this context what it implies is that unless you are around the office every day you may be passed over for promotion or a higher salary. If you are among a handful of such employees that are telecommuting, you will probably have to make sure you are not forgotten by the firm.

Some view telecommuting as the 21st-century version of "piecework," an exploitative type of employment practice (common in the 19th-century) in which employees worked in their homes and were paid based on the number of units produced. This is not a particularly bright perspective, but it does raise several questions. Should employers have to pay part of your utilities, rent, or mortgage if they intend to have you use your home for their benefit? Should they supply you with a computer and such other items as you might need to work at home? Are employers liable for your injuries while working at home? These are a few of the issues raised in the literature that views telecommuting as a throwback form of exploitation of workers.

As for telecommuting's "freeing" the worker, this conception is misleading. The employee who works without a supervisor can be monitored quite easily by keeping close tabs on either the computer being used or the volume of work being completed. It is probably likely that many firms in the future will automatically monitor work stations as an indication of productivity. This is not an attractive idea but one that corporations will doubtless find hard to resist.

ICT AND TRANSPORT

Aside from the journey to work, there are several other areas of transportation where the application of advanced ICT has the potential of decreasing the amount of travel and transport that takes place. We examine some of these applications here. Many ICT applications arc in a field generally referred to as "intelligent transport systems" (ITS), which seeks to improve the flow and safety aspects of transport (it will be discussed further in Chapter 21).

In this section, we look at the influence of ICT on personal travel as well as on transport as it relates to business flows to individuals as well as other businesses. These business-related flows are often referred to as e-commerce.

E-Commerce

Many individuals today take advantage of e-services, of which there are numerous examples, including e-shopping, e-banking, e-education (more often called distance education), e-entertainment, and e-government services. E-shopping could include anything from pizza to automobiles. The Toyota Prius hybrid automobile was initially offered for sale only over the Internet in the United States. On the lower end of the scale, it is likely that much e-shopping has represented a switch from the use of telephones to the use of the computer. On the upper end, some of these services did not exist in a communications context some 20 years ago, e.g., e-banking. E-banking is something that has also caught on in part because it is very attractive to employers, and this clearly replaces the need to go to one's bank on payday. The downloading of movies directly to your TV or the television-enabled computer is in the process of replacing the trip to the video store. Perhaps no area has seen more e-commerce than the travel area. E-tickets secured over the Internet (with the airlines' tacit endorsement) have nearly replaced consumers' need to interact with travel agents, who are desperately trying to hang on via the cruise business. Most government services used to require one's physical presence to accomplish most functions. This is slowly changing, and some localities are even experimenting with the idea of e-voting, although certain technical problems still exist in this area that need to be overcome. Nearly all of these services were nonexistent a little more than a decade ago.

Of course, one could suggest that many other services have come along that have not been mentioned here. That is true. Nearly every utility from cable TV to telephone, electricity, water, and many others can be paid via the Internet in most communities. Of course, these were usually paid by simply mailing in the payment in an earlier day. They may involve the substitution of the computer for the local mail carrier, but most of the world still receives "snail mail," and the marginal cost of submitting bill payments by mail is relatively small.

This raises the question of exactly how important is e-commerce that involves businesses interacting with consumers ("B-to-C"). According to the United Nations Conference on Trade and Development (2003), such commercial trade represented approximately $43.5 billion in 2002 in the United States and $28.3 billion in Europe. Although we don't know the total retail sales in Europe, in the United States e-commerce represented 1.34% of total retail sales (in Europe, probably a like amount), and of course, the total and proportion are growing substantially each year.

How significant is all this in terms of the sustainability of transport and travel? Will such e-commerce dampen the need to travel in many cases? Button et al. (2006, p. 121) have stated, "While it is possible to deliver some goods online (airline tickets and music), most goods and services ultimately have to in some way be produced, shipped, and consumed." This would suggest that e-commerce involving consumers will not make a major contribution to transport sustainability.

E-commerce involving the interaction of businesses ("B-to-B") is a much larger activity. In this case, the United Nations unit noted above suggested that B-to-B e-commerce in the United States represented $995 billion in 2002, or nearly 15% of B-to-B sales there (the comparable value of such transactions in 2002 was about $200 billion in Europe). Other regions of the world are lower, but the Asia-Pacific area is at about $120 billion. Clearly this is a growing area of commerce around the world.

Alexander Graham Bell is credited with inventing the telephone, in 1876. By as early as 1884 grocery stores had already begun advertising shopping by phone, and pictorial ads were appearing by the early 1900s (see Figure 18.1). There was no charge for delivery, typically accomplished the same day by a delivery boy who either walked or rode a bike. The whole process was undoubtedly more sustainable than any of the e-commerce taking place today—yet apparently no one thought to call it t-commerce!

How much of today's e-commerce is new activity, and how much of it is simply a substitution of Internet sales for sales by mail or the telephone? We really don't know. The main economic impact of this activity may have nothing to do with transport sustainability at all, instead simply enabling new businesses in other parts of the world to interact with businesses they did not interact with before. The practice of reverse bidding, in which a firm simply notes what it needs on the Internet and then chooses the winning bid for the items, from willing suppliers, will most likely keep prices well in check. At the same time, the goods will still need to be shipped, and we may thus see little reduction in transport costs and inputs. On the contrary, we may even see an increase in transport inputs as more remote areas become part of the worldwide supply chain for these materials.

So, what can we suggest about the impacts of e-commerce on transport sustainability? In terms of local and national B-to-C commerce, the impact will likely be modest. The goods ordered by the individual will still have to be delivered via some transport mode. On the other hand, the B-to-B area may on balance be detrimental to transport sustainability, although the overall economic impact on prices may outweigh the negative externalities that the additional e-commerce generates.

Personal Travel

Some of the potential travel savings for individuals from ICT were suggested earlier in that many travel tasks can be replicated more inexpensively by ICT. As earlier

Reno, Nevada
1909

Lima, Ohio
1900

FIGURE 18.1. Examples of early advertising trying to get customers to use the telephone for grocery shopping.

noted, a great number of governmental services have gone online. In the United States, for example, if you want a tax form as you prepare your annual federal or state income tax return, you can readily download and print it, whereas formerly the same task would have required you to visit your local post office or other distributors of such forms. Similarly, if you want the daily news nowadays there is no need to go out and pick up a newspaper—you can simply surf the Internet and access news of every kind at any time of day. Trips to the library are becoming less and less necessary with the exploding growth of the Internet. Libraries recognize this trend, and many are morphing into local community centers.

Telephones have always enabled us to keep in touch with our families. The current level of technology in computers and the Internet allows for real-time interaction. Does this remove the need to travel near and far to visit one's relatives? Probably not.

It is possible for academics to regularly interact with other academics in distant countries. At the risk of being criticized for inserting a personal anecdote, this writer must note that he undertook research and wrote a research paper with a scholar in Europe without ever meeting that individual prior to publication of the paper—something that would have been nearly impossible 20 years ago. That coauthor subsequently invited me to present a lecture in her country. Although the ability to collaborate on the paper via the Internet was a positive point, the subsequent trip undoubtedly cancelled any transport "sustainability" advantage that accrued from that interaction, the latter being possible only because of the earlier experience.

This anecdote raises a very real question, namely, Does virtual interaction of the type facilitated by the Internet lead to enough familiarity to actually induce travel that would not have taken place otherwise? Most indications are that it does.

Video Conferencing

One substitute for some types of long-distance business travel is to make use of video conferencing. Anyone who has participated in a video conference is probably well aware of its shortcomings. Of these, perhaps one of the most irritating is the slight delay in the audio signal that leads to speakers in different locations talking at the same time. As the distance increases between the various speakers, this problem becomes more acute. If the conference is taking place in a North American–European setting, then additionally there are significant local time differences, which means that the American participants have just arrived at work, while, for the Europeans, lunch is already over or, worse yet, they are about to leave for the day. Despite the drawbacks, video conferences involving small sets of participants have definite potential for decreasing the need to travel.

Certain large-scale meetings within a country or region with only minor time differences also have potential for the productive use of video conferences, even in cases where the only thing to be accomplished is hearing a presentation and possibly taking some questions from the audience. Of course, video conferences may be usefully employed for a variety of other activities, such as discussing possible joint research projects, making corporate presentations, interviewing for jobs, attempting to place one's graduates in jobs, or delivering recommendations regarding potential contingency plans. Some of these things are perhaps best handled, however, in a video conference with relatively few participants in attendance.

CONCLUSIONS

In this chapter we have examined telecommuting and its relationship to sustainable transport. Several research questions related to telecommuting were explored, and the findings were for the most part encouraging, that is, telecommuting appears to contribute to sustainable transport in nearly every case. A brief review of the potential "market" for telecommuting is less encouraging in terms of its impact on traffic congestion, fuel use, and the like. If the market is under 20 million—and this projection includes many 1-day-a-week telecommuters—then the impact of this activity may prove to be modest.

This chapter also touched on why employers and employees might find telecommuting attractive. Naturally the employer's reasons largely derive from the bottom line of its income statements. Employees who believe that telecommuting is of interest to them often embrace it for all the wrong reasons. The discussion here has attempted to summarize the pros and cons of telecommuting from the perspective of both groups, employers and the employed.

There are many positive attributes to telecommuting in a sustainable transport world, but it would be misleading to assign it more than a secondary role. Although some research is encouraging, California may not be typical of most of the United States (or the world, for that matter). Even if it is, we should not overestimate the number of drivers telecommuting will take off the highway.

We have also examined the potential impacts of e-commerce on the transport of goods and services, reflecting as it does a growing area that many have viewed as something possibly leading to various communications substitutes for travel. We have reached a different conclusion: while e-commerce may serve as a substitute for certain types of commercial trips, these are not very numerous, and therefore we see e-commerce as being of little help to sustainable transport. To the extent that e-commerce encourages additional long-distance transport related to the global economy, it may even result in more transport than took place heretofore.

Finally we have looked at video conferencing to see if it offers any potential for decreasing the amount of travel that takes place. One thing that is apparent is that the last decade has seen considerable growth in electronic communications as well as considerable growth in international travel. This suggests that video conferences and various other types of electronic communications, such as e-mail, may actually be generating incremental demand for long-distance travel and transport rather than serving as a substitute for it.

CHAPTER 19

The Potential of Alternative Fuels

The Hydrogen Economy is within sight. How fast we get there
will depend on how committed we are to weaning ourselves
off of oil and other fossil fuels.
—JEREMY RIFKIN (2002)

The global warming problem and problems with local air quality are attributable in large part to the consumption of gasoline by the world's motor vehicle fleet. While these environmental problems impact the sustainability of transport, that sustainability is also adversely affected by the finite nature of the petroleum stocks from which gasoline is refined. All of this would suggest that it might be best to consider the development and use of alternative fuels that are renewable and, ideally, do not contribute to global or local environmental problems.

BACKGROUND

In the latter part of the 19th century the automobile was under development in the United States, England, and France. There was no agreement on what the power source would be for these "horseless carriages," but the leading candidates at the time were the steam engine, electricity derived from lead batteries, and gasoline burned in internal combustion engines. Steam had several things going for it: faster acceleration and greater power (attributable to its high torque), smooth and flexible speed and power control, and the ability to burn cheaper fuel. It also carried such problems as slow startup times, the need for water to be added to the boiler frequently, the need to replace the boilers, and problems of freezing (Jamison, 1970, p. 46). Although most of these problems would be solved during the years that followed, there was still the need for a fuel to create the steam. Electric cars were also attractive, relatively quiet, but had a limited range of 25–30 miles. The last of these candidates, the gasoline-fueled internal combustion engine, was to win out—in large part because of the discovery of huge reserves of petroleum that reduced the price of gasoline to the point that no other fuel could compete with it (Greene, 1996).

As a direct consequence of this fortuitous (for it) set of circumstances, the internal combustion engine has dominated the motor vehicle industry for the past 100 years. However, during the 1960s a growing awareness arose about the air quality problems created by the automobile. The U.S. Senate held hearings in 1967 on electric vehicles and alternatives to the internal combustion engine, and in 1968 there were hearings on the steam engine as an alternative to the internal combustion engine (Jamison, 1970). These hearings also initiated an interest in alternative fuels, but it was the OPEC oil embargo of 1973–1974 that truly stimulated the greatest interest in fuels that could lessen our dependence on petroleum.

During the OPEC embargo the price of petroleum doubled, although it fell shortly afterward. The Iran–Iraq war that raged throughout the 1980s again created fuel shortages, and again the price of petroleum doubled. Although prices remained high during most of the conflict, the oil market collapsed in 1986 and global oil prices fell. They doubled again, from $17.50 to $33 per barrel, during the Persian Gulf war of 1990–1991 but then dropped again when Saudi Arabia and the United Arab Emirates increased production to make up for the decreased output of Iraq and Kuwait (Greene, 1996, p. 23). These intermittent interruptions in fuel supplies have escalated to the status of a national security issue, and many would like to see North America, as well as Europe, permanently out from under this recurrent energy supply threat.

Today the air quality problems created by the internal combustion engine persist and have even worsened. Environmental concerns have broadened with the growing recognition that carbon dioxide emitted by the transport sector is in large part responsible for what has become commonly recognized as the threat of climate change, more specifically global warming. The potential for petroleum embargoes has lessened, but it has not gone away. There is also the stark fact that global petroleum reserves are being depleted at a rate that exceeds the rate at which new reserves are being discovered.

In December 1997 certain members of OPEC announced an increase in petroleum production. This and a relatively mild winter in Europe and North America drove down the price of gasoline to its lowest (inflation-adjusted) level in 10 years and its second-lowest price in 25 years. Even states with comparatively higher fuel prices (e.g., California) saw a notable drop in price in 1998 (see Figures 19.1 and 19.2). The OPEC announcement came during the Kyoto climate change meeting in which countries were trying to set carbon emission goals for the coming 10–12 years. Low fuel prices and a vigorous economy in North America and Europe stimulated increased travel and fuel consumption, which was counter to the direction one would like to see at the time.

As the summer of 2000 approached, fuel prices began to increase significantly due to cutbacks in production by OPEC as well as increased summer demand, pipeline failures, refinery shutdowns, and a host of other problems. Gasoline prices in

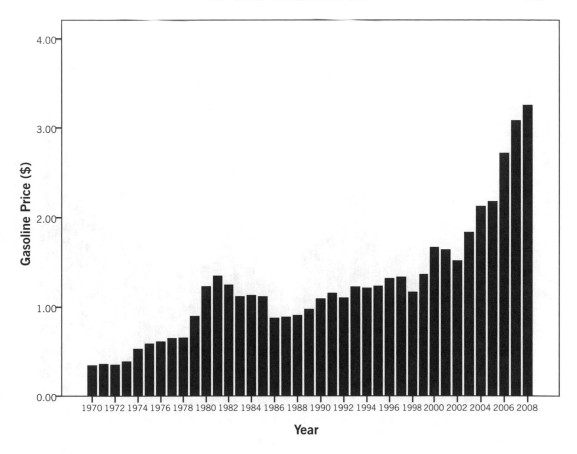

FIGURE 19.1. California gasoline prices, 1970–2008. *Source*: California Energy Commission, 2009).

the Midwest, where they were the highest, ranged from $2.00 to $3.00 a gallon. Prices fell after 2001, only to begin climbing again in 2003, 2004, 2005, and 2006, fueled in part by the war in Iraq. Gasoline prices in the United States during the first 8 months of 2008 were higher than they have ever been (see Figure 19.3), even inflation-adjusted.

This lengthy historical introduction to a chapter on new and alternative fuels was needed to place the topic in perspective. An alternative fuel to gasoline should ideally have several attributes.

1. It should be based on a renewable source or at least be relatively ubiquitous so as not to create concerns of the type we have seen in the past 40 years (e.g., fuel shortages).
2. It should be nonpolluting in terms of local air quality.
3. It should not contribute to climate change.
4. It should be low in price if it is to compete with gasoline.

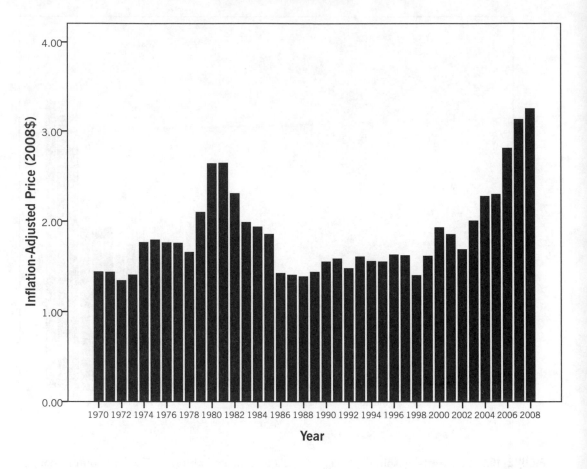

FIGURE 19.2. California gasoline prices adjusted for inflation, 1970–2008. *Source*: California Energy Commission, 2009).

It would be possible to conclude this chapter now by simply stating that none of the alternative fuels available satisfies these criteria, but this option would not get us very far. Instead, let us examine some of the alternative fuels that are available and see how closely they come to satisfying all the requirements. This chapter will look only at fuels. There are various technologies for using fuels differently or employing other energy sources (e.g., fuel cells, electric and hybrid vehicles), but these will be examined in the next chapter.

THE POSSIBLE ALTERNATIVE FUELS

One of the best early discussions of alternative fuels can be found in Gordon (1991). Although nearly 20 years old, that discussion is still a good source of information on alternative fuels. Gordon's presentation discusses the following fuels:

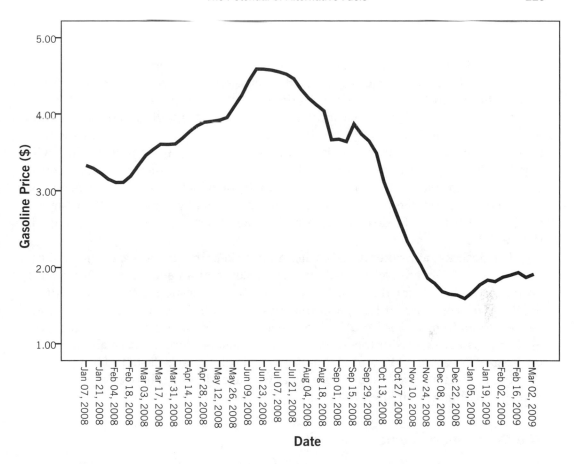

FIGURE 19.3. U.S. average weekly gasoline prices, January 2008–March 2009. *Source*: EIA, 2009.

- Methanol
- Ethanol (from corn)
- Ethanol (from woody biomass)
- Compressed natural gas (CNG)
- Liquefied petroleum gas (LPG, or propane)
- Biodiesel fuel
- Solar energy
- Hydrogen
- Reformulated gasoline
- Oxygenates (MTBE/ETBE)

Gordon examines these alternative fuels by using several criteria, including consumer cost and market availability, engine modifications that would be necessary to use these fuels, resource base and secure supply, fuel properties and safety matters, greenhouse gas attributes and emissions, and the impact of existing government policies. There is no doubt that these criteria are important in the rapid shift to an alternative fuel. However, it is possible to envision this shift as a move in the national interest and as a result one in which, over a few years, barriers to the adoption of the fuel could be eliminated. As a result, there are certain points that will be dismissed for purposes of the present discussion. It is assumed here that if the cost of the product is excessive or if its distribution to consumers is made difficult by the absence of sufficient distribution centers, then this will be resolved by federal actions or subsidies. Engine modifications are already known for most of these fuels; so, this is not a major problem, although it is recognized that the fuel will slowly move into the vehicle fleet in the same manner in which emission control devices moved into the fleet at the time of their introduction. Finally, we need not be concerned about the presence of existing government policies and their impact on the identification of a desirable alternative fuel. Where policies must be changed, they will be.

The desirable attributes noted earlier must be kept in mind as we examine alternative fuels. There are concerns about the existence of an adequate resource base and a secure supply for the fuel. There should be no question that the fuel will be available for centuries (at least) and that any nation adopting it should not be concerned about "embargoes" and the like. Fuel properties have to be of some concern, as do the safety aspects of these. Finally, there must be some concern about greenhouse gas emissions and other air quality aspects of the fuels. It should be apparent that the concerns expressed are with what we have identified here as the "sustainability" attributes of an alternative fuel.

The Conventional Fuels

To put this discussion into the proper context, we first need to discuss the fuels currently in use that are derived from crude oil sources, namely, gasoline and diesel fuels. We should be aware of the positive and negative attributes of both. We follow this with a discussion of the several alternative fuels: methanol, ethanol, biodiesel fuel, compressed natural gas, liquefied petroleum gas, solar energy, and hydrogen. We will not examine reformulated or oxygenated fuels independently, as these are modified forms of gasoline that will be discussed with that fuel.

Gasoline

The chief fuel in use today is gasoline. It is a liquid composed of a few hundred different hydrocarbons. The components of its exhaust (earlier presented in our discussion of urban air quality in Chapter 4) include such emissions as carbon monoxide, hydrocarbons, nitrogen oxides, and sulfur oxides. Some countries (though not the United States or Canada) still have lead in their gasoline, which is an additional exhaust pollutant of special concern. It was common practice through most of the 20th century to add lead to gasoline in order to increase its octane level and in some cases to prevent engine knock. For obvious health reasons, this is no longer done in the United States, and most of the European Union nations have also banned this practice.

Oxygenated supplements, which may include ethanol, methanol, methyl t-butyl ether (MTBE), and ethyl t-butyl ether (ETBE), among others, were added to gasoline to reduce carbon monoxide and hydrocarbon emissions, to lower emissions from older vehicles, and to increase the octane rating of the gasoline.

When these oxygenates are added to the gasoline, it is often referred to as reformulated gasoline, and it usually has less evaporative emissions and sulfur, which also reduces nonmethane hydrocarbons, carbon monoxide, and nitrogen oxide emissions. Formaldehyde, one of the air toxics, is also lower in reformulated gasoline. The oxygenates actually make the gasoline burn cleaner, and for this reason there are fewer tailpipe emissions.

Several years ago it was found that MTBE was leaking from underground storage tanks and pipelines across the country, with the leakage finding its way to ground water supplies. This experience has led several states to ban the use of MTBE (see Table 19.1). In its place the states may use either ETBE or ethanol, which is a major ingredient of ETBE.

Diesel Fuel

Another one of the energy products of crude petroleum refining is diesel fuel, which because of its high thermal efficiency is used primarily in commercial and heavy-duty vehicles such as trucks and buses. In general, it costs less than gasoline, but its

TABLE 19.1. State Bans against the Use of MTBE

State	MTBE ban or ban schedule	MTBE consumption (% U.S. total as of December 2002)
California	Ban started January 1, 2004.	31.7
Colorado	Ban started April 30, 2002.	0
Connecticut	Ban started October 1, 2003.	3.4
Illinois	Ban started July 2004	0
Indiana	Limited to 0.5% of volume since July 23, 2004.	0
Iowa	Limited to 0.5% of volume since July 1, 2004.	0
Kansas	Limited to 0.5% of volume since July 1, 2004.	0
Kentucky	Ban started January 1, 2006.	0.8
Maine	Goal to phase out use of MTBE; not a ban.	0
Michigan	Ban started June 1, 2003.	0
Minnesota	Ban started July 1, 2005.	0
Missouri	Limited to 0.5% of volume since July 1, 2005.	1.1
Nebraska	Limited to 1.0% of volume since July 13, 2000.	0
New York	Ban started January 1, 2004.	7.5
Ohio	Ban started July 1, 2005.	0
South Dakota	Limited to 0.5% by volume.	0
Washington	Ban started December 31, 2003.	0

Source: Energy Information Administration (2006).

price is often determined by local supplies. Usually diesel emissions contain fewer hydrocarbons and nitrogen oxides and higher levels of particulate matter. However, a primary concern with regard to this fuel is sulfur emissions.

For many years diesel-fueled vehicles were exempt from the emission standards of the U.S. Environmental Protection Agency, primarily because gasoline-powered motor vehicles were so much more plentiful that they constituted by far the chief source of air quality problems in American cities. Given the substantial progress that has been made in controlling emissions from gasoline-powered vehicles, however, diesel-powered vehicles have come under increased scrutiny in recent years. The EPA proposed and finalized rules for emissions from heavy-duty trucks in 2000; these rules call for a 97% reduction of sulfur in diesel fuel. Earlier rules were issued for light- and heavy-duty trucks, and the rules promulgated 2000 were in addition to those previously established.

The new rules also include specifications for the manufacture of more efficient engines, which in turn should reduce fuel use as well as carbon dioxide emissions. With regard to sulfur, the former rules allowed for sulfur content in diesel fuels of 500 ppm, whereas the new rules call for a level of 15 ppm. Nitrogen oxides should be reduced by 95% and particulate matter should be reduced by 97% under the 15 ppm standard, also called the ultra-low-sulfur diesel standard. Full implementation of the standard is to be completed by December 1, 2010.

The Alternative Fuels

The following fuels have a non-crude oil origin and are generally referred to as alternative fuels. Some of these fuels have a fossil fuel origin (e.g., compressed natural gas), and from a sustainability point of view this should be viewed as a shortcoming since all fossil fuels are nonrenewable.

Methanol

Methanol is an alcohol that may be produced from natural gas, coal, or biomass (e.g., urban waste). Of these sources, natural gas is the most common; coal is the least desirable since the manufacturing process produces substantial amounts of carbon dioxide; and the waste approach has some appeal since it at least represents a renewable fuel source. In general this fuel is used as M85, a blend of 85% methanol and 15% hydrocarbons, but it is also used as 100% methanol, or M100, in some areas.

Although emissions from methanol are similar to those from gasoline, it does not perform as well in cold weather conditions. It is toxic and burns with an invisible flame, which raises numerous safety problems. It also has the disadvantage of producing less energy than gasoline, which decreases fuel economy by about 50%. In addition to these problems it tends to cost more than gasoline, although increased levels of production could drive the price down somewhat. All things considered, it is not a very desirable fuel except for the possible use of urban waste for production. However, this does not seem to be sufficient to lead to its widespread use. When municipal electric power generators began using urban waste, there were numerous instances of insufficient supplies, something that could also occur with waste used for methanol production.

Ethanol

Ethanol is known to most people in the United States as a component of gasohol (a blend that is 90% gasoline and 10% ethanol in its most common form). Ethanol, or grain alcohol, is an oxygenated fuel derived from the fermentation of biomass. This fuel appeared in the 1970s when it was added to gasoline, as suggested above, in an attempt to stretch supplies of that fuel. Typically ethanol is derived from corn or sugar cane; the former is primarily used in the American Midwest, while the latter is used in Brazil.

There is also an E85 blend of 85% ethanol and 15% gasoline that has begun to catch the attention of environmentalists. This fuel blend can be used in flexible-fuel vehicles (FFVs). A study by *Consumer Reports* (Consumer Union, 2006) evaluated this fuel and noted:

1. The fuel emits fewer pollutants capable of producing smog than gasoline.
2. It provides fewer miles per gallon than gasoline (8–15% less).
3. It costs more.
4. It is hard to find retailers of the fuel outside the Midwest.
5. Government support for FFVs that could use the fuel has resulted in more gasoline consumption.

These points are perfectly clear except perhaps for the last two which may need clarification. As of 2006 there are only about 1,600 E85 retailers in the United States.

The FFV point also requires a little more of an explanation. Flexible-fuel vehicles, as the name implies, may use different fuels (i.e., gasoline or E85). Since they can use an alternative fuel, the manufacturers of these vehicles actually get government tax credits for producing them, which artificially lowers the price of the vehicles sold to consumers. As a result, consumers are buying the FFVs because of their lower price (among other reasons) and never using anything in them except gasoline, which is cheaper and, as suggested above, may be easier to find than an E85 retailer. Increases in the price of gasoline since 2006 have lessened this problem.

Brazil began its ethanol program during the 1970s with the stated goals of reducing oil imports, assisting its sugar industry, and creating more employment opportunities. The program was considered to be the most ambitious national effort ever undertaken in the alternative fuels area. Two products were manufactured: a gasohol composed of 20% ethanol and 80% gasoline and a 100% alcohol (hydrated alcohol). By 1988 alcohol cars represented more than half of the vehicles in Brazil (IEA, 1995, p. 284). Shortly after 1988 the world price of sugar escalated dramatically, and producers of the sugar cane-based ethanol shifted their production to sugar as an end crop, which created an immediate problem for those with the 100% alcohol vehicles.

Today pure alcohol cars are less common than gasohol/gasoline vehicles in Brazil. These vehicles are for the most part flexible-fuel vehicles that can run on either ethanol or gasoline. Car sales in Brazil in July 2008 were nearly 90% "flex-fuel" vehicles.

Among the several advantages of ethanol are its ability to burn in internal combustion engines with only minor modifications; its biomass origin, which makes it a renewable resource; its lower yield of greenhouse gas emissions; its decreasing cost of production; its lower level of toxicity than gasoline; and the fact that its hydrocarbon emissions are less photochemically reactive and therefore less likely to create urban ozone. While these are all desirable qualities, there are some negative attributes to this fuel that all but offset these qualities. First, the biomass origin of this fuel may not be as attractive as it appears. The planet is on the way to a population of approximately 9 or 10 billion by the end of the 21st century, and most academics believe the planet can support a population of this magnitude. However, it is quite reasonable to ask whether arable land will be dedicated to the production of food in the future or ethanol biomass stocks.

Second, it could also be argued that ethanol production will inevitably drive up the price of various foods that currently use corn as an input, including all types of livestock, from chickens to cattle, and various cereals. In addition, if production of other crops is suppressed in favor of corn for ethanol, this phenomenon will drive up the price of those agricultural commodities, owing to less supply. There is considerable anecdotal evidence that that phenomenon occurred during the 2007–2008 surge in agricultural commodity prices, which followed in the wake of tremendous increases in ethanol production (see Figure 19.4).

Third, if we use conventional methods to produce ethanol, the planting, cultivation, fertilization, harvesting, and distillation are all energy-intensive activities. Some analyses suggest that substantial amounts of land and agricultural activity would have to be dedicated to biomass production. One study of the latter suggests that turning over the current production of barley, corn, oats, sorghum, and seven other crops to biomass production in the United States would create enough ethanol to power the nation's motor vehicle fleet for only 62 days, which is about 17% of the national motor vehicle fuel demand for a year (Pearson, 1999). The study did not examine sugar, which would temporally extend ethanol supplies, but most estimates suggest that biomass fuels could not provide more than 20–30% of the transport energy needs of the United States (IEA, 1995, p. 284). This projection suggests that the United States might need to become a net *importer* of ethanol, which would not exactly be in the national interest.

One point of clarification is necessary regarding the greenhouse gases associated with the use of ethanol. It is generally stated that using ethanol as a fuel results in no carbon dioxide emissions. This is obviously not the case. However, if the fuel has come from plants that would have died and released carbon dioxide into the atmosphere at that time, then it is said that the fuel is greenhouse gas neutral. Others have noted that the planting, cultivating, and harvesting of the plant biomass is often done with equipment that uses gasoline. If we are looking at the "total greenhouse gas cost," we must recognize that these gasoline emissions should be attrib-

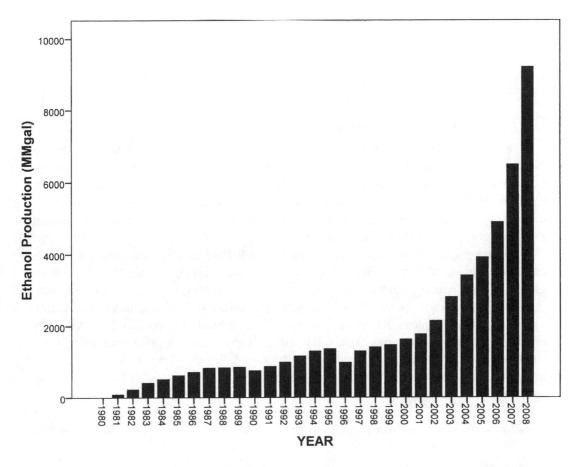

FIGURE 19.4. U.S. ethanol production, 1980–2008. *Source*: Energy Information Administration (EIA, 2008).

uted to ethanol. Of course, it would be possible to use ethanol as the fuel for these activities, but this would reduce the net yield of ethanol and increase the price of the fuel.

Ethanol does have some other negative attributes, many of which could probably be resolved with some effort. For example, it can be corrosive and damaging to some metals, and it can be highly flammable but difficult to ignite in cold weather. At the same time, it does not provide the energy that one would get from a comparable quantity of gasoline and therefore ethanol-fueled vehicles would require larger fuel tanks or more frequent fueling.

Overall, ethanol seems to come with too many drawbacks that make it a good second choice but not a fuel that is likely to replace gasoline except as an additive that would stretch petroleum reserves and as an oxygenate to allow fewer emissions from the use of gasoline.

Nevertheless, there should be little doubt that ethanol will have a major place in future transport energy supplies. It will most likely be made from cellulosic materials (leaves, stalks, wood pulp, and some grasses). It will not replace gasoline but will probably join it and other alternative fuels as an energy source for transport. A study by Oak Ridge National Laboratory (Perlack et al., 2005) suggests it may replace as much as 30% of the oil consumption of the United States by 2030.

Compressed Natural Gas (CNG)

CNG is a hydrocarbon gas mixture that is primarily made up of methane (80–90%). Nontoxic and highly flammable, it is used as a transport fuel in diverse countries, notably Canada, the United States, and New Zealand. This gas is placed in a tank in the vehicle under pressure. However, this is also a drawback of the fuel since there are not a large number of refueling locations available and the capital investment for CNG compressors is quite significant.

In general, CNG is viewed as a cleaner fuel than gasoline or diesel. It generates lower levels of carbon dioxide than other fuels, but it emits more methane than gasoline. In terms of other emissions, as compared with gasoline it emits substantially less carbon monoxide (70% less), nitrogen oxides (87% less), and nonmethane organic gases (89% less; Khare & Sharma, 2004). It tends to produce high levels of energy in comparison to most fuels. It is difficult to discuss its price since this varies considerably from place to place, but the average price in 2006 was about $1.90 per gallon of gasoline equivalent (GGE) (see Table 19.2). It is also viewed as a relatively safe gas since it would vent to the atmosphere if its tank were ruptured.

Overall, CNG is a good alternative fuel to gasoline except for two factors: (1) it is difficult to find refueling stations in most parts of the country, and (2) it is a fos-

TABLE 19.2. Number of Vehicles in Use by Fuel Type and Fuel Prices

Fuel type	Vehicles, 1995	Vehicles, 2006	Fuel price per gallon, 2006 (energy equivalent basis)
Gasoline	201,530,021	244,165,686	$2.84
Diesel			$2.98
LPG	172,806	164,846	$2.88
CNG	50,218	116,131	$1.90
LNG	603	2,798	$2.50
M85	18,319	0	
M100	386	0	
E85	1,527	297,099	$2.43
E95	136	0	
Electricity	2,860	53,526	

Note. Gasoline vehicles for 1995 and 2006 include all vehicles, gasoline, diesel, and those using alternative fuels.
Sources: EIA, 2008; FHWA, 2007; U.S. Department of Energy, 2009.

sil fuel and therefore nonrenewable. There are also some parts of the United States where natural gas can be seasonally scarce.

Liquefied Petroleum Gas (LPG)

LPG gas is a combination of primarily propane and butane in liquid form. The actual composition varies from place to place, based on ambient temperatures. It is stored under pressure and usually takes up less space than CNG. It tends to be used as a fuel in Italy, the Netherlands, the United States, and parts of Asia and Oceania.

Its emission attributes are similar to those of CNG. It does not have the energy levels of gasoline, and it requires up to 30% more fuel to go the same distance as a gasoline-powered vehicle. Its price varies considerably from place to place, but its national average in 2006 was $2.88 per GGE. It is not as safe as some other fuels since it is heavier than air; if it leaks, it tends to pool in low-lying areas and can be ignited.

The major drawback of LPG as an alternative fuel is the somewhat limited supplies of this gas. However, LPG fueled vehicles are the second leading alternative fuel vehicle after ethanol fueled vehicles in the United States as of 2008 (see Table 19.3).

Biodiesel

A relatively new alternative fuel is biodiesel. It is produced from ethanol or methanol reacted with vegetable or animal fats (see Demirbas, 2008). The resulting fuel has the physical attributes of diesel fuel. Biodiesel has lower carbon monoxide and hydrocarbon emissions than diesel but more nitrogen oxides. Most of its other attributes are close to those of diesel fuel, although it emits no sulfur or aromatic hydrocarbons. There is some disagreement regarding emissions of particulate matter from biodiesel-fueled vehicles at this time.

Solar Power

A renewable resource that would generate no emissions or noise is solar power. Solar cars often resemble a table on wheels. The table is covered with solar panels that convert sunlight to electricity, which is passed along to an electric motor that powers the vehicle. These vehicles have led to numerous races in various parts of the world. Two of the more popular of these is the World Solar Challenge in Australia, between Darwin and Adelaide, and the North American Solar Challenge between Plano, Texas, and Calgary, Alberta, Canada. The October 1997 winner of the former race was a TU Delft solar car from the Netherlands that covered the 3021 kilometers (1,877 miles) in 33 hours and at an average speed of 90.87 kilometers per hour (55.97 miles per hour). The North American Solar Challenge features university solar car designs and racing teams. The University of Michigan's Solar Car Team won the latter race in July 2008 with an average speed of 72.58 kilometers per hour (45 miles per hour). It would appear that the technology is fairly standardized, albeit the vehicles in these races are unusual in that they are covered with solar or photovoltaic panels. As a practical matter, there is no commercially available car today that runs only on solar power. Nevertheless, solar power has a promising role to play in transport, and we will return to this later.

Hydrogen

Hydrogen, as many high school graduates know, can be derived from water by splitting the water into its hydrogen and oxygen components, and when energy is derived in this manner it is a renewable resource. This fuel has a lower flammability limit than gasoline and produces minimal nitrogen oxide and hydrocarbon emissions (the latter due primarily to lubricants) and no emissions of carbon monoxide or sulfur oxides. The primary emissions from using hydrogen as a fuel are oxygen and water vapor, relatively harmless in the quantities that would be produced. Hydrogen is also nontoxic and disperses quickly upon release, reducing the probability of a fire following a motor vehicle crash.

On the negative side, hydrogen can be made with fossil fuels as an energy source, and it would not be a renewable fuel if produced in this manner. Using fossil fuels would seem to make little sense, considering our sustainable transport objectives. At the same time, the United States has abundant quantities of coal, and carbon dioxide sequestration methods have advanced to the point where producing hydrogen in this manner is being given some attention (Doctor & Molberg, 2004).

The primary problems with hydrogen in the past have been how to transport and distribute it to refueling centers and then how to place it in the vehicle. Although hydrogen could be stored as a liquid, a compressed gas, or as a metal hydride, all of these options appear to generate costs that significantly increase the price of the fuel. Then, too, the engines of hydrogen-powered vehicles would differ significantly from the internal combustion gasoline engine.

There are other problems related to the use of hydrogen as a vehicle fuel, all of which are related to the loss of hydrogen to the atmosphere during refueling or the refilling of tanks at refueling stations. The problem is that we do not know what the impact of such hydrogen releases will be on the atmosphere, bearing in mind that hydrogen is not a naturally occurring gas (see Tromp et al., 2003).

A final problem with hydrogen is simply its production and distribution cost. Expressed in its simplest form, we need a relatively inexpensive way to produce and transport hydrogen. At present hydrogen is produced from natural gas by using a steam reforming process. The assumption at one point was that this would be done in large centralized production facilities, resulting in some serious distribution costs. Today the assumption seems to be that the natural gas will not be centrally produced, significantly reducing distribution costs since pipelines for natural gas already exist.

The U.S. Department of Energy (2006, 2008b) is attempting to get the cost of hydrogen to approximately the $5.90 per gallon of gasoline equivalent. This is an attainable goal since current pricing is around $5.00–$6.00 per gallon of gasoline equivalent (Green Car Congress, 2005), which is competitive with a gasoline price of $1.90 untaxed. However, it is almost impossible to talk about the price of gasoline since it has fluctuated wildly over the past couple of years. It creates a problem for any alternative fuel that it must be able to compete with gasoline in terms of price. However, if hydrogen becomes competitive and the consumption of gasoline begins to fall, then prices for gasoline will also fall. This, in turn, will have an impact on the price of hydrogen.

It is important to note that although capital costs are incorporated in the target prices, transport and storage costs are not. Adding these would only increase the total costs. It is possible that these costs will decrease further, but most experts believe that the use of hydrogen as a fuel will not occur until about 2030 (Ramesohl & Merten, 2006).

CONCLUSIONS

From a sustainable transport perspective, the most logical fuel system would be a solar–hydrogen system. If the hydrogen for such a system could be derived from electrolysis of water, this process would yield a truly sustainable transport fuel. Some support for such a solar–hydrogen transport energy system is found in the work of Nadis and MacKenzie (1993), MacKenzie (1994), and Sperling (1995). At the same time, one must admit that solar–hydrogen is nowhere near market-ready at this time. Nevertheless, this seems like the direction in which society should be moving unless some significant events occur that substantially alter the situation.

The use of coal and carbon dioxide sequestration as well as electrolysis of water may ultimately prove to be feasible. Those goals are something to work toward, and research should continue on all aspects of both approaches.

There are obviously situations where something else might have to be tried quickly. In such cases, a short-term shift to natural gas (CNG) is worth considering. It is *more* sustainable than petroleum; it is a nonrenewable fossil fuel, but its reserves are considerably larger. This fuel would be even more attractive if more of its emissions could be captured. Apart from CNG, there are alternative uses that can be made of gasoline that would extend its life and reduce emissions, for example, as the fuel in fuel cells, which would yield more energy. Although this does not seem to be a prudent course to take, there are circumstances where this may appear to be a promising alternative.

At the time of this writing some of the major advocates of hydrogen have begun to be less forceful—or perhaps more realistic—about the adoption of that fuel in the near term. Indeed, many are seeing a future where the alternatives are not seriously being considered. The situation has been summarized rather effectively by Sperling and Cannon (2004b), and they conclude that alternative fuels have failed. They attribute this failure to three errors. The first of these is underestimates regarding the level of potential oil reserves. The second is the assumption that gasoline could not be improved, which turned out to be false since both gasoline and diesel were reformulated to burn cleaner (and the internal combustion engine was also improved to reduce emissions). And third, the statements made about the environmental and economic benefits of the alternative fuels were exaggerated. One could argue at length about these statements, but they are fundamentally true.

The reality is that there is still an abundance of oil in North America, albeit in the form of oil sands and oil shales. It may not be the type of oil we want to use, given its environmental externalities, but it is there. Do we really expect the petroleum industry to shut its doors and go away? No, ultimately the industry will figure out how to get at these nonconventional sources of oil in such a way that it satisfies the environmental regulators and perhaps even some of the environmentalists. It isn't just inertia, it is also the existing distribution system that adds considerable appeal to continuing the status quo.

This is not meant to suggest that we will lack alternative fuels in use in the future. We will have them, but they will be found in a mix of fuels that will be used in motor vehicles. In addition, we will have a mix of vehicles that will be available to consumers, some of which will use fuel cells, others natural gas, and there will be an abundance of hybrids. If we are talking about the future in terms of 2025 or 2030, this brief description typifies the environment that will exist then and in which gasoline will probably continue to be the primary fuel.

CHAPTER 20

New Vehicles, Fuel Cells, and Catalytic Converters

At the other extreme, it is equally possible to conclude that most progress made to date has been the result of technological innovation and change and that it is logical to presume that technological change is the only promising path by which to approach sustainable mobility in America.

—MARTIN WACHS (2004)

Beginning in the late 1800s inventors began trying to develop a personal transportation vehicle that could be operated by an individual singly. Three separate types of power systems were in contention for supplying the necessary motive force, namely, electric–battery systems, steam engines, and the internal combustion engine. In this chapter we briefly review these early historical developments, note the early triumph of the internal combustion engine, and explore the vehicle propulsion technologies that have suddenly appeared at the beginning of the 21st century. Still in early development are fuel cells that promise even more efficiency in terms of fuel economy, which is the primary driving force behind these developments and the basis of our interest in them as a key element in the revolution toward more sustainable transport.

A related technological development is the catalytic converter, which radically decreases the harmful emissions emanating from the use of petroleum-based fuels. These emissions also work against a sustainable transport system. We review the development of this technology and suggest the direction that it will take in the future.

THE ELECTRIC CAR: BATTERY-POWERED

Electric vehicles came into production in the United States in 1891. The batteries of the day were not able to hold much of a charge, and as a result the vehicle was not as attractive as the steam-powered automobiles that were also emerging at the time. Later the market share of electric vehicles began to increase, and by 1900 it had nearly caught up with the "steamers." According to several sources, in 1900 electrics represented 38% of the production as compared to the "steamer's" share at 40%, while internal combustion vehicles were a distant third at 22% (Drake, 1995, p. 243; MacKenzie, 1994, p. 33; Scott, 1993, p. 9; Shacket, 1983; Sperling, 1995, p. 156). Ironically, by 1915 gasoline-powered motor vehicles dominated the automobile fleet, and by 1930 electric cars and steam cars were curiosities.

The internal combustion engine dominated the automobile market for most of the 20th century. When the United States became concerned about air quality in the 1960s, attention soon focused on the emissions produced by these vehicles. Anticipating that emissions reductions would soon be mandated (as they were in the Clean Air Act of 1970), the industry began to look at ways in which it could achieve reductions in these pollutants. One possible solution was to shift to electric vehicles, and this technology was reexamined at that time. In the interim the catalytic converter was developed, and the industry recognized that it could meet the emissions reduction targets without changing the power source. Plans for electric vehicle development were set aside.

The OPEC oil embargo of 1973, which resulted in a significant increase in gasoline prices at the time, stimulated interest once again in electric cars. World oil prices fluctuated during the 1980s, and by the latter part of that decade these prices were at record lows and "gasoline regained the dubious distinction of being the lowest cost liquid other than water" (Drake, 1995, p. 246).

Environmental concerns and some developments in technology led General Motors to release the GM Impact electric vehicle. This vehicle was able to provide rapid acceleration and travel 70 city miles or 90 highway miles between charges on the energy equivalent of 1.5 gallons of gasoline (Drake, 1995, p. 246). The Impact's commercial successor was the EV1, which was sold for a brief period of time in California and Arizona. It was later leased but was withdrawn from the market in 1999.

Electric vehicles use batteries as their power source, and this results in zero tailpipe emissions, but the vehicles do have to be recharged. This recharging can involve the use of electricity from hydroelectric facilities, wind energy, or fossil fuel-fired power plants. If the two former sources are used, the vehicle remains clean; if fossil fuels are used, then the vehicle may be less environmentally attractive. At the same time, if the vehicle is recharged during periods of low demand for electric power but nevertheless at times when the power must be available, it becomes less clear whether this is environmentally damaging. The answer probably rests with whether demand for recharging in the low-demand hours reaches levels necessitating additional power production. At that point the additional capacity brought on-line should be considered "avoidable" (i.e., were it not for electric vehicles), and the pollution generated (if any) would have to be assigned to the electric vehicles in any environmental accounting system.

Electric vehicles also have some other drawbacks that should be noted. Obviously, the recharging limits the range of the vehicle. The exact range depends on traffic conditions, and unexpected traffic jams may very well result in the vehicle's losing its charge at rather inconvenient times and locations. Some electric vehicles may have heavy battery packs, and in order to keep the weight of the battery from becoming excessive, lower-weight materials are used on other parts of these vehicles whenever possible. The impact of these lightweight materials on safety have not been the subject of much research, although the general impact of weight reductions has been examined (NHTSA, 1997). It was thought that physical geography could play a role in terms of where it is feasible to use this vehicle; the belief was that the batteries would not work in cold or frigid environments. However, experiments with heated batteries under these conditions suggest they will function in those environments. Nevertheless, sales and marketing efforts for the new electric vehicles did not target these areas.

Of course, research and development continued on the electric car and batteries into the 1990s. In October 1997 a Solectria Sunrise midsize four-passenger prototype electric vehicle powered by a nickel–metal hydride battery pack (manufactured by General Motors Ovonics) traveled the 216 miles between Boston and New York on a single charge at normal highway operating speeds. After a recharge of a few hours, the vehicle made the return trip to Boston. Improvements in batteries and other developments, for example, insulating the battery against cold temperatures, could extend the consumer and geographic markets of electric vehicles.

In the meantime Honda Motors released the Honda EV (electric vehicle) Plus as part of the 1996 model year. This vehicle had a top speed of just above 131 kilometers per hour (80 miles per hour) and a range of 205 kilometers (125 miles). It was powered by a 40-kilowatt brushless DC motor and 24 12-volt Ovonic nickel–metal hydride batteries. The vehicle had four seats (the General Motors EV1 was a two-seater) and the amenities expected in contemporary automobiles, such as power steering, power brakes, power windows, and air conditioning, as well as the expected safety equipment, for example, antilock brakes and air bags. If the vehicle had a negative attribute, it had to be its purchase price of $53,999. Honda set up a reasonably good leasing program that made the vehicle competitive with an average new car valued at $20,000. Battery charger units were also made available on generous terms. The company hoped to lease 300 vehicles over the next few years prior to mass marketing the car; however, the model was withdrawn from the market in 1999, possibly in response to the introduction of Honda's first hybrid vehicle, the Insight. Over its brief life (1996–1999), there were only 325 of the Honda EV Plus vehicles sold or leased (Healy, 2000).

Six of the top 10 "greenest" vehicles in 1998 were electric. It should be recognized that a vehicle's greenness (meaning the least negative environmental impact) is based on tailpipe emissions, for the most part. By 2000 only 3 of the top 10 so-

TABLE 20.1. The 10 Greenest Vehicles of 2000

Vehicle	Model and fuel	Emission standard	Green score
GM EV-1	Electric	ZEV	52
Honda Civic GX CNG	1.6L 4, auto (CNG)	SULEV	52
Nissan Altra	Electric	ZEV	50
Honda Insight	1.0L 3, manual	ULEV	48
Toyota RAV4 EV	Electric	ZEV	47
Toyota Camry CNG	2.2L 4, auto (CNG)	ULEV	42
Ford Ranger Pickup EV	Electric	ZEV	40
Nissan Sentra	1.8L 4, auto	SULEV	39
Chevrolet Metro/Suzuki Swift	1.3L 4, manual	LEV	38
Toyota Echo	1.5L 4, manual	LEV	37

Source: Reprinted from DeCicco and Kleisch (2000). Copyright 2000 by the American Council for an Energy-Efficient Economy. Reprinted by permission.
Note. ZEV, zero-emission vehicle; SULEV, super ultra low-emission vehicle; LEV, low-emission vehicle. Green scores are based on tailpipe pollution and global warming impacts. Although the GM EV-1 appeared on the 2000 model list, it was actually withdrawn from the market in December 1999.

called greenest vehicles were electric (see Table 20.1). Other vehicles were not displacing the electric vehicles so much as the electric vehicles were being removed from the market, as suggested by the experience with the GM EV1 and the Honda EV Plus. By 2003 all of the electric vehicles in the United States had been withdrawn from the market (see Table 20.2). By 2008 hybrids dominated the list of the greenest vehicles (Table 20.3).

The Market for Electric Cars

In spite of the limited success of Honda's EV Plus, the GM EV1, and other electric cars, it would seem that there should be a substantial market for electric cars, given their recent increases in range. However, it is unlikely that the market will take full advantage of that range. The more likely market is what is generally referred to as

TABLE 20.2. Brief History of Electric Vehicle Sales

Electric vehicle	Year introduced	Sold or leased through May 2003	Status as of June 2005
Ford Ranger compact pickup	1998	1,500	Discontinued 2002.
GM EV1 two-seat coupe	1997	755	Discontinued 1999.
Toyota RAV4 sport utility vehicle	1997	1,333[a]	Discontinued 2003.
GM Chevrolet S-10 compact pickup	1997	500	Discontinued 1999.
Honda EV Plus	1996	325	Discontinued 1999.
Chrysler minivan	1993	249	Discontinued 1999.
Nissan Altra EV station wagon	1998	56	Discontinued 2003.

Source: Data from Healy (2000).
[a]Estimated.

TABLE 20.3. The 12 Greenest Vehicles of 2008

Vehicle	Model and fuel	Emission standard	Green score
Honda Civic GX	1.8L 4 auto CNG	PZEV	57
Toyota Prius (Hybrid)	1.5L 4 auto CVT	PZEV	53
Honda Civic Hybrid	1.3L 4 auto CVT	PZEV	51
Smart Fortwo Convertible/Coupe	1.0L 3 auto stk (P)	ULEV II	49
Toyota Yaris	1.5L 4 manual	ULEV II	46
Nissan Altima Hybrid	2.5L 4 auto CVT	PZEV	46
Toyota Corolla	1.8L 4 manual	ULEV II	45
Mini Cooper/Clubman	1.6L 4 manual (P)	LEV II	44
Ford Focus	2.0L 4 manual	PZEV	44
Toyota Camry Hybrid	2.4L 4 auto CVT	PZEV	44
Honda Civic	1.8L 4 manual	ULEV II	44
Honda Fit	1.5L 4 manual	LEV II	44

Source: Reprinted from *www.greenercars.org/highlights_greenest.htm*. Copyright 2008 by the American Council for an Energy-Efficient Economy. Reprinted by permission.
Note. LEV II, low-emission vehicle with 25% less carbon monoxide and 88% less nitrogen oxides of LEV (replaced LEV in 2004); ULEV II, ultra-low-emission vehicle with 20% less carbon monoxide and 88% less nitrogen oxides than ULEV (replaced ULEV in 2004); PZEV, nearly zero emission vehicle; same as SULEV but must maintain that standard for 15 years. Green scores are based on tailpipe emissions and global warming impact.

neighborhood electric vehicles (NEVs), which basically means that the vehicles will be used for relatively short, local trips in smaller urban areas or subareas of larger metropolitan areas. This market would include those interested in driving to work relatively short distances. Attempts to increase the market for electric vehicles in general by increasing the range of the vehicle seem something of a waste of effort. Most drivers in smaller urban areas are concerned about whether they have sufficient gasoline for a trip, but if the tank is full they may completely disregard the exact amount of fuel they have available because they will not come close to using it all. The same is also true of a fully charged electric vehicle; it will generally have more than a sufficient amount of electric charge for any urban trip of interest to the driver. At the same time, there do have to be opportunities to refuel in the gasoline case and recharge in the electric case. Perhaps developing this infrastructure is where industry and governments should focus their future attention.

HYBRID VEHICLES

Hybrid vehicles were developed in response to the major shortcoming of the electric car powered only by batteries: the possibility that the vehicle will lose its charge, leaving the inattentive driver stranded. Hybrid vehicles, or more specifically hybrid electric vehicles, use a small-sized internal combustion engine along with a battery-powered electric drive motor. Hybrid electric vehicles may be of a series or parallel type. A series vehicle uses its engine to drive a generator to charge batteries that power an electric drive motor. On the other hand, a parallel vehicle uses both its engine and an electric motor to drive the vehicle. Both systems significantly reduce emissions and improve fuel efficiency.

Although hybrid vehicles can involve any two types of fuels, they are usually electric with the associated gasoline system, as noted above. This creates a problem for hybrids that electric vehicles do not have. If the internal combustion system is present, then the vehicle ceases to be a zero-emission vehicle. Therefore, if the objective is to minimize emissions, hybrids may not be the way to go. If, on the other hand, the objective is to extend petroleum stocks, then this may be the direction to take; but is it the best solution for this? Probably not. If the hybrids are simply to fill an interim need between rather efficient internal combustion engines and improved battery-based electric cars, then one must certainly ask whether major investment in this technology is merited.

As early as 1994 MacKenzie (1994) noted efforts under way by GM and Ford in the United States to develop hybrids. There were also similar efforts under way in Japan, Canada. and Germany. Researchers differ significantly in the attention they give to hybrids. Sperling (1995) gives them considerably more attention than MacKenzie (1994). Duleep (1997) took a conventional mid-size car rated at 28 miles per gallon and costing $19,500 (in 1995 dollars) and modified it. He noted that a 13% ($2,550) price increase could yield an advanced conventional gasoline vehicle that could achieve 53.2 miles per gallon, or a 90% improvement in fuel efficiency. On the other hand, a hybrid vehicle with battery could achieve 65.3 miles per gallon, or a 133% improvement in fuel efficiency, but it would cost an additional 29% ($5,700). Increasing hybrid vehicles' efficiency beyond this amount becomes considerably more expensive.

Toyota Prius

The preceding discussion indicates that, while there may be a market for hybrid vehicles, developments over the past few years have for the most part placed hybrids on the sidelines. This is not exactly the case. In December 1997 Toyota began marketing its hybrid (part electric, part gasoline) automobile called the Prius (pronounced pre-us). Initially, the vehicle was marketed only in Japan at a price of about $17,500. This was about $4,000–$9,000 less than production costs, according to most estimates. The vehicle could seat four and came with an automatic transmission. Toyota anticipated producing 1,000–1,200 vehicles a month, but initial orders in December for 3,500 vehicles led most dealers to stop accepting orders until production levels could increase in the summer of 1998.

During the summer of 2000, Toyota announced that it would market the Prius in the United States only over the Internet. This seemed like a risky venture in a country where even those who know nothing about cars like to look under the hood and kick the tires. The vehicle had a manufacturer's suggested retail price of $20,450, including destination charges. Toyota reevaluated this marketing approach toward the end of 2000 and began selling the vehicle through its U.S. dealerships. As of 2008 the Prius dominates the hybrid vehicle market.

Although not a clean car in the environmental sense, it generates about half of the emissions of current gasoline-based vehicles. It also differs from other vehicles in that it will get better gas mileage within cities (52 miles per gallon) than on the open highway (45 miles per gallon). These are not overwhelming figures, but the one real advantage of this vehicle is that it uses a fuel (gasoline) that has an established distribution system (of gasoline service stations). Lack of such a system is a major barrier to just about every type of alternative fuel being considered.

Honda Insight

Honda introduced its hybrid vehicle, the Honda Insight, during the spring of 2000. It was a two-seat vehicle that came only with a standard transmission, probably two major drawbacks in the U.S. market in comparison to the Prius. The Insight hybrid connected a 6-horsepower electric motor to a 67-horsepower gasoline-powered internal combustion engine. When braking, the energy produced (previously lost in most vehicles) was captured and used to recharge the battery pack that powered the vehicle's electric motor. The electric motor was used during acceleration, resulting in no additional increase in fuel consumption. The vehicle's gasoline engine would shut off during idling but would start automatically when the driver shifted the vehicle into gear and engaged the clutch. Priced at about $19,295 including destination charges, Honda should have expected it would have a difficult time competing with some larger vehicles that sell for less. At the same time, its advertised 113 kilometers per gallon of gasoline (61 miles per gallon, city; 70, highway) rating should have made it attractive to some consumers. It did not, and in 2005 Honda ceased production of the Insight and allowed hybrid versions of some of its other vehicles, notably the Civic and Accord, to replace it. As of 2009, only the Honda Civic was available in a hybrid model.

Honda will release a new version of the Insight with the 2010 model year. This new hybrid has the name of the earlier model, but otherwise it appears to be a completely new vehicle. This hybrid seats five passengers, has four doors, and features an automatic transmission. Its price of less than $20,000 should enable it to compete with the Toyota Prius. It is expected to have an overall fuel economy of 41 miles per gallon. In addition, the vehicle has a fuel economy enhancement system, referred to as Eco-Assist, which allows the driver to increase fuel economy by altering his or her driving style (Consumers Union, 2009).

General Motors Volt

The 2011 model year will see the Chevrolet division of General Motors releasing the Chevrolet Volt. This vehicle is viewed as typical of the new generation of hybrids. It will be propelled by an electric motor and have a small gasoline engine that will extend the car's range. Its unique attribute is that it will be possible to recharge the battery by connecting it to electric power sources in the home (*The Economist*, 2008). This plug-in capability will most likely typify hybrids of the next decade.

The 2009 Model Year

Increases in the price of fuel have led to additional sales of hybrids, and these sales are expected to increase over the next several years, although economic conditions have impacted this trend (see Figure 20.1). The 2009 model year has no fewer than 27 different hybrids, ranging from compact vehicles to SUVs (see Table 20.4). Currently Honda and Toyota seem to have the "greenest" automobiles, whether we are looking at the air pollution measure or the carbon footprint of the vehicle. This "footprint" measures greenhouse gas emissions from motor vehicles: carbon dioxide, nitrous oxide, and methane. Although the American firms initially focused on hybrid pickup trucks, they have now begun producing cars. However, their fuel economy figures are not very impressive. The sport-utility vehicles, two-wheel drive and four-wheel drive, are one area where the American and Japanese manufacturers compete, and in this case the miles per gallon figures are comparable.

Numerous other manufacturers will be getting into the hybrid vehicle business on a larger scale in the next few years if their statements are to be believed. From a transport sustainability point of view, one should not lose sight of the fact that these vehicles still use gasoline as their major fuel. Although these vehicles represent a substantial improvement in miles per gallon when compared with non-hybrid vehicles, they are still using a finite resource.

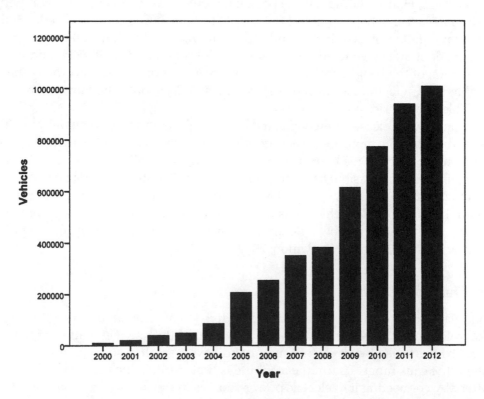

FIGURE 20.1. U.S. Hybrid Vehicle Sales, 2000–2007, and Forecasts, 2008–2012. Copyright by J. D. Power and Associates. U.S. hybrid sales/forecast. Reprinted by permission.

TABLE 20.4. Hybrid Vehicles, as of 2009 Model Year

Vehicle model	MPG city	MPG highway	Annual fuel cost	Carbon footprint	Air pollution score (10 max.)
Toyota Prius	48	45	$628	4.0	8
Honda Civic Hybrid	40	45	$689	4.4	9
Nissan Altima Hybrid	35	33	$851	5.4	NA
Ford Escape Hybrid FWD	34	31	$906	5.7	8
Mazda Tribute Hybrid 2WD	34	31	$906	5.7	8
Mercury Mariner Hybrid FWD	34	31	$906	5.7	8
Toyota Camry Hybrid	33	34	$851	5.4	8
Ford Escape Hybrid 4WD	29	27	$1,034	6.6	8
Mazda Tribute Hybrid 4WD	29	27	$1,034	6.6	8
Mercury Mariner Hybrid 4WD	29	27	$1,034	6.6	8
Toyota Highlander Hybrid 4WD	27	25	$1,115	7.1	8
Chevrolet Malibu Hybrid	26	34	$999	6.3	6
Saturn Aura Hybrid	26	34	$999	6.3	6
Saturn Vue Hybrid	25	32	$1,034	6.6	6–7
Lexus GS 450h	22	25	$1,409	8.0	NA
Chevrolet Silverado 15 Hybrid 2WD	21	22	$1,378	8.7	6
GMC Sierra 15 Hybrid 2WD	21	22	$1,378	8.7	6
Chevrolet Tahoe Hybrid 2WD	21	22	$1,378	8.7	6
GMC Yukon 1500 Hybrid 2WD	21	22	$1,378	8.7	6
Lexus LS 600h L	20	22	$1,542	8.7	8
Dodge Durango HEV	20	22	$1,378	8.7	NA
Chrysler Aspen HEV	20	22	$1,378	8.7	NA
Cadillac Escalade Hybrid 2WD	20	21	$1,448	9.2	6
Chevrolet Silverado 15 Hybrid 4WD	20	20	$1,448	9.2	6
GMC Sierra 15 Hybrid 4WD	20	20	$1,448	9.2	6
Chevrolet Tahoe Hybrid 4WD	20	20	$1,448	9.2	6
GMC Yukon 1500 Hybrid 4WD	20	20	$1,448	9.2	6

Source: *www.fueleconomy.gov/feg.*

One way of decreasing reliance on gasoline is to increase the role of the electric motor in such vehicles, as with the Chevrolet Volt, or to develop new fuels that can be used in such vehicles. Both of these are seeing some development, with moves afoot to develop plug-in hybrid vehicles and hybrids that can run on diesel or bio-fuels.

FUEL CELLS

One of the major developments over the past several years is the continuing improvement in fuel cells. Fuel cells are similar to electric batteries in that they convert fuel directly into electricity. The cells electrochemically combine hydrogen and oxygen and release as much as 90% of the chemical energy produced as electricity. In this chemical process there is very little heat produced, and this is part of the reason for the efficiency of the process. The major byproduct formed (aside from electricity) is water.

Vehicles that include fuel cells generally have a fuel tank as well as an electric motor. There may also be a battery and other apparatus for power boosts. The fuel of fuel cells may be just about anything, including gasoline, methanol, natural gas, petroleum products, or hydrogen. Hekkert et al. (2005) note that the use of natural gas in this context would reduce carbon dioxide emissions by 40%. If a fuel other than hydrogen is used, then the vehicle needs a reformer to convert the fuel into hydrogen.

The system works by moving hydrogen gas to a negative electrode, or anode, and moving air to the positive electrode, or cathode. "The hydrogen molecules separate, with the stream of electrodes, or electricity, directed along a wire to the electric motor. The remaining hydrogen protons (positive ions) are pulled through an electrolyte and combine with oxygen that has been delivered as air to the cathode" (Sperling, 1995, p. 83).

Aside from their high level of efficiency, fuel cells result in significantly lower levels of nitrogen oxides, hydrocarbons, carbon monoxide, and particulate matter for most fuels. Gordon (1991, p. 103) places the emissions from 1,600 fuel cell vehicles at the level of one 1990 gasoline-powered automobile, although the fuel used is not stated. If hydrogen is used as a fuel, then the vehicle emits none of these; nor does it emit carbon dioxide, the principal greenhouse gas.

On the downside there may be emissions if the hydrogen fuel is produced outside the vehicle from fossil fuels, that is, as input to the production process. If hydrogen fuel is produced by using solar energy and water, then there are no emissions.

If fuel cells have any major shortcomings, the most notable is probably their excessive weight. This perception resulted in the belief that they might be best used in heavier vehicles, and to date fuel cells have primarily been used to power buses and trucks. There is a possibility of fuel cells being used in light rail in the future, but they are currently too expensive for that application.

The differences in fuel cells are related primarily to the electrolyte technology that they use, including the PEM (proton-exchange membrane) type, in which the electrolyte is made from a solid polymer; solid oxide, with a ceramic electrolyte; phosphoric acid, with a liquid electrolyte; and alkaline, also with a liquid electrolyte. The PEM type of electrolyte technology is the most promising one for use in vehicles (Sperling, 1995, p. 87).

In October 1997 the U.S. Department of Energy and the consulting firm of Arthur D. Little announced they had developed a fuel cell capable of deriving electricity from gasoline through a new method that decreased pollution by 90% while it doubled the energy per gallon produced by existing vehicles. The major pollutant would be carbon monoxide, based on media reports to date.

The Little firm transferred these activities to a new firm, Nuvera Fuel Cells, which has used fuel cells in forklifts, tractors, and stand-alone power modules.

One point of clarification should be made regarding hydrogen vehicles and fuel cell vehicles. A hydrogen vehicle is one that would use hydrogen as a fuel. Although the fuel cell vehicle also uses hydrogen as a fuel, normally it produces this on board from another fuel, often gasoline. These two types of vehicles should not be viewed as the same.

CATALYTIC CONVERTERS

The federal Clean Air Act of 1970 set new vehicle emission standards that called for a reduction in emissions of 90% by 1975–1976 as compared to 1970 levels. Carbon monoxide was to decrease from 46 grams per vehicle mile to 0.41 grams per vehicle mile. Hydrocarbons were to drop from 4.7 grams per vehicle mile to 3.4 grams per vehicle mile, while nitrogen oxide was to drop from 6 grams per vehicle mile to 0.40 grams per vehicle mile (Flink, 1990, p. 387). These are substantial reductions by any measure, and thus the automobile industry was able to get an extension of the deadline to 1977. The approach taken to meeting the new standards was to install catalytic converters on new cars, and the majority of American cars introduced in 1975 had catalytic converters. Were it not for California's ZEV (zero-emissions vehicle) mandate, that history might close the book on the catalytic converter. However, failure of the ZEV mandate (as discussed in Chapter 13) led to a negotiated solution to produce some LEVs (low-emission vehicles) during the interim period.

LEVs (actually transitional LEVs, LEVs, and ultra LEVs) have been made possible primarily by improving the catalytic converter. General Motors found that adding small additional amounts of such catalysts as palladium, rhodium, or platinum increased the efficiency of the catalytic converter. Other actions such as increasing the surface area of the converter, or making it thinner (thus enabling it to heat faster), or placing it closer to the engine (but not too close) all increased the device's efficiency. Of course, the costs of these changes had to be a concern, but surprisingly, for the most part, they were not unreasonable. Transitional LEV status could be obtained for about $72 additional, LEV status would cost from $100 to $200, and ultra-LEV status would run from $100 to $1500, depending on the changes needed (Wald, 1998).

CONCLUSIONS

This chapter has briefly examined fuel systems that are alternatives to the internal combustion system used by most motor vehicles today—or at least supplements to that system. Beginning with electric vehicles, it was noted that these would have substantially improved the national vehicle fleet's fuel consumption and emissions record. At the same time, there were some concerns about the origins of the electric power that was used to charge the batteries of electric vehicles: If this were of a fossil fuel origin and generated purely for electric vehicles, this might not be an attractive avenue to follow. If, on the other hand, these vehicles were charged during off-peak period in terms of power demand, the marginal environmental cost of the fossil fuel might be nearly zero. Nevertheless, these vehicles never quite caught on (possibly owing to their high prices and limited range between charges), and by 2003 they were virtually nonexistent on the American landscape after being recalled or cancelled by their manufacturers.

There are indications that electric cars may reappear on the market in the United States. Ford has announced its intention to introduce an all-electric four-door sedan in 2011. Chrysler has four all-electric vehicles in the design stage. One of these, the Dodge Circuit EV, has a range of 150–200 miles (241–322 kilometers) on a single charge. Toyota expects to market a small battery-operated car in the United States in 2012 (Carty, 2009).

Hybrid vehicles are generally electric vehicles with internal combustion engines, as noted. These vehicles can significantly reduce pollution and fuel use, but so long as they require gasoline in any quantity they would appear to be academically interesting but not necessarily what society should endorse for the long run. At this point in time, if the motor vehicle fleet began switching to hybrid gasoline–electric vehicles, it is doubtful that this would do much to extend petroleum reserves since adoption of these vehicles would take some time and many drivers would not be able to afford to make the transition quickly. However, the threat of immediate petroleum shortages materializing is not so great as once perceived.

Fuel cells appears to offer far more potential than has been realized to date. It is interesting to see gasoline being considered here, but once again the problems of emissions and long-term supply problems should raise some concerns. Putting more effort into solar–hydrogen fuel cells as the long-term solution to this problem has considerable merit. This effort will not be easy or inexpensive, but we must look ahead to a universally available fuel that would meet the future energy needs of the planet. Certainly solar power offers that potential, and using it to generate hydrogen would solve most of our current environmental problems as well as problems with future fuel supply. The use of fuel cells in most of the motor vehicle fleet is likely decades away, probably not achievable until 2030–2040. Nevertheless, it is a technology that deserve continued heavy investments in research and development over time.

CHAPTER 21

Intelligent Transport Systems

> In recent years there have been major efforts throughout the
> developed world to apply our new technological capabilities
> in computing, sensing, and communication to improve road
> transport. The effort in the United States has been dubbed
> the intelligent transportation system program.
> —WILLIAM L. GARRISON AND JERRY D. WARD (2000)

Initially there was an Intelligent Vehicle Highway Systems (IVHS) program, but that gave way to intelligent transport systems with the recognition that perhaps ITS technology might be applicable also to transport modes other than highways and motor vehicles. We now have clusters of technology that focus on selected problem areas. This chapter reviews some of the technology developed in this area within the context of sustainable transport.

The Transportation Research Board defines Intelligent Vehicle Highway Systems as "the application of advanced information processing and communications, sensing, and control technologies to surface transportation," noting that the objective is "to promote more efficient use of the existing highway and transportation network, increase safety and mobility, and decrease the environmental costs of travel" (TRB, 1993, p. 5). Several of the problems with sustainable transport are problems that can be resolved by IVHS or, more recently, ITS. This chapter surveys the broad areas where ITS is being applied, provides illustrations of these applications, and then evaluates its relative success in solving some of the problems of transport sustainability.

Reasons for moving in this technological direction rest on the belief that the current transport system is about as large as it is going to get, particularly in urban areas. If you accept that premise then in order to improve the flow of traffic, reduce congestion, and increase safety we must be able to communicate more with the driver than is possible with the occasional passive road sign. In other words, we need to increase efficiency.

ITS TECHNOLOGIES

In general there are six recognized areas of ITS activity. The first set of three is primarily technology-oriented, while the second set is applications-oriented. The technology areas are examined first below.

Advanced Traffic Management Systems (ATMS)

The ATMS area includes technologies designed to monitor, control, and manage traffic flow on streets and highways. Examples of such systems include centralized traffic control facilities that monitor traffic at critical sites throughout the urban area and control congestion using ramps, signals, and other devices to these ends; message boards that convey information to drivers regarding traffic conditions and alternate routing; priority routing for emergency vehicles; programmable directional traffic control systems; and automatic systems for dispatching tow, service, and emergency vehicles to crash sites. These are already well established in certain urban areas, featuring interactive traffic signals that can change in response to the specific levels of traffic or even individual disabled vehicles in an intersection, as opposed to a signal on a timer.

Advanced Traveler Information Systems (ATIS)

ATIS includes technologies that are useful to travelers in planning as well as related to improving the convenience and efficiency of travel. Examples of this technology within the vehicle might include onboard map displays that feature roadway signs intended to communicate information to the driver, systems to interpret digital traffic data, and driving hazard systems that report on road conditions. Outside the vehicle, trip planning services and route and headway information for public transit services are the most common functions provided.

Advanced Vehicle Control Systems (AVCS)

AVC systems are intended to assist drivers in controlling their vehicles, relieving them of certain tasks through use of various electronic, mechanical, or communication devices. These may be in the vehicle or on the roadway.

This area is perhaps more advanced in people's minds than it is in real operations. Included here would be systems referred to as adaptive cruise control, which slows cruise-controlled vehicles if they get too close to other vehicles; systems to enhance viewer vision at night or during storm events; systems that warn the driver when the vehicle has left its lane; systems (often called collision avoidance systems) that prevent vehicles from running into one another; and automated highway systems that control vehicle movement in certain lanes thus increasing highway capacity and safety.

ITS APPLICATION AREAS

The specific application areas for ITS are generally organized around three activities or types of systems, namely, advanced public transportation systems, commercial vehicle operations, and advanced rural transportation systems.

Advanced Public Transportation Systems (APTS)

The APTS area uses advanced technologies to improve the attractiveness and economics of public transit operations. These technologies, which affect both vehicles and drivers, aid in coordinating operations and making better information available to system users. Examples of this technology include fleet monitoring systems, dispatching systems, onboard displays, real-time displays at transit stops, intelligent fare collection systems, and ride share and high-occupancy-vehicle databases and information systems.

Commercial Vehicle Operations (CVO)

CVO applications are intended to assist the operations of commercial vehicles, whether on land or sea (e.g., motor carriers, buses, or ships). Applications in these areas generally replace activities that may interfere with the flow of commercial vehicles through the reduction of administrative barriers. Among the functions served are toll collections, vehicle weighing, permit acquisition, and the like. Notable activities in these areas include weigh-in-motion systems, electronic placards and bills of lading, automatic vehicle location systems (most of which use global positioning systems), and communications systems installed vehicles that enable them to communicate directly with central dispatchers.

Advanced Rural Transportation Systems (ARTS)

These systems are generally implemented in rural areas, which because of their lower population densities and lesser transport demand, are sometimes overlooked or neglected. The principal ARTs applications at present are systems that assist with route guidance, communications, emergency signaling, incident detection, as well as automatic vehicle location systems and road warning systems.

These six enumerated areas, are not so much targeted areas for future development of these applications but rather a classification of the work already being done by them. The lines demarcating certain areas are sometimes tenuous, but the distinctions offered are instructive. However, the established categories are not necessarily a function of need—except insofar as one views the activities of inventors and entrepreneurs as responding to need.

A different approach to this classification of ITS would have been obtained had we gone to governmental organizations and simply asked the question, Which of your current problems can technology have the greatest impact in resolving? This was essentially the approach employed by the Finnish National Road Administration, or Finnra (Kulmala & Noukka, 1998), which in assessing Finland's long-term transport plan for 2010 determined that ITS could play a pivotal role in helping that nation reach its objectives. Looking at the six major objectives and the capabilities of ITS, it was determined that the latter could help with all of the objectives but certain objectives were more important than others (see Table 21.1). Table 21.1 reflects the perception that ITS can definitely make traffic and transport more efficient and safer. It can also help with managing transport demand and the efficient use of the transport infrastructure, but increasing cooperation between modes or ensuring mobility and accessibility are less relevant to its particular strengths.

Finnra followed the prioritization of its objectives for ITS by sending a list of specific potential ITS functions to numerous experts in the field. The experts were to score (from –1 to 3) each potential ITS function in terms of the perceived capability of ITS to successfully address each of the six objectives; the median score (usually rounded) on each assessment appears in Table 21.2. Functions are ranked in order by the overall scores they received. Incident management was viewed as the most accomplishable ITS function, especially as it relates to efficiency and safety. Several functions are important in the safety area. Broadly speaking, these either relate to weather information or, in what we typically call "smart cars," consists in modifying the vehicle's actions (e.g., speeding up or slowing down) to avoid potential hazards or incidents. Often these functions are important *only* in the safety area. Few ITS capabilities can do much for intermodal cooperation except to make information more widely available about options. Similarly, there isn't much that ITS capabilities can do for mobility and accessibility as well. The one item that stands out is demand-responsive public transit. Although this mode uses ITS in many cases, it is probably incorrect to include it here.

TABLE 21.1. The Weights of Finnra's Objectives for ITS

1. Ensure efficiency of traffic and transport	30%
2. Improve traffic safety	30%
3. Manage demand more efficiently	15%
4. Use infrastructure more efficiently	15%
5. Improve cooperation between modes	5%
6. Ensure mobility and accessibility	5%

Source: Reprinted from Kulmala and Noukka (1998). Copyright 1998 by UKIP Media & Events Ltd. Reprinted by permission.

TABLE 21.2. Potential of ITS Functions to Fulfill Finnra's Objectives (Median Scores)

ITS function	Efficiency	Safety	Demand management	Efficient useof infrastructure	Modal cooperation	Mobility and accessibility
Incident management	2	2	0.5	1	0	0
Pretrip information on other modes	1	1	1	1	2	1
Park-and-ride facilities	1	1	1	1	2	1
Guidance to alternative routes	1	1	1	2	0	0
Pretrip weather information	1	2	0.5	0	1	0
Pretrip info on incidents, congestion	1	1	1	1	1	0
Roadside information about weather	1	2	0	0	0	0
Local warnings about weather	1	2	0	0	0	0
Weather-controlled speed limits	1	2	0	0	0	0
Congestion/area tolls for motor vehicles	1	0	1	2	1	0
Information about congested locations	1	1	0	1	0	0
Roadside info on incidents, congestion	1	1	0	1	0	0
Demand-responsive public transit	1	0	1	1	1	2
Signal control at junctions	1	1	0	1	0	0
Network signal control	1	1	0	1	0	0
Lane control at special locations	1	1	0	1	0	0
Lane control in tunnels	1	1	0	1	0	0
Lane control on motorways	1	1	0	1	0	0
Terminal/stop timetable information	1	0	1	1	1	1
Alternative mode information	1	0	1	1	1	0
Roadside dynamic parking information	1	0	1	1	1	0
Dynamic speed adaptation	0	2	0	0	0	0
Intelligent headway control	0	2	0	0	0	0
Collision warning systems	0	2	0	0	0	0
Collision avoidance systems	0	2	0	0	0	0
Vision enhancement	0	2	0	0	0	0
Driver state monitoring	0	2	0	0	0	0
Automatic speed enforcement	0	2	0	0	0	0

Source: Reprinted from Kulmala and Noukka (1998). Copyright 1998 by UKIP Media & Events Ltd. Reprinted by permission.

ITS AND SUSTAINABLE TRANSPORT

It is not immediately apparent how ITS has a role to play with regard to sustainable transport as defined here. Recall once again that our current systems are considered nonsustainable because they deplete finite petroleum reserves, pollute both the local and global environments, result in excessive human fatalities and injuries, and encourage too much traffic congestion.

ITS is unlikely to have much of an impact on the finite nature of petroleum reserves. On the other hand, there are aspects of ITS that increase the efficiency with which fuel is used, including navigational systems that avoid needless "searching" behavior by drivers, systems that provide drivers with information regarding the availability of parking, and various route-finding technologies. The overall impact of these on extending the life of petroleum is probably minor but nonetheless real.

Of course, any ITS system that saves on fuel use by its very nature also decreases local air pollutants and global greenhouse gases. Again, we may not be talking significant amounts, but ITS will help to some extent.

However, the main contribution of ITS to sustainable transport, as defined here, is in the area of motor vehicle crashes and the resulting fatalities and injuries. We have already seen major ITS developments in these areas, with the introduction of various automatic restraint systems for passengers and air bags that instantly inflate on impact, which help minimize injuries from such crashes. But by far the most exciting technologies are those that prevent accidents from occurring in the first place—for example, ITS systems that can adjust the speed of your vehicle to existing traffic conditions or keep your vehicle at a safe distance from other vehicles. If your vehicle is about to collide with another vehicle, there is technology that can forewarn you of that and even technology that enables your vehicle to take over and avoid such collisions. Other systems can monitor your body and wake you if you doze off at the wheel. Or, if night weather conditions are bad, there is technology that effectively improves your vision. Finally, there are systems of automatic speed enforcement that can prevent excessive speeding, which is known to account for many crashes.

Various weather information services made possible by ITS are available, and, to the extent that this information leads people to cancel trips when learning of poor driving conditions, this may result in the saving of lives and reductions in injuries. In other cases state highway weather information systems may lead those on the highways to change their routes because conditions are bad on the route they are using. In still other cases highway departments that monitor speed levels closely and count vehicles remotely may also have sensors in the pavement that can detect hazardous pavement conditions, for example, snow or ice. Through advanced ITC this information could be communicated to vehicles on the highway and the vehicles could adjust their speed to these conditions and so inform the driver. These advanced systems, many just on the drawing boards, are intended to prevent crashes, and this prospect must surely be a fundamental part of a sustainable transport system.

There has been no discussion here of the growing number of baby boom drivers who will soon be reaching old age. For a while there was a general consensus that we would see a resurgence of public transit ridership as this age group reached its "golden years." This belief has since been weakened somewhat by a number of points. First, this age group, at least in the United States, is one that has grown up and grown old with the automobile. They are unlikely to be willing to hang up their car keys and switch to a new mode just because of their age. Second, public transit appears to be losing elements of prior support, so that it is unlikely that this mode will provide anything near the level of mobility or accessibility that it did previously. Clearly, if we are unable to get people out of their cars and into public transit, the reality is that they are going to be driving their automobiles.

Statistics on automobile crashes show that motor vehicle crash rates are highest for both the young and the elderly. We may be able to control fatalities of the former group through such regulatory measures, as stronger drunk driving laws or increasing the age for beginning drivers, but these measures are less applicable to the aged. Consequently, we must do more to increase the safety of the vehicles they use. This appears to be an area where ITS can usefully contribute to improvements in the future.

With regard to congestion, there are a number of ways in which ITS can be helpful. There are roadside or radio systems that inform drivers of congested situations and recommend alternative routes to avoid these. In the event of highway crashes there are systems that can detect these and inform drivers "upstream" that they may want to consider alternative routes under these circumstances as well.

Of course, one of the ITS areas of growing importance in relation to congestion is congestion pricing or tolls. There are basically two types of such facilities. The first charges drivers to use an alternative (frequently parallel) route that has much less traffic because of the fee. This enables one to travel at higher speeds, and the value drivers place on their travel time may make this a reasonable expenditure. The second sets fees for use of a facility simply to increase the cost of transport, to increase transport funds for a state or city, and as a result decrease the volume of traffic on it. It is difficult to say how widespread congestion pricing will become as a way of decreasing traffic volumes. Wachs has argued there are political risks associated with congestion pricing and that no political constituency will consistently fight to increase it. "Advocates of congestion pricing will have to settle for smaller victories during the foreseeable future. Eventually many small victories could add up to a new approach to highway management and finance, but don't count on it happening any time soon" (Wachs, 1994, p. 19).

Some ITS Cases

It may be worthwhile simply to illustrate some of the ITS products that have already been introduced. Examples from the areas of AVCS (automated vehicle control), ATMS (congestion pricing), and ATIS (weather warning systems and navigation systems) will be reviewed here.

The San Diego Automated Highway

There is a 7.6-mile section of Interstate 15 north of San Diego in California that has been made into an automated highway (see Kasindorf, 1997). This system was first demonstrated successfully in August 1997. In rural areas it requires automated vehicles that include onboard cameras and sensors that keep the vehicle within the lane markings and warn of drivers passing or following too closely. In urban areas the vehicle switches to an under-the-bumper sensor system that tracks magnets embedded in the roadway, approximately one every 4 feet and costing $1 each. This system was developed by American Honda Motor Company. An alternative guiding system has been developed by Ohio State University that involves the use of radar and magnetic strips in the road. The cost of the system is one of the attributes that many highway officials find especially appealing: It would cost less than $10,000 a mile, as compared to a new highway, which would cost $1–$10 million a mile.

Developers of the system argue that it has the potential to significantly increase safety since the crash avoidance systems should eliminate the 90% of the crashes that result from human error. Drive times would also be more predictable. Vehicles on these systems would also likely use less fuel and pollute less, and what is most important is that vehicle spacing could be precisely controlled, which would enable much higher densities and volumes on the systems without the attendant risks that these phenomena currently entail. Similar systems are under development elsewhere; Japan first tested such a system in 1995.

Congestion Pricing

Certainly there is nothing new about collecting money from the users of highway transportation facilities. This was common on early private roads as well as on the national road of the United States during the early 19th century. The difference between the charges then and the charges now is that nowadays people can be charged to travel variable amounts on facilities that have less traffic. Still, this *could* be done even without ITS. However, today this process of charging and collecting fees is very much influenced by ITS. Let us look briefly at southern California's State Route 91 (SR-91) in Orange County.

The SR-91 project involved the construction of four new express lanes in the median strip of an existing freeway. ITS was implemented in this project in several ways. First, the toll charged is intended to provide users with a free flow of traffic, and the rate charged varies depending on the rate of the flow (which ranged from $0.25 to $2.50 during the spring following the lanes' opening on December 27, 1995). Second, vehicles using the facility must first secure a transponder, which is placed near the center of the front windshield of the vehicle. As the vehicle passes under overhead receivers, the driver's account is charged for the trip. Third, if the vehicle includes three or more passengers, it is allowed to pull into a special lane that credits any charges back to the account; this lane may also be used by buses.

State troopers patrol the special lanes, just to assure against cheating to avoid the charges.

The facility revealed was built by the California Private Transportation Company, a private corporation that now operates the express lanes. The fees collected go toward retiring the company's debt and covering its operating costs, which includes among other things contractual payments made to the California Highway Patrol to police the facility. The state retains ownership of the underlying rights-of-way.

A similar facility exists south of San Diego, California, on Interstate 15. The so-called FasTrak system there also uses lanes constructed on the median, transponders, and variable tolls that are based on traffic volumes at the time of use.

Weather Information Systems

When the state highway department sends out trucks to put down chemicals in response to a snowfall, the typical cost is $100,000. Obviously there is a need for accurate decision making regarding the use of snow removal equipment. For many years the highway departments and departments of transportation used local weather forecasts to determine what actions they should take with regard to snow and specifically when they should take them. For areas of northern North America as well as Europe, this is potentially a multimillion-dollar problem.

For the past several years we have been seeing an increase in road weather information systems (RWISs). These systems enable highway maintenance units to have far more information available to them. An RWIS may include accurate sensors embedded in the pavement to sense surface and subsurface temperatures, dew point, and the percentage of ice versus snow. These systems may also include wind speed and direction, barometric pressure, and the type of precipitation falling. Some enhanced sites may include video cameras for verification of weather conditions suggested by the data, which is usually sent to a central facility for analysis. If the system detects dangerous conditions, it automatically activates the highway advisory radio.

As of 1998, 44 states in the United States have RWIS systems. Colorado has 150 RWIS sites alone, which it finds necessary for traveler safety in the event of sudden changes in weather conditions. The system also helps with general routing decisions during adverse weather (Hansen, 1998). It also helps to decrease vehicular crashes, as weather conditions play a role in an estimated two-thirds of all highway crashes!

In-Car Navigation Systems

In-car navigation systems come in many varieties. The earliest of these consisted of a CD-ROM that included a digital map of the city of interest. More recent systems have digital information that may be updated from the Internet and have a voice-directed in-car navigation system developed by Pioneer. Their Raku-Navi unit is activated by the vehicle's ignition being turned on. The system will first ask for the driver's destination. Once the driver gives this information, the system will offer graphic information on a 5.6-inch television screen as to the best route, or it will issue voice commands that relay the same information (*Traffic Technology International*, 1998b). Technology is moving rapidly in this area—so much so that investments in systems installed by the vehicle manufacturer may be an unwise choice.

Usually these devices include in-car navigation systems or GPS gear for determining the vehicle's location. It should be obvious that, unless it is immediately disabled, this could also be an excellent antitheft device. It has frequently been used in this manner, according to various news reports. In cases where the driver loses track of his or her parked vehicle, some manufacturers have produced portable car-and-pocket systems.

Some major automobile manufacturers in the United States have developed systems that include cell phones and GPS. The driver simply "phones home" to the manufacturer, which in turn locates the "lost" vehicle and informs the driver where to find it. This system also uses a geographic information system (GIS) on the manufacturer's end along with the GPS readings. Other systems that employ GIS devices paired with a facilities database can readily supply the user information on nearby restaurants and shopping facilities. Information specific to each locality, for example, local weather conditions or traffic information, can also be passed along via such a system.

There are other systems that inform the manufacturer whenever a vehicle's air bags have been deployed. In this case, the manufacturer can contact the vehicle occupants to see whether emergency vehicles need to be dispatched, a measure that can obviously assist in reducing injured fatalities from accidents, particularly in remote areas.

As for the other navigation-based systems, if they significantly decrease the amount of driver "search behavior," then they will result in less fuel being wasted and fewer pollutants being emitted. On the other hand, in a partial offset, it might also encourage drivers to go into more distant areas unfamiliar to them and in the end generate incrementally more travel.

CONCLUSIONS

There is far more going on in ITS than one can hope to cover here (see Stough, 2001), but most of it appears to have only minor impacts on sustainable transport. The greatest contribution is from those systems that lessen motor vehicle fatalities and injuries. Second are systems that reduce congestion in some corridors. Third are those systems that increase the efficiency of certain transport systems and their operation.

While all of these technological changes will facilitate traffic flow and make it safer, there is some question as to whether this is what we really want to do. Put another way, every major transport improvement over the past 200 years ended up resulting in an increase in the total amount of travel taking place. Is it likely that ITS when implemented will result in this same type of impact? Will it in the end generate additional travel? It may, but that travel should be safer and more efficient than it has ever been before, so perhaps the negative impacts of additional travel will not be as great as they are now.

PART III

SUMMARY AND CONCLUSIONS

CHAPTER 22

Summary, Conclusions, and the Current Status of Sustainable Transport

> At one level, public policymaking on sustainable transport is straightforward, as it is more or less taken for granted that . . . people will respond with the expected changes in behaviour. When the results of the policy fall short of expectation, the people are blamed. Individuals regularly refuse to behave in ways that policymakers would prefer.
>
> —DAVID BANISTER (2005)

As this final chapter is written in the spring of 2009, one can say that sustainability and sustainable transport have become popular subjects of media attention. Cities around the world are suddenly trying to become more sustainable; the same can also be said of university campuses (Torr & Havlick, 2004). Major corporations are becoming more aware of the topic, and the petroleum industry is beginning to look at renewable fuels. We will look at some of these developments later, but let us first summarize the key policy and planning aspects of what has been discussed in this volume.

SUMMARY AND CONCLUSIONS

We have come quite far in our discussion of planning and policy surrounding sustainable transport and travel. Part of the reason why can be attributed to our asserting a workable definition of sustainable transport in Chapter 1. We did not approach this task from the perspective of "What is a sustainable transport system?" If you put 100 experts in a room and asked them that question, you would end up with 100 definitions. Instead, we used an approach that basically posed the question "What is it that *prevents* a transport system from being sustainable?" That approach yielded

263

the pentad that we have referred to numerous times since in this volume, namely, finite and diminishing fuel reserves, excessive injuries and loss of life on the current highway system, local atmospheric problems resulting in problems for human health, global atmospheric problems leading to climate change, and excessive traffic congestion on the transport system. The formal definition derived was: *A sustainable transport system is one that provides transport and mobility with renewable fuels while minimizing emissions detrimental to the local and global environment and preventing needless fatalities, injuries, and congestion.* There are academics who disagree with this approach, but they cannot argue that such phenomena as plant damage or wild animal deaths keep a transport system from being sustainable. They may also have genuine concerns about equity, but is it reasonable to believe these concerns can be resolved by a sustainable transport system? Is a sustainable transport system, as defined, attainable? Probably not, but we can get very close to this ideal.

In Chapter 2 we gave the reader a brief history of the problem of sustainability in the transport sector. We concluded that all of the earlier transport systems were nonsustainable once they were used excessively: that conclusion applied equally to ships of the 18th century, railroads of the 19th century, and automobiles of the 20th century. The key takeaway logical insight is that a variety of transport modes and fuels must be involved in any sustainable transport system.

In Chapter 3 we focused on how climate change is resulting from excessively high emissions of greenhouse gases. We identified these greenhouse gases and their transport origins in many cases. We then examined the major impacts of global warming: higher average temperatures and a rise in the level of the oceans. The nature of the resulting impacts on each of the various transport sectors was identified. A Transportation Research Board report that appeared in 2008 is the most comprehensive treatment of the impacts of climate change on transport that has appeared to date, and readers should be aware of it (TRB, 2008). A brief policy summary of the failure of the United States to act on climate change was also presented in this chapter.

Some scientists still believe that climate change is part of a natural cycle and that humans are not the primary cause of or contributor to this problem. This writer disagrees with that assessment. However, even if there were some merit to their position, is it reasonable for the nations of the world to continue pumping carbon dioxide into the atmosphere at very high levels? The precautionary principle would dictate that if there is a possibility that these emissions are detrimental to the environment, even in the absence of solid scientific evidence, it is imperative that action be taken. Thus, limiting these emissions has merit regardless of one's position on climate change. Those who argue that the costs of limiting carbon dioxide emissions will be detrimental to the economy are not taking into account the positive economic impacts of the new technologies that will need to be developed in this area.

Where things stand with regard to urban air quality was discussed in Chapter 4. The various pollutants were introduced and their negative impacts, primarily on human health, were reviewed. Existing CAFE standards were revealed along with the reductions that these have brought to motor vehicle emissions. From a policy point of view, there is not much more that can be done with the criteria pollutants without excessive costs being incurred. This is not as bad as it sounds since phenomenal reductions have been achieved since the 1970s. On the other hand, although vehicle emissions per vehicle have dropped significantly, the increase in vehicle miles traveled and the gradual growth of the nation's vehicle fleet result in high total emissions from the transport sector, and this must be addressed.

Petroleum, the automotive fuel source of choice, was the subject of Chapter 5. The consumption that has taken place during the past 100 years was discussed along with possible production over the rest of this century. World reserves of conventional oil exceed all that has been used to date, but now there are many new users of oil in the world and it is unlikely that this energy source will last beyond the mid-century mark.

There may be some who believe we have overstated the seriousness of the nonrenewable fuels problem. Although we continue to find additional petroleum reserves, these new finds are relatively small in comparison to previous ones. There are also nonconventional sources of petroleum, but these come with their own special energy and environmental costs attached; so, we should consider these costs very carefully before attempting to develop them on a large scale. Even if petroleum reserves were to expand significantly, the major growth occurring in the size of the world's vehicle fleet, particularly in such countries as China and India, will place tremendous demands on these resources. We must try to move away from petroleum as the primary fuel for the world's vehicles.

Chapter 6 focuses on motor vehicle crashes and safety, noting the deplorable situation in the United States. Though the safety record is much worse elsewhere in the world, for a developed country to be losing more than 40,000 people a year and 3 million people in the last century to motor vehicle fatalities is unacceptable. We examined the costs of crashes, identified the groups most impacted (chief among them, young men), and the causes of accidents. It appears that U.S. policy in this area is to make crashes *survivable*, whereas others believe the goal should be to *prevent them*. We spent some time suggesting what planners can do to decrease fatalities by using Sweden's Vision Zero approach as a guide.

Even if we can resolve the preceding four problems, we still have a major fifth problem on our hands, namely, congestion. In Chapter 7 we examined urban traffic congestion, which has been at critical levels for more than a half-century. We began by defining congestion and identifying its causes. We expect a certain level of congestion for special events, but we would like to see it reduced. We examined several indicators or measures of congestion, which is necessary if we are to evaluate progress. We reviewed several potential tools and critiqued their value in reducing congestion. Some of these are technological solutions, while others can be implemented by policy advisers and planners. If the solutions are simple, they may have already been proposed and tried. In other cases there is some belief that although the actions may not solve the congestion problem they might contribute to the eventual solution. Such actions or means include telecommuting, congestion pricing, and some intelligent transport systems. We do see some merit in the vehicle density argument put forth in Chapter 7.

Chapter 8 serves as a brief introduction to the possible solutions described in Part II of this volume. These solutions fall broadly into the areas of pricing, planning, policy, education, and of course technology. Each of these is discussed in the second half of the book.

The *full* costs of transportation and travel are rarely recognized. Chapter 9 summarizes these, ranging from the obvious—the cost of fuel—to the esoteric—the military costs of maintaining a presence in the Middle East. In between these extremes are other costs that should be given serious thought by policymakers, such as the costs of various pollutants to society as a whole. Even if these are not incorporated in the price of fuel in some manner, programs to explain these to the public would certainly be worthwhile.

The various ways of introducing additional pricing mechanisms into the transport realm are discussed in Chapter 10. Some of these have already been introduced—highway congestion pricing in California, congestion taxes of the sort implemented in London, and taxes on parking. Less common are pollution and characteristic taxes. The most obvious way of pricing transport is through a fuel tax that would have the double role of increasing the cost of travel and funding the maintenance and/or construction of highways. Policymakers shy away from increasing these taxes at the state or federal level, but in view of the other price increases we have seen for fuel, this reluctance is misguided. Hardly anyone would lose many votes in the next election by supporting a nickel tax on a gallon of gasoline for highway maintenance. Nevertheless, certain U.S. presidential candidates in 2008 failed to support additional tax levies on fuel and instead proposed waiving the existing federal tax for the summer months of that year.

Urban form—the *shape* of a city—is one of the least understood aspects of urban planning. It is not clear how it affects travel in most cases because research in the area has been undertaken differently by nearly every researcher in the field. In Chapter 11 we summarized the history of land use and transport planning to emphasize the haphazard way in which our "understanding" developed in this area. We cautioned planners not to automatically opt for "new-urbanism" approaches to urban planning, because these actually rest on a very shaky foundation. Instead, better use of traditional techniques of land use control such as zoning and fewer waivers of this mechanism are recommended.

The use of indicators in planning for sustainability is presented in Chapter 12. Although one could write an entire book on indicators of transport sustainability, we thin out the field and focus on those related to the five factors reflect the identified as most crucial in our definition of the term, namely, fuel use, fatalities and injuries, local air quality, global climate change, and congestion. We also demonstrate that all of these are highly related to vehicle miles traveled, or VMT. Therefore, if planners really want to increase the sustainability of travel and transport, they must monitor this variable if no other. We also suggest how the indicators identified could be used by planners in a very practical way.

There is a tendency for individuals, institutions, or governments to believe that the problems of transport sustainability are beyond their ability to have much of an impact. Chapter 13 summarizes the various actions and policies that can be undertaken by individuals, cities and towns, states, multistate regions, and nations. The actions vary from individuals walking more and purchasing "green" cars to protocols and treaties of the Montreal or Kyoto type. Some specific programs are reviewed as examples.

Speed and speed policies are the focal points of Chapter 14. If controlling vehicle miles traveled represents the most important variable in moving toward transport sustainability, the speed at which those miles are accumulated is a major tool in the hands of the policymaker. Yet, they seem unwilling to use this tool. Fatalities and the severity of injuries increase as the speeds of vehicles involved in collisions increase. For internal combustion engines, emissions and fuel use increase at both the lowest and highest speeds. Hybrid vehicles restrict this problem to higher speeds so long as they use electric engines for low speeds. Ironically, congestion can be caused by vehicles traveling at *high* speeds. Thus, it is highly important for policymakers to take more of an interest in speed and speed limit policies. One area where they could take immediate action is to discourage advertising that seeks to sell automobiles based solely on their speed attributes.

Many nations have developed policies on transport sustainability. Chapter 15 includes summaries of some of these, not as active policies but as illustrations of what has been tried. Some of the actions are somewhat draconian and would probably not be acceptable in the United States or Canada, but others may be worth considering. Several specific policies and programs are discussed here as well. In many cases these have been tried in the United States and seem to have had not much of an impact. Others might be worth a second try. The idea here is not to prescribe but to suggest.

We make the argument in Chapter 16 that just about all travel demand management is sustainable travel demand management. We look at some of the common techniques in this realm from a sustainability perspective. Included in the discussion are traffic calming, vehicle replacement/retirement programs, feebates, car pooling and van pooling, cash-out programs, transit vouchers, and the merits of eliminating company cars. All of these activities would contribute positively to a more sustainable transport system.

We did not become a nation of automobile drivers overnight. Detroit and Madison Avenue worked diligently to "educate" us into our current dilemma. Thus, it's time that we were reeducated. Perhaps we need to counter automakers' advertising with educational programs in the same way that we have countered cigarette advertising with public service announcements and messages. For example, everyone is familiar with the message "Warning: The Surgeon General Has Determined That Cigarette Smoking Is Dangerous to Your Health" that must appear on all packages of cigarettes as well as on all cigarette print advertising. However, there is nothing comparable that warns about the dangers of driving fast in response to speed-oriented automobile advertising. Chapter 17 proposes that we give some thought to educating the public about the hazards of speed as well as the environmental problems of using the automobile.

Telecommuting, information and communication technology, and e-commerce are examined in Chapter 18 in terms of their potential impact on transport. We have long been of the opinion that certain types of technology can substitute communications for travel and that is what we look at here. Unfortunately, there is not much here to be optimistic about. Telecommuting or teleworking has not lived up to expectations because there are so few types of jobs that can be done remotely. ICT and e-commerce have grown substantially, but it is not at all clear how much the Internet has been a substitute for the telephone, how much it has led to less travel, and how much it has generated additional travel and transport. In the business world with the advent of globalization more goods are moving greater distances, stimulated in part by developments in ICT. However, one should not expect any major contribution from these sectors in solving the specific problems of nonsustainability in transport.

Another area in which technology plays a major role is in the development of alternative fuels. Unfortunately, there is not much in the way of light at the end of this tunnel. We are fairly certain of the fuels that are possible, and these are discussed at length in Chapter 19. It is more than likely that the fuels of 2030 will be the fuels of today, but with greater shares coming from nongasoline sources. The one exception to this statement is the potential use of hydrogen in fuel cells. We would like to see this produced using solar energy, but there would still be storage and distribution problems for this fuel.

A key technological breakthrough in the recent past has been the hybrid motor vehicle, which is discussed in Chapter 20. This vehicle significantly increases the miles per gallon of any fuel used. We believe that hybrids will dominate the market during the next decade and that these will eventually be capable of using numerous types of fuel. This is not to say that the fuel cell will be unimportant—only that it will just take longer to dominate the market.

Chapter 21 examines what have come to be called intelligent transport systems, whose most important contributions to sustainable transport lies in the area of vehicle safety and driving behavior. We are already seeing such useful innovations as car navigation systems using GPS, self-parking vehicles, video cameras that enable drivers to see blind spots, and so forth. Still other innovations are thus far available only as prototypes, such as automated guideways, vehicles that forewarn one of hazards or potential crashes, and vehicles that may communicate with one another regarding traffic and environmental conditions. We expect countless innovations in this area in the future.

If we were writing this volume for all the nations of the world, we would have included more discussion about the role of the economy and economic development in the sustainability of nations and their transport systems in the developing world. Some countries will inevitably gravitate toward a nonsustainable transport system—despite all the pollution, congestion, and other problems inherent in such systems—in order to give them an immediate higher level of mobility and hopefully the economic resources needed to make their transport system more sustainable in the long run. This volume has focuses exclusively on the United States, Canada, the United Kingdom and certain other EU countries that are relatively homogeneous economically (see Black, 2002, for a more extended discussion of the rate of economic levels in mobility).

Additionally, this volume has not examined certain other areas related to transport sustainability explicitly, including freight transport (see Black, 2007) and sustainable tourism (see Black, 2004). In the case of freight transport, most of the major problems are tied to globalization and international trade and are beyond the scope of this volume (as well as the interest of most domestic planners and policymakers). As for sustainable tourism, much of that literature pertains to areas outside the United States and Canada and would also be of little interest to planners and policymakers here.

RECENT ACTIONS

During the summer of 2008 the price of gasoline in the United States briefly reached an average price of more than $4.50 a gallon. This is the highest average price ever recorded for gasoline in the United States surpassing even the inflation-adjusted price reached in 1981 in response to the OPEC oil embargo of that year. The higher prices have had some positive impacts, based on anecdotal evidence: an increase in carpooling, more transit ridership, more combining of trips or trip chaining, deferring some trips, and purchasing fewer vehicles that use large amounts of fuel (e.g., SUVs). It remains to be seen whether these crisis conditions will persist long enough to become trends, but this seems unlikely as of mid-2009. Decreases in the price of fuel since mid-2008 have led to a decline in purchases of more fuel-efficient vehicles. On the other hand, this decline could be attributable to the general downward trend in the economy of the United States and elsewhere.

The economic recession of 2007–2009 has had a very dramatic impact on the domestic automobile manufacturers in the United States: General Motors, Chrysler, and Ford. Although billions of taxpayer dollars were funnelled into both General Motors and Chrysler in a failed effort to keep the firms solvent, post-bankruptcy both companies will need to more accurately assess and address the needs of consumers with attractive car models that sell. Although the two firms are playing catchup at this point and producing hybrid vehicles, the economy remains so precarious that their long-term future remains very much clouded.

Honda Motors has released the Honda FCX to a small number of consumers in California. This is a hydrogen-powered fuel cell vehicle. Rather than using gasoline or natural gas as a fuel stock for making hydrogen on board, this vehicle uses hydrogen stored in a fuel tank. The vehicle has a driving range of 270 miles. It will probably see primary use in California, which so far has 26 refueling stations, but only 6 are open to the public (Yvkoff, 2009). There are probably less than a dozen such stations outside of that state. Although there probably won't be many of these vehicles produced and sold (or more likely leased), it is amazing that the vehicle is available this soon.

Prior to its government-sponsored bankruptcy reorganization, General Motors was developing a Saturn hybrid (the electric–gasoline) Aura model that would allow owners to plug the vehicle into a home wall socket for charging its battery overnight. It is quite likely that the vehicle would never need to use its gasoline engine in most circumstances. A release date for the vehicle has not been announced at this writing, and in fact GM was set to dispose of its Saturn division as of mid-2009 as a part of its downsizing; so, the fate of this project remains uncertain.

With regard to our belief that more could be done to educate the driving public, we were pleased to see Allstate Insurance begin placing full-page advertisements in major news magazines that state: "The #1 killer of teenagers does not have a trigger. It has a steering wheel." The advertisement has several additional paragraphs of information and references to Allstate's website. It is actually a commendable effort by Allstate to reduce teenage fatalities resulting from motor vehicle accidents through increased public awareness.

Various technical innovations are being developed in the vehicle safety area. ITS technologies that allow vehicles to "communicate" (i.e., trade input) with other vehicles about road conditions, approaching emergency vehicles, traffic accidents, and congestion were demonstrated during the spring of 2007. It will take at least 15 years for these technologies to be found in the nation's automobile fleet once they are adopted by manufacturers, but these are all positive developments currently in progress.

In addition, recent data would suggest that Americans are driving less. Over the period 1980–2005 vehicle miles driven rose an average of 2.7% annually. For the period 2005–2007 this rate of growth declined to only 0.3% annually, on average. Even the 2000–2005 rate showed some decrease, with a growth rate of only 1.9% per year. Reasons cited for the decrease include increased gasoline prices, additional public transit options, comparatively fewer women willing to join ranks of motorists, and revitalized city centers that resulted in intraurban relocation of workers nearer their jobs. We would place the heaviest emphasis on fuel price increases.

If consumers begin to expect more options, then market forces can go a long way toward solving some of the problems that are keeping transport from being sustainable. If fuel prices remain at current levels or increase, we will begin to see competitive alternatives flourish. We don't know if this will occur. It is virtually impossible to forecast fuel prices over the long term. It might be wise to consider undertaking a policy that increases fuel taxes whenever fuel prices begin to drop. While never politically popular, such a tax policy would keep us on the right path toward longer-term sustainability.

There are some indications that attractive public transit options are proliferating around the United States. If we are ever going to manage the congestion problem, we must have this alternative mode available for use. Little attention has been given to public transit here. In large part this is due to the fact that a doubling of transit capacity would at best double transit ridership. In the case of the United States, this progression from 3% to 6% of all trips would not, in and of itself, solve the sustainability problem—but it would certainly contribute to the solution.

Overall, I am optimistic about the future of sustainable transport in the United States. There are admittedly negative trends afoot, but these are not altogether insurmountable. We see no immediate success in bringing carbon dioxide emissions under control except possibly in California. Beyond the transport sector there are technologies for carbon sequestration available, but we do not foresee their widespread use anytime soon. We also hear political candidates in the United States talking about cap-and-trade systems for carbon dioxide, which is clearly good news. Technologies for controlling other emissions abound, but controlling vehicle miles traveled will be necessary if these emissions are going to be successfully eliminated in the coming years.

This discussion brings us back to the behavioral aspects of the problem. We need a concerted effort to educate the public on the need to drive less. It should probably also be recognized that the period of "peak mobility" has passed in the United States and Canada. In 1999 Professor Andrew Gillespie of the University of Newcastle in the United Kingdom correctly observed that "the nations of the world spent most of the 20th century encouraging people to be more mobile, and now we must encourage them to be less mobile." If there is a single goal that we should all strive for that will make transport more sustainable, it is simply to "bit the bullet" and start driving less.

References

Aarts, L., & van Schagen, I. (2006). Driving Speed and the Risk of Road Crashes: A Review. *Accident Analysis and Prevention, 38*, 215–224.

Albion, R. G. (1965). *Forests and Sea Power: The Timber Problem of the Royal Navy, 1652–1862*. Hamden, CT: Archon Books.

Anderson, W. P., Kanaroglou, P. S., & Miller, E. J. (1996). Urban Form, Energy and the Environment: A Review of Issues, Evidence and Policy. *Urban Studies, 33*(1), 7–35.

API (American Petroleum Institute). (2009). Retrieved from: .

Apogee (1994). *The Costs of Transportation: Final Report*. Boston: The Conservation Law Foundation.

Arnott, R. (1998). Economic Theory and the Spatial Mismatch Hypothesis. *Urban Studies, 35*(7), 1171–1185.

AWST (*Aviation Week and Space Technology*). (1990). Intense Heat Disrupts Flights at Sky Harbor Airport in Phoenix. *Aviation Week and Space Technology, 133,* 56.

Badoe, D. A., & Miller, E. J. (2000). Transportation–Land Use Interaction: Empirical Findings in North America, and Their Implications for Modeling. *Transportation Research D, 5,* 235–263.

Bae, C.-H. C., & Mayeres, I. (2005). Transportation and Equity. In K. P. Donaghy, S. Poppelreuterr, & G. Rudinger (Eds.), *Social Dimensions of Sustainable Transport: Transatlantic Perspectives* (pp. 164–194). Aldershot, UK: Ashgate.

Bamford, P. W. (1956). *Forests and French Sea Power 1660–1789*. Toronto: University of Toronto Press.

Banister, D. (2005). Overcoming barriers to the implementation of sustainable transport. In P. Rietveld & R. R. Stough (Eds.), *Barriers to Sustainable Transport, Institutions, Regulation and Sustainability*. London and New York: Spon Press.

Banninga, G. (1999). *Static and Dynamic Analysis of Average Worktrip Travel Times for a Large Set of U.S. Cities*. Unpublished PhD dissertation, Indiana University, Bloomington.

Barnett, T. P., Adam, J. C., & Lettenmaier, D. P. (2005). Potential Impacts of a Warming Climate on Water Availability in Snow-Dominated Regions. *Nature, 438,* 303–309.

Bartis, J. T., LaTourrette, T., Dixon, L., Peterson, D. J., & Cecchine, G. (2005). *Oil Shale Development in the United States: Prospects and Policy Issues*. Santa Monica, CA: RAND Corporation.

Beckerman, W. (2003). *A Poverty of Reason: Sustainable Development and Economic Growth.* Oakland, CA: Independent Institute.

Bezdek, R. H., & Wendling, R. M. (2005). Potential Long-Term Impacts of Changes in U.S. Vehicle Fuel Efficiency Standards. *Energy Policy, 33,* 417–419.

Black, W. R. (1987). An Investigation of the Ownership of Railroad Right-of-Way: The Case of Indiana. *Transportation Research Record, 1154,* 4–10.

Black, W. R. (1990). Global Warming: Impacts on the Transportation Infrastructure. *TR (Transportation Research) News,* No. 150, 2–8, 34.

Black, W. R. (1996). Sustainable Transportation: A U.S. Perspective. *Journal of Transport Geography, 4*(3), 151–159.

Black, W. R. (1999, June–September). ALTERNAT: A Tool for Evaluating the Costs of Alternative Transportation Projects. *Rivista Geografica Italiana, 106*(2–3).

Black, W. R. (2000). Socio-Economic Barriers to Sustainable Transport. *Journal of Transport Geography, 8,* 141–147.

Black, W. R. (2001). An Unpopular Essay on Transportation: The 2000 Fleming Lecture. *Journal of Transport Geography, 9,* 1–11.

Black, W. R. (2002). Sustainable Transport and Potential Mobility. *European Journal of Transport and Infrastructure Research, 2,* 179–196.

Black, W. R. (2003). *Transportation: A Geographical Analysis.* New York: Guilford Press.

Black, W. R. (2004). Sustainable Transport and Its Implications for Tourism. In L. M. Lumsdon & S. J. Page (Eds.), *Tourism and Transport: Issues and Agenda for the New Millennium* (pp. 57–68). Amsterdam: Elsevier.

Black, W. R. (2007). Sustainable Solutions for Freight Transport. In T. R. Leinbach & C. Capineri (Eds.), *Globalized Freight Transport: Intermodality, E-Commerce, Logistics and Sustainability* (pp. 189–216). Aldershot, UK: Edward Elgar.

Black, W. R., Munn, D. L., Black, R. J., & Xie, J. (1995). *Modal Choices: An Approach to Comparing the Full Costs of Transportation Alternatives.* Bloomington: Department of Geography and the Transportation Research Center, Indiana University.

Blowers, A. (Ed.). (1993). *Planning for a Sustainable Environment: A Report by the Town and Country Planning Association.* London: Earthscan.

Boarnet, M., & Crane, R. (2001). The Influence of Land Use on Travel Behavior: Specification and Estimation Strategies. *Transportation Research A, 35,* 823–845.

Bowie, N. N., & Walz, M. (1994). Data Analysis of the Speed-Related Crash Issue. *Auto and Traffic Safety, 1,* 31–38.

British Code of Advertising, Sales Promotion and Direct Marketing (2005). Retrieved from: *www.asa.org.uk/NR/rdonlyres/AE1CB9D7098147928FF1C27A39DA917E/0/CAP-Code.pdf.*

Burchell, R. W., Lowensteain, G., Dolphin, W. R., Galley, C. C., Downs, A., Seskin, S., et al. (2002). In TRB, *Costs of Sprawl—2000.* TCRP Report 74. Washington, DC: National Research Council, Transportation Research Board.

Bureau of Transportation Statistics. (1999). *National Transportation Statistics, 1999.* Washington, DC: U.S. Department of Transportation.

Bureau of Transportation Statistics. (2004). *Transportation Statistics Annual Report.* Washington, DC: U.S. Department of Transportation.

Burnham, J. C. (1961, December). The Gasoline Tax and the Automobile Revolution. *Mississippi Valley Historical Review.*

Burwell, D. G., Bartholomew, K., & Gordon, D. (1991). Energy and Environmental Research Needs. In TRB, *Transportation, Urban Form, and the Environment.* Special Report 231. Washington, DC: National Research Council, Transportation Research Board.

Business Week. (2005, September 12). Let That Be a Warning: What Katrina Can Teach about Handling Natural Disasters and Energy Better. *Business Week*, pp. 42–43.

Button, K. J. (1984). Road Pricing—An Outsider's View of the American Experience. *Transport Reviews, 5*, 73–98.

Button, K. J. (1993a). *Transport Economics* (2nd ed.). Aldershot, UK: Edward Elgar.

Button, K. J. (1993b). *Transport, the Environment and Economic Policy*. Brookfield, VT: Edward Elgar.

Button, K. J., Stough, R., Bragg, M., & Taylor, S. (2006). *Telecommuications, Transportation and Location*. Cheltenham, UK: Edward Elgar.

California Department of Consumer Affairs. (undated). *Smog Check Consumer Assistance Program Application Package*. Sacramento, CA: Bureau of Automotive Repair.

Caltrans. (2006). *Valuing Accidents*. Office of Transportation Economics. Retrieved May 10, 2007, from *www.dot.ca.gov/hq/tpp/offices/ote/Benefit_Cost/benefits/accidents/value_estimates.html*.

Cambridge Systematics. (2005). *Traffic Congestion and Reliability: Trends and Advanced Strategies for Congestion Mitigation*. Prepared for the Federal Highway Administration, Cambridge, MA.

Campbell, C. J. (1997). *The Coming Oil Crisis*. Essex, U.K.: Multiscience Publishing Co. and Petroconsultants SA.

Carty, S. S. (2009, January 12). Electric Cars Rule at Auto Show. *USA Today*, p. B1.

Centre for Sustainable Transportation. (1998). *Definition and Vision of Sustainable Transportation*. Toronto: Author.

Changnon, S. A., & Glantz, M. H. (1996). The Great Lakes Diversion at Chicago and Its Implications for Climate Change. *Climatic Change, 32*, 199–214.

Clinton, W. J., & Gore, a., Jr. (1993). *The Climate Change Action Plan*. Washington, DC: U.S. Government Printing Office.

Commission of the European Community. (1993a). *The Future Development of the Common Transport Policy*. Brussels: European Commission.

Commission of the European Community. (1993b). *Green Paper on the Impact of Transport on the Environment*. Brussels: European Commission.

Consumers Union. (2006, October). The Ethanol Myth. *Consumer Reports*, pp. 15–19.

Consumers Union. (2009, April). New Cars: Profiles. *Consumer Reports*, pp. 38–71.

Council on Environmental Quality. (1974). *The Costs of Sprawl*. Washington, DC: Real Estate Research Corporation.

Crane, R. (2000). The Influence of Urban Form on Travel: An Interpretative Review. *Journal of Planning Literature, 15*, 3–23.

Daly, H. E. (1992). *Steady State Economics*. Washington, DC: Island Press.

Daly, H. E., & Farley, J. (2004). *Ecological Economics: Principles and Applications*. Washington, DC: Island Press.

Davis, S. C. (1995). *Transportation Energy Data Book: Edition 15*. ORNL-6856. Oak Ridge, TN: Oak Ridge National Laboratory.

Davis, S. C. (1997). *Transportation Energy Data Book: Edition 17*. ORNL-6919. Oak Ridge, TN: Oak Ridge National Laboratory.

DeCicco, J., & Kliesch, J. (2000). *ACEEE's Green Book: The Environmental Guide to Cars and Trucks, Model Year 2000*. Washington, DC: American Council for an Energy-Efficient Economy.

Deffeyes, K. S. (2001). *Hubbert's Peak: The Impending World Oil Shortage*. Princeton: Princeton University Press.

Delucchi, M. A. (1995). Bundled Private Sector Costs of Motor Vehicle Use: Report No. 6 in the Series. In *The Annualized Social Costs of Motor Vehicle Use in the U.S., Based on*

1990–1991 Data. Davis: Institute for Transportation Studies, University of California at Davis.

Demirbas, A. (2008). *Biodiesel: A Realistic Fuel Alternative for Diesel Engines*. London: Springer-Verlag.

Department of Environment. (1994). *Sustainable Development: The U.K. Strategy*. London: Her Majesty's Stationery Office.

Dickerson, S. M. (1995). *Challenges of Environmental Sustainability in Transport Policies: The European Model*. Unpublished MA thesis, Indiana University, Bloomington.

Dill, J. (2004). Estimating Emissions Reductions from Accelerated Vehicle Retirement Programs. *Transportation Research Part D, 9*, 87–106.

Doctor, R. D., & Molburg, J. C. (2004). Clean Hydrogen from Coal and CO_2 Capture and Sequestration. In D. Sperling & J. S. Cannon (Eds.), *The Hydrogen Energy Transition: Moving Toward the Post Petroleum Age in Transportation* (pp. 93–104). Amsterdam and Boston: Elsevier.

Dowdeswell, J. A. (2006). The Greenland Ice Sheet and Global Sea-Level Rise. *Science, 311*, 963–964.

Downs, A. (1992). *Stuck in Traffic: Coping with Peak-Hour Traffic Congestion*. Washington, DC: The Brookings Institution, and Cambridge, MA: The Lincoln Institute for Land Policy.

Drake, D. A. (1995). Technology, Economics, and the ZEV Mandate: A Vehicle Manufacturer's Perspective. In D. Sperling & S. A. Shaheen (Eds.), *Transportation and Energy: Strategies for a Sustainable Transportation System*. Washington, DC: American Council for an Energy-Efficient Economy.

Duleep, K. G. (1997). Evolutionary and Revolutionary Technologies for Improving Automotive Fuel Economy. In J. DiCicco & M. Delucchi (Eds.), *Transportation, Energy, and Environment: How Far Can Technology Take Us?* (pp. 157–178). Washington, DC: American Council for an Energy Efficient Economy, 243–254.

Dumas, A., Greene, D. L., & Bourbeau, A. (2007). North American Feebate Analysis Model. In D. Sperling & J. S. Cannon (Eds.), *Driving Climate Change: Cutting Carbon from Transportation* (pp. 107–127). Boston: Elsevier.

Dunphy, R. T. (1991). *12 Tools for Improving Mobility and Managing Congestion*. Washington, DC: Urban Land Institute.

duVair, P., Wickizer, D., & Burer, M. J. (2002). Climate Change and Potential Implications for California's Transportation Systems. In USDOT, *The Potential Impacts of Climate Change on Transportation* (pp. 125–134). Washington, DC: Center for Climate Change and Environmental Forecasting.

ECMT (European Conference of Ministers of Transport). (1993). *Transport Policy and Global Warming*, Paris: ECMT/OECD.

ECMT (European Conference of Ministers of Transport). (2000). *Traffic Congestion in Europe, Round Table 110*. Paris: ECMT/OECD.

EIA (Energy Information Administration). (2000). *Annual Energy Review, 2000*. Washington, DC: Author.

EIA (Energy Information Administration). (2005). *Emissions of Greenhouse Gases in the United States 2004*. Washington, DC: Author.

EIA (Energy Information Administration). (2006a). *International Energy Outlook 2006*. Washington, DC: Author.

EIA (Energy Information Administration). (2006b). *Annual Energy Review, 2006*. Washington, DC: Author.

EIA (Energy Information Administration). (2006c). *International Energy Annual 2006*. Washington, DC: Author.

EIA (Energy Information Administration). (2008). *Annual Energy Review, 2008*. Washington, DC: Author.

EIA (Energy Information Administration). (2009). *Retail Gasoline Historical Prices*. Retrieved from: *www.eia.doe.gov/oil_gas/petroleum/data_publications/wrgp/mogas_history.html*.

Elvik, R. (2001). Area-Wide Urban Traffic Calming Schemes: A Meta-Analysis of Safety Effects. *Accident Analysis and Prevention, 33*, 327–336.

Emanuel, K. (2005). Increasing Destructiveness of Tropical Cyclones over the Past 30 Years. *Nature, 43614*, 686–688.

Enright, D. (2001). *The Wicked Wit of Winston Churchill*. London: Michael O'Mara Books Limited.

EPA (U.S. Environmental Protection Agency). (1996). *Indicators of the Environmental Impacts of Transportation*. EPA 230-R-96-009. Washington, DC: Author.

EPA (U.S. Environmental Protection Agency). (2001). *National Air Quality and Emissions Trends Report, 1999*. EPA 454/R-01-004. Research Triangle Park, NC: Office of Air Quality Planning and Standards Research, EPA.

EPA (U.S. Environmental Protection Agency). Sea Level. Retrieved from *yosemite.epa.gov/oar/global warming.nsf/content/Climate Futures ClimateSeaLevel.html*.

EPA (Environmental Protection Agency). (2009). *National Ambient Ambient Air Quality Standards*. Retrieved from: *www.epa.gov/air/criteria.html*.

Eurostat. (1999). *Transport in Figures: Statistical Pocket Book, 1999*. Luxembourg: European Commission.

Evans, L. (2003). Transportation Safety. In R. W. Hall (Ed.), *Handbook of Transportation Science* (pp. 67–112). Boston: Kluwer Academic.

Evans, L. (2006). The Dramatic Failure of U.S. Traffic Safety Policy. *TR (Transportation Research) News*, No. 242, 28–31.

Ewing, R. (1997). Is Los Angeles-Style Sprawl Desirable? *Journal of the American Planning Association, 63*, 107–126.

Fallon, I., & O'Neill, D. (2005). The World's First Automobile Fatality. *Accident Analysis and Prevention, 37*, 601–603.

Feitelson, E. (1996). Sustainable Transport Policy. In Ministry of the Environment, *Towards Sustainable Development in Israel* (pp. 79–86). Jerusalem: The State of Israel.

Feitelson, E. (2002). Introducing Environmental Equity Concerns into the Discourse on Sustainable Transport. In W. R. Black & P. Nijkamp (Eds.), *Social Change and Sustainable Transport* (pp. 141–147). Bloomington: Indiana University Press.

Feitelson, E., & Rotem, O. (2004). The Case for Taxing Surface Parking. *Transportation Research D, 9*, 319–333.

Fellows, N. T., & Pitfield, D. E. (2000). An Economic and Operational Evaluation of Urban Car-Sharing. *Transportation Research Part D, 5*, 1–10.

Ferguson, E. (1995). Recent Nationwide Declines in Carpooling. *Nationwide Personal Transportation Survey, Travel Mode Special Reports*, Washington, DC: FHWA, U.S. DOT. pp. 1–49.

Ferguson, E. (2000). *Travel Demand Management and Public Policy*. Aldershot, UK: Ashgate.

Ferguson, E. (2004). Zoning for Parking as a Policy Process: A Historical Review. *Transport Reviews, 24*, 177–194.

Fergusson, M., & Taylor, D. (1999). *Greening Vehicle Excise Duty*. London: Institute for European Environmental Policy.

Ferrão, P., & Amaral, J. (2006). Assessing the Economics of Auto Recycling Activities in Relation to European Union Directive on End of Life Vehicles. *Technological Forecasting and Social Change, 73*, 277–289.

FHWA (Federal Highway Administration). (1996). *Highway Statistics 1995*. Washington, DC: U.S. Department of Transportation.

FHWA (Federal Highway Administration). (1997). *Highway Statistics, 1996*. Washington, DC: U.S. Department of Transportation.

FHWA (Federal Highway Administration). (1998). *Synthesis of Safety Research Related to Speed*. Publication No. FHWA-RD-98-154. Retrieved from *www.fhwa.dot.gov/tfhrc/safety/pubs/speed/speed.htm*.

FHWA (Federal Highway Administration). (2006). *Highway Statistics 2005*. Washington, DC: U.S. Department of Transportation.

FHWA (Federal Highway Administration). (2007). *Highway Statistics, 2006*. Washington, DC: U.S. Department of Transportation.

FHWA (Federal Highway Administration). (2008). *Highway Statistics, 2007*. Washington, DC: U.S. Department of Transportation.

Fielding, G. J. (1994). Private Toll Roads: Acceptability of Congestion Pricing in Southern California. In TRB, *Curbing Gridlock: Peak-Period Fees to Relieve Congestion* (pp. 380–404). Special Report 242, Vol. 2. Washington, DC: Transportation Research Board, National Academy Press.

Flink, J. J. (1990). *The Automobile Age*. Cambridge, MA: MIT Press.

Fogel, R. W. (1964). *Railroads and American Economic Growth: Essays in Econometric History*. Baltimore, MD: The Johns Hopkins University Press.

Ford Motor Company. (2000). *Connecting with Society*. Retrieved from: *www.ford.com*

Forman, R. (Ed.). (2002). *Road Ecology: Science and Solutions*. Washington, DC: Island Press.

Frantz, D., & Collins, C. (1999). *Celebration, USA: Living in Disney's Brave New Town*. New York: Henry Holt & Company.

Friedrich, R., & Bickel, P. (Eds.). (2001). *Environmental External Costs of Transport*. New York: Springer.

Friel, B. (2005, June 25). Curbing the Carnage. *National Journal*, pp. 2040–2045.

Funk, K., & Rabl, A. (1999). Electric versus conventional vehicles: Social costs and benefits in France. *Transportation Research Part D: Transport and Environment, 4*, 397–411.

GAO (U.S. General Accounting Office). (1995). *Global Warming: Limitations of General Circulation Models and Costs of Modeling Efforts*. GAO/RCED-95-164, Washington, DC: Author.

GAO (U.S. Government Accounting Office). (2009). *Climate Change Science: High Quality Greenhouse Gas Emissions Data Are a Cornerstone of Programs to Address Climate Change*. GAO-09-423T. Washington, DC: Author.

Garrison, W. L. (1999). *Changing Large Technical Systems*. Paper presented at the Conference on Social Change and Sustainable Transport, Nation Science Foundation–European Science Foundation. University of California at Berkeley.

Garrison, W. L., & Ward, J. D. (2000). *Tomorrow's Transportation: Changing Cities, Economies and Lives*. Boston: Artech House.

Gelbspan, R. (1997). *The Heat Is On*. Reading, MA: Addison-Wesley.

German, J. (1997). Federal Test Procedure Revisions and Real-World Emissions. In J. DeCicco & M. Delucchi (Eds.), *Transportation, Energy, and Environment: How Far Can Technology Take Us?* (pp. 51–73). Washington, DC: American Council for an Energy-Efficient Economy.

Giuliano, G. (1994). Equity and Fairness Considerations of Congestion Pricing. In TRB, *Curbing Gridlock: Peak-Period Fees to Relieve Congestion* (pp. 250–279). Special Report 242, Vol. 2. Washington, DC: National Research Council, Transportation Research Board.

Giuliano, G., & Narayan, D. (2003). Another Look at Travel Patterns and Urban Form: The U.S. and Great Britain. *Urban Studies, 40*(11), 2295–2312.

Glasby, G. P. (2002). Sustainable Development: The Need for a New Paradigm. *Environment, Development and Sustainability, 4*, 333–345.

Gordon, D. (1991). *Steering a New Course: Transportation, Energy, and the Environment*. Washington, DC: Island Press.

Gordon, D. (1995). Sustainable Transportation: What Do We Mean and How Do We Get There? In D. Sperling & S. A. Shaheen (Eds.), *Transportation and Energy: Strategies for a Sustainable Transportation System* (pp. 1–11). Washington, DC: American Council for an Energy-Efficient Economy.

Gordon, P., & Richardson, H. W. (1997). Are Compact Cities a Desirable Planning Goal? *Journal of the American Planning Association, 63*, 95–106.

Green Car Congress. (2005). *DOE raises hydrogen cost target*. Retrieved from: .

Greene D. L. (1990). CAFE or PRICE?:An Analysis of the Effects of Federal Fuel Economy Regulations and Gasoline Price on New Car MPG, 1978–89. *The Energy Journal, 11*, 37–57.

Greene, D. L. (1996). *Transportation and Energy*. Lansdowne, VA: Eno Foundation.

Greene, D. L. (1998). Why CAFÉ Worked. *Energy Policy, 26*(8), 595–613.

Greene, D. L., Hopson, J. L., & Li, J. (2003). *Running Out of Oil: Analyzing Global Oil Depletion and Transition Through 2050*. ORNL/TM-2003/259. Oak Ridge, TN: Oak Ridge National Laboratory.

Greene, D. L., Jones, D. W., & Delucchi, M. A. (Eds.). (1997). *The Full Costs and Benefits of Transportation: Contributions to Theory, Method and Measurement*. Berlin, Heidelberg, and New York: Springer-Verlag.

Greene, D. L., & Wegener, M. (1997). Sustainable Transport. *Journal of Transport Geography, 5*, 177–190.

Greene, D. L., Patterson, P. D., Singh, M., & Li, J. (2005). Feebates, rebates and gas-guzzler taxes: A study of incentives for increased fuel economy. *Energy Policy, 33*, 757–775.

Gudmundsson, H. (2003). Making concepts matter: Sustainable mobility and indicator systems in transport policy. *International Social Science Journal, 55*(2), 155–217.

Hadaller, O. J., & Momenthy, A. M. (1993). Characteristics of Future Aviation Fuels. In D. L. Green & D. J. Santini (Eds.), *Transportation and Global Climate Change* (pp. 233–282). Washington, DC: American Council for Energy-Efficient Economy.

Hagerstrand, T. (1970). What about People in Regional Science? *Papers of the Regional Science Association, 24*, 7–21.

Hagman, D. G. (1975). *Urban Planning and Land Development Control Law*. St. Paul, MN: West Publishing.

Hansen, J. (1998). Ground Truth: Integration of Weather Information in ITS Deployment. *Traffic Technology International*. Annual Review.

Harbord, B. (1997, October–November). Success over "Stop-Start": Results of the M25 "Controlled Motorway" Pilot. *Traffic Technology International*, pp. 57–60.

Harmon, H. H. (1976). *Modern Factor Analysis*. Chicago: University of Chicago Press.

Hatfield, C. B. (1997). Oil Back on the Global Agenda (Commentary). *Nature, 387*, 121.

Healy, J. R. (2000, June 2). California May Soften Electric Car Mandate. *USA Today*, C1.

Heanue, K. (1997). *Transportation S&T Strategy Partnership Initiatives*. A presentation to the National Science and Technology Council, Transportation Research and Development Committee, September 25, Washington, DC.

Hekkert, M. P., Hendriks, F. H. J. F., Faaij, A. P. C., & Neelis, M. L. (2005). Natural Gas as an Alternative to Crude Oil in Automotive Fuel Chains Well-to-Wheel Analysis and Transition Strategy Development. *Energy Policy, 33*, 579–594.

Hickman, J. C. (1999). *The British Navy and the Depletion of English Oak*. Unpublished MA thesis, Department of Geography, Indiana University, Bloomington.

Howitt, A. M., & Altshuler, A. M. (1999). The politics of controlling auto air pollution. In J. R. Meyer, J. A. Gómez-Ibáñez, W. B. Tye, & C. Winston (Eds.), *Essays in transportation economics and policy* (pp. 223–256). Washington, DC: Brookings Institution Press.

Hubbert, M. K. (1956, June). Nuclear Energy and Fossil Fuels. *Proceedings* of the spring meeting of the American Petroleum Institute, San Antonio, pp. 7–25; also Shell Development Company Publication No. 95.

Hubbert, M. K. (1981). The World's Evolving Energy Systems. *American Journal of Physics, 49,* 1007–1029.

Hughes, P. (1993). *Personal Transport and the Greenhouse Effect.* London: Earthscan.

IEA (International Energy Agency). (1995). *World Energy Outlook 1995.* Paris: OECD/IEA.

IEA (International Energy Agency). (2005). CO_2 *Emissions from Fuel Combustion, 1971–2003.* Paris: OECD/IEA.

Institute for Research in Public Safety. (1975). *Tri-Level Study of the Causes of Traffic Accidents, Vol. 1. Research Findings.* Prepared for the National Highway Traffic Safety Administration. Bloomington: Institute for Research in Public Safety.

Insurance Institute for Highway Safety. (1980). Right Turn on Red Laws Raise Intersection Toll. *Status Report,* Vol. 15, No. 18, December.

IPCC. (1995). Impacts, adaptations, and mitigation. In *Climate Change 1995: Scientific Technical Analyses. Contribution of Working Group II to the Second Assessment of the Intergovernmental Panel on Climate Change* [R. T. Watson, M. C. Zinyowera, and R. H. Moss (eds.)]. Cambridge, UK: Cambridge University Press.

IPCC. (2001a). Impacts, adaptation and vulnerability. In *Climate Change 2001: Contribution of Working Group III to the Third Assessment Report of the Intergovernmental Panel on Climate Change* [B. Metz, O. Davidson, R. Swart and J. Pan (eds.)]. Cambridge, UK, and New York: Cambridge University Press.

IPCC. (2001b). Mitigation. In *Climate Change 2001: Contribution of Working Group II to the Third Assessment Report of the Intergovernmental Panel on Climate Change* [J. J. McCarthy, O. F. Canziani, N. A. Leary, D. J. Dokken, and K. S. White (eds.)]. Cambridge, UK, and New York: Cambridge University Press.

IPCC. (2001c). Summary for policymakers (SPM) and technical summary (TS). In *Climate Change 2001: Contribution of Working Group I to the Third Assessment Report of the Intergovernmental Panel on Climate Change.* Cambridge, UK, and New York: Cambridge University Press.

IPCC. (2007). Summary for policymakers. In *Climate Change 2007: The Physical Basis. Contribution of Working Group I to the Fourth Assessment Report of the Intergovernmental Panel on Climate Change* [S. Solomon, D. Qin, M. Manning, Z. Chen, M. Marquis, K. B. Averyt, M. Tignor, and H. L. Miller (eds.)]. Cambridge, UK, and New York: Cambridge University Press.

ITOPF (International Tanker Owners Pollution Federation). (2008). *Oil Tanker Spill Statistics: 2008.* Retrieved from: *www.itopf.com/informationservices/dataandstatistics/statistics/documents/Statpack200.8_001.pdf.*

Jamison, A. (1970). *The Steam-Powered Automobile: An Answer to Air Pollution.* Bloomington: Indiana University Press.

Johnstone, N., & Karousakis, K. (1999). Economic Incentives to Reduce Pollution from Road Transport: The Case for Vehicle Characteristics Taxes. *Transport Policy, 6,* 99–108.

Joksch, H. C. (1993). Velocity Change and Fatality Risk in a Crash. *Accident Analysis and Prevention, 25,* 103–104.

Kanafani, A. (1983). *The Social Cost of Road Transport.* Berkeley: Institute for Transportation Studies, University of California.

Kasindorf, M. (1997, July 23). Automated Highway Is a "No Hands" Success. *USA Today*, p. 3A.

Kavalec, C., & Setiawan, W. (1997). An Analysis of Per Mile Pollution Fees for Motor Vehicles in California's South Coast. *Transport Policy, 4*, 267–273.

Keijzers, G. (1996). The Netherlands Approach to Sustainable Development in the Transportation Sector. In Ministry of the Environment, *Towards Sustainable Development in Israel* (pp. 109–117). Jerusalem: State of Israel.

Khare, M., & Sharma, P. (2003). Fuel Options. In D. Hensher & K. J. Button (Eds.), *Handbook of Transportation and the Environment* (pp. 159–183). New York: Elsevier.

Khattak, A. J., & Rodriguez, D. (2005). Travel Behavior in Neo-Traditional Neighborhood Developments: A Case Study in the USA. *Transportation Research A, 39*, 481–500.

Knight, R. J. B. (1993). *Shipbuilding Timber for the British Navy: Parliamentary Papers, 1729–1792.* New York: Scholar's Facsimiles and Reprints.

Kulesa, G. (2002). Weather and Aviation: How Does Weather Affect the Safety and Operations of Airports and Aviation, and How Does FAA Work to Manage Weather-Related Effects? In USDOT, *The Potential Impacts of Climate Change on Transportation* (pp. 199–208). Washington, DC: Center for Climate Change and Environmental Forecasting.

Kulmala, R., & Noukka, M. (1998, February–March). Rating the Objectives: Finland's ITS Strategy to 2010. *Traffic Technology International*, 78–82.

Lave, C. A. (1990). Things Won't Get a Lot Worse: The Future of U.S. Traffic Congestion. *ITS Review* (Institute of Transportation Studies, University of California), *14*, 4–8.

Lay, M. G. (1992). *Ways of the World: A History of the World's Roads and of the Vehicles That Used Them.* New Brunswick, NJ: Rutgers University Press.

Leden, L., Wikstrom, P.-E., Garder, P., & Rosander, P. (2006). Safety and Accessibility Effects of Code Modifications and Traffic Calming of an Arterial Road. *Accident Analysis and Prevention, 38*, 455–461.

Lemmen, D. S., & Warren, F. J. (Eds.). (2004). *Climate Change Impacts and Adaptation: A Canadian Perspective.* Ottawa, ON: Climate Change Impacts and Adaptation Directorate, National Resources of Canada.

Lewyn, M. (2002). Sprawl, Growth Boundaries and the Rehnquist Court. *Utah Law Review, 1*, 47.

Litman, T. (1995). *Transportation Cost Analysis: Techniques, Estimates and Implications.* Vancouver, BC, Canada: Victoria Transport Policy Institute.

Litman, T. (1999a). *Evaluating Transportation Equity.* Victoria, BC, Canada: Victoria Transport Policy Institute.

Litman, T. (1999b). *Sustainable Transportation Indicators.* Retrieved from *www.islandnet. com/~litman/sti.htm*.

Lomax, T., Turner, S., & Shunk, G. (1997). *Quantifying Congestion, Vol. 1.* Washington, DC: National Cooperative Highway Research Program, Transportation Research Board, National Academy Press.

Longerbone, D. B. (2000). *The Impact of Household Responsibility Characteristics on Working Women's Commute Times.* Unpublished MA thesis, Department of Geography, Indiana University, Bloomington.

MacKenzie, J. J. (1994). *The Keys to the Car: Electric and Hydrogen Vehicles for the 21st Century.* Washington, DC: World Resources Institute.

MacKenzie, J. J. (1995, October 27). *Alternative Fuels to Reduce Petroleum Consumption, Global Warming Gases, and Urban Air Pollution.* Paper presented at the Symposium on Challenges and Opportunities for Global Transportation in the 21st Century, John A. Volpe Transportation Systems Center, Cambridge, MA.

MacKenzie, J. J., Dower, R., & Chen, D. T. (1992). *The Going Rate*. Washington, DC: World Resources Institute.

Maddison, D., Pearce, D., Johansson, O., Calthrop, E., Litman, T., & Verhoef, E. (1996). *Blueprint 5: The True Costs of Road Transport*. London: Earthscan.

Mather, K. F. (1947). The availability of petroleum: Today and tomorrow. In W. E. Pratt & D. Pratt (Eds.), *World geography of petroleum* (p. 342). American Geographical Society Special Publication No. 31. Princeton: Princeton University Press.

Matson, T. M., Smith, W. S., & Hurd, F. W. (1955). *Traffic Engineering*. New York: McGraw-Hill.

McCubbin, D. R., & Delucchi, M. (1999, September). The Health Costs of Motor Vehicle Related Air Pollution. *Journal of Transport Economics and Policy, 33*(Part 3), 253–286.

Menabe, S., & Wetherald, R. T. (1967). Thermal Equilibrium of the Atmosphere with a Given Distribution of Relative Humidity. *Journal of Atmospheric Science, 24*, 241–259.

Meyer, M. D. (1994). Alternative Methods for Measuring Congestion Levels. In TRB, *Curbing Gridlock: Peak-Period Fees to Relieve Congestion* (pp. 32–61). Special Report 242, Vol. 2. Washington, DC: National Research Council, Transportation Research Board.

Meyer, M. D. (1999). Demand Management as an Element of Transportation Policy: Using Carrots and Sticks to Influence Travel Behavior. *Transportation Research Part A, 33*, 575–599.

Middleton, W. D., & Wolinsky, J. (Eds.). (2001, March). The North American Passenger Rail Market. *Railway Age*.

Miles-McLean, R., Haltmaier, S. M., & Shelby, M. G. (1993). Designing Incentive-Based Approaches to Limit Carbon Dioxide Emissions from the Light Vehicle Fleet. In D. L. Greene & D. J. Santini (Eds.), *Transportation and Global Climate Change* (pp. 109–126). Washington DC: American Council for an Energy-Efficient Economy.

Millard-Ball, A., Murray, G., ter Schure, J., Fox, C., & Burkhardt, J. (2005). *Car-Sharing: Where and How It Succeeds*. Transit Cooperative Research Program, TCRP Report 108. Washington, DC: Transportation Research Board.

Miller, P., & Moffet, J. (1993). *The Price of Mobility—Uncovering the Hidden Costs of Transportation*. Washington. DC: Natural Resources Defense Fund.

Milly, P. C. D., Dunne, K. A., & Vecchia, A. V. (2005). Global Pattern of Trends in Streamflow and Water Availability in a Changing Climate. *Nature, 438*, 347–350.

MIT & CRA (Massachusetts Institute of Technology and Charles River Associates Incorporated). (2001). *Mobility 2001: World Mobility at the End of the Twentieth Century and Its Sustainability*. Prepared for the World Business Council for Sustainable Development. Cambridge, MA: MIT Press.

Mitchell, R. B., & Rapkin, C. (1954). *Urban Traffic: A Function of Land Use*. New York: Columbia University Press.

Mokhtarian, P. L. (1997). The Transportation Impacts of Telecommuting: Recent Empirical Findings. In P. Stopher & M. Lee-Gosselin (Eds.), *Understanding Travel Behavior in an Era of Change* (pp. 91–106). New York: Pergamon Press.

Mokhtarian, P. L., Salomon, I., & Choo, S. (2005). Measuring the Measurable: Why Can't We Agree on the Number of Telecommuters in the U.S.? *Quality and Quantity, 39*(4), 423–452.

Morrison, S. A. (1986). A Survey of Road Pricing. *Transportation Research 20A*, 87–97.

Mullen, M. A., Wilson, J. H., Jr., Gottsman, L., Noland, R. B., & Schroeer, W. L. (1997). *The Emissions Impact of Eliminating National Speed Limits: One Year Later*. Transportation Research Record No. 1587, 113–120.

Mumford, L. (1957). *The Highway and the City*. New York: Harcourt, Brace & World.

Nader, R. (1966). *Unsafe at Any Speed.* New York: Pocket Books.

Nadiri, M. I., & Mamuneas, T. P. (1998). *Contributions of Highway Capital to Output and Growth in the U.S. Economy and Industries.* Report prepared for the Federal Highway Administration, U.S. Department of Transportation, Washington, DC.

Nadis, S., & MacKenzie, J. J. (1993). *Car Trouble.* Boston: Beacon Press.

NASA (National Aeronautics and Space Administration). (2006). 2005 Warmest Year in over a Century. Retrieved from *www.nasa.gov/vision/earth/environment/2005_warmest.html.*

Newman, P. W. G., & Kenworthy, J. R. (1989). Gasoline Consumption and Cities: A Comparison of U.S. Cities in a Global Survey. *Journal of the American Planning Association, 55,* 24–36.

Newman, P. W. G., & Kenworthy, J. R. (1999). *Sustainability and Cities: Overcoming Automobile Dependence.* Washington, DC: Island Press.

New York Times. (1899, September 14). Fatally Hurt by Automobile. Page 1.

NHTSA (National Highway Traffic Safety Administration). (1989). *The Economic Cost to Society of Motor Vehicle Accidents.* Washington, DC: Author.

NHTSA (National Highway Traffic Safety Administration). (1997). *The Effect of Decreases in Vehicle Weight on Injury Crash Rates.* DOT HS 808 575. Washington, DC: Author.

NHTSA (National Highway Traffic Safety Administration). (2002). *The Economic Impact of Motor Vehicle Crashes 2000.* Washington, DC: U.S. Department of Transportation. Also available at .

NHTSA (National Highway Traffic Safety Administration). (2008, December). Early Estimate of Motor Vehicle Traffic Fatalities from January to October 2008. *Traffic Safety Facts.* DOT HS 811 054. Washington, DC: Author.

NHTSA (National Highway Traffic Safety Administration). (2009). *Traffic Safety Facts.* Washington, DC: NHTSA National Center for Statistics and Analysis, June. Also available at: *wwwnrd.nhtsa.dot.gov/Pubs/811172.pdf.*

Niles, J. (2002). Telecommunication Substitution for Transportation: A presentation during a meeting of the STAR/STELLA project. Arlington, VA: National Science Foundation, January 15.

O'Brien, C. (1999, March). *Children and Sustainable Transportation: Evidence to Encourage Social Change.* Paper presented at the National Science Foundation Conference on Social Change and Sustainable Transport, Berkeley, CA.

OECD (Organisation for Economic Co-operation and Development). (1983). *Effects of Traffic and Roads on the Environment in Urban Areas.* Paris: Author.

OECD (Organization for Economic Co-operation and Development). (1998). *Indicators for the Integration of Environmental Concerns into Transport Policies: Part I. Policy Context and Indicator Development,* and *Part II. Measured Indicators.* Paris: Author.

Ogden, J. M., & DeLuchi, M. A. (1993). Solar Hydrogen Transportation Fuels. In D. L. Greene & D. J. Santini (Eds.), *Transportation and Global Climate Change* (pp. 189–241). Washington, DC: American Council for an Energy-Efficient Economy.

Owen, W. (1956). *The Metropolitan Transportation Problem.* Garden City, NY: Doubleday.

Pearce, D., Markandya, A., & Barbier, E. S. (1989). *Blueprint for a Green Economy.* London: Earthscan.

Pearson, B. (1999). *An Estimation of Potential Production of Agri-Based Ethanol.* Unpublished PhD dissertation, Department of Geography, Indiana University, Bloomington.

Perlack, R. D., Wright, L. L., Turhollow, A. F., Graham, R. L., Stokes, B. J., & Erbach, D. C. (2005). *Biomass as Feedstock for Bioenergy and Bioproducts Industry: The Technical Feasibility of a Billion-Ton Annual Supply.* Oak Ridge, TN: Oak Ridge National Laboratory and the U.S. Department of Agriculture.

Phillips, C. R. (1986). *Six Galleons of the King of Spain*. Baltimore, MD: The Johns Hopkins University Press.

Pigou, A. C. (1920). *Wealth and Welfare*. London: MacMillan.

PCSD (President's Council on Sustainable Development). (1995). *Status Update, April 1995*. Washington, DC: U.S. Government Printing Office.

PCSD (President's Council on Sustainable Development). (1996). *Sustainable America: A New Consensus*. Washington, DC: U.S. Government Printing Office.

Quinet, E. (2004). A Meta-Analysis of Western European External Costs Estimates. *Transportation Research D, 9*, 465–476.

Railway Age. (2005, October). Railroads Rise to the Challenge. *Railway Age, 206*, 10, 29–33.

Ralph Nader Study Group. (1972). *Small on Safety*. New York: Grossman.

Ramesohl, S., & Merten, F. (2006). Energy System Aspects of Hydrogen as an Alternative Fuel in Transport. *Energy Policy, 34*, 1251–1259.

Rey, J. R., Polzin, E. E., & Bricka, S. G. (1994). An Assessment of the Potential Saturation in Men's Travel. In Federal Highway Administration, *Nationwide Personal Transportation Survey, Demographic Special Reports* (pp. 1–63). Washington, DC: U.S. Department of Transportation.

Rietveld, P., & van Ommeren, J. (2002). Company Cars and Company Provided Parking. In W. R. Black & P. Nijkamp (Eds.), *Social Change and Sustainable Transport* (pp. 201–208). Bloomington: Indiana University Press.

Rifkin, J. (2002). *The Hydrogen Economy*. New York: Tarcher/Putnam.

Roberts, P. (2004). *The End of Oil: On the Edge of a Perilous New World*. Boston: Houghton Mifflin.

Roland, N. (2009). Obama Kills Development of Hydrogen Fuel Cell Vehicles. *Automotive News*. Retrieved from: .

Root, A. (2001). Can Travel Vouchers Encourage More Sustainable Travel? *Transport Policy, 8*, 107–114.

Rosenberg, N. J., Easterling, W.E., III, Crosson, P. R., & Darmstader, J. (Eds.). (1989). *Greenhouse Warming: Abatement and Adaptation*. Washington, DC: Resources for the Future.

Ross, M. (1994). Automobile Fuel Consumption and Emissions: Effects of Vehicle and Driving Characteristics. *Annual Review of Energy and Environment, 19*, 75–112.

Ross, M., Patel, D., & Wenzel, T. (2006). Vehicle Design and the Physics of Traffic Safety. *Physics Today, 59*, 49–54.

Ross, M., & Wenzel, T. (1997). Real-World Emissions from Conventional Passenger Cars. In J. DeCicco & M. Delucchi (Eds.), *Transportation, Energy, and Environment: How Far Can Technology Take Us?* (pp. 21–49). Washington, DC: American Council for an Energy-Efficient Economy.

Rouwenthal, J., & Verhoef, E. (2006). Basic Economic Principles of Road Pricing: From Theory to Applications. *Transport Policy, 13*, 106–114.

Rummel, R. J. (1988). *Applied Factor Analysis*. Evanston, IL: Northwestern University Press.

Sandqvist, T. (1992, March). *Growing Up with and without a Family Car*. Paper presented at the National Science Foundation Conference on Social Change and Sustainable Transport, Berkeley, CA.

Santos, G. (2005). Urban Congestion Charging: A Comparison between London and Singapore. *Transport Reviews, 25*, 511–534.

Schade, J., & Schlag, B. (2003). Acceptability of Urban Transport Pricing Startegies. *Transportation Research F, 6*, 45–61.

Schipper, L. (1996). *Sustainable Transport: What It Is, Whether It Is*. Paper presented at the

Towards Sustainable Transportation Conference of the Organisation of Economic Co-operation and Development, Vancouver, BC, Canada.

Schipper, L., & Ng, W. S. (2006). China Motorization Trends, Consequences, and Alternatives. *TRB 85th Annual Meeting Compendium of Papers CD-ROM*. Washington, DC: Transportation Research Board.

Schipper L., Steiner, R., & Meyers, S. (1993). Trends in Transportation Energy Use, 1970–1988: An International Perspective. In D. L. Greene & D. J. Santini (Eds.), *Transportation and Global Climate Change* (pp. 51–89). Washington, DC: American Council for an Energy-Efficient Economy.

Schrank, D. L., & Thomas, T. J. (2009). 2009 Urban Mobility Report, College Station: Texas Transportation Institute, July.

Scott, A. J. (Ed.). (1993). *Electric Vehicle Manufacturing in Southern California: Current Developments, Future Prospects.* Los Angeles, CA: Lewis Center for Regional Policy Studies.

Senate Department for Urban Development. (2007). *Mobility in the City—Berlin Transport in Figures.* Retrieved from: *www.stadtentwicklung.berlin.de/verkehr/verkehr_in_zahlen/en/nachhaltigkeit/index.shtml.*

Shacket, S. R. (1983). *The Complete Book of Electric Vehicles.* Northbrook, IL: Domus Books.

Shiftan, Y., & Burd-Eden, R. (2001). Modeling Response to Parking Policy. *Transportation Research Record, 1765*, 27–34.

Shinar, D. (1998). Speed and Crashes: A Controversial Topic and an Elusive Relationship. In TRB, *Managing Speed* (pp. 221–276). Washington, DC: National Research Council, Transportation Research Board, National Academy Press.

Shoup, D. C. (1997). Evaluating the Effects of Cashing out Employer-Paid Parking: Eight Case Studies. *Transport Policy, 4*, 201–216.

Simmons, M. R. (2005). *Twilight in the Desert: The Coming Saudi Oil Shock and the World Economy.* New York: Wiley.

Sissine, F. (1996). *The Partnership for a New Generation of Vehicles (PNGV).* Report to Congress. Washington, DC: Congressional Research Service.

Sitarz, D. (1994). *Agenda 21: The Earth Summit Strategy to Save Our Planet.* Boulder, CO: Earthpress.

Smerk, G. M. (1991). *The Federal Role in Urban Mass Transportation.* Bloomington: Indiana University Press.

Smith, S. V. (2000). Jury Verdicts and the Dollar Value of Human Life. *Journal of Forensic Economics, 13*, 169–188.

Speer, L. J. (2009). Renault: Subsidies needed for e-cars. *Automotive News Europe*, February 16. Retrieved from: .

Sperling, D. (1995). *Future Drive: Electric Vehicles and Sustainable Transportation.* Washington, DC: Island Press.

Sperling, D., & Cannon, J. S. (2004a). *The Hydrogen Energy Transition: Moving toward the Post Petroleum Age in Transportation.* Amsterdam and Boston: Elsevier.

Sperling, D., & Cannon, J. S. (2004b). Hydrogen Hope or Hype. In D. Sperling & J. S. Cannon (Eds.), *The Hydrogen Energy Transition: Moving toward the Post Petroleum Age in Transportation* (pp. 235–239). Amsterdam: Elsevier.

Sperling, D., & Gordon, D. (2009), *Two Billion Cars: Driving toward Sustainability*, New York and Oxford: Oxford University Press.

Stewart, J. Q. (1942). A Measure of the Influence of Population at a Distance. *Sociometry, 5*, 63–71.

Still, B., & Simmonds, D. (2000). Parking Restraint Policy and Urban Vitality. *Transport Reviews, 20,* 291–316.

Stouffer, S. A. (1940). Intervening Opportunities: A Theory Relating Mobility and Distance. *American Sociological Review, 5,* 845–867.

Stough, R. (Ed.). (2001). *Intelligent Transport Systems: Cases and Policies.* Northhampton, MA: Edward Elgar.

Subramanian, R. (2006). *Motor Vehicle Traffic Crashes as a Leading Cause of Death in the United States, 2003.* Research Note, DOT HS 810 568. Washington, DC: National Highway Traffic Safety Administration.

Sullivan, E. C. (2003). Implementing Value Pricing for U.S. Roadways. *European Journal of Transport and Infrastructure Research, 3,* 401–413.

Taylor, D., & Tight, M. (1997). Public Attitudes and Consultation in Traffic Calming Studies. *Transport Policy, 4,* 171–182.

Texas Transportation Institute. (2009). Retrieved from: *mobility.tamu.edu/ums/congestion_data/.*

The Economist. (2008, November). A Global Love Affair: A Special Report on Cars in Emerging Markets.

Thornes, J. E. (1992). The Impact of Weather and Climate on Transport in the U.K. *Progress in Physical Geography, 16,* 187–208.

Titus, J. (2002). Does Sea Level Rise Matter to Transportation along the Atlantic Coast? In USDOT, *The Potential Impacts of Climate Change on Transportation* (pp. 133–150). Washington, DC: Center for Climate Change and Environmental Forecasting.

Torr, W., & Havlick, S. W. (2004). *Transportation and Sustainable Campus Communities: Issues, Examples, Solutions.* Washington, DC: Island Press.

Traffic Technology International. (1998a, April–May). Congestion Evaporation. *Traffic Technology International,* p. 16.

Traffic Technology International. (1998b, February–March). Navigation Positions. *Traffic Technology International,* p. 13.

Traffic Technology International. (1998c, February–march). To Cut Congestion, Close the Roads. *Traffic Technology International,* p. 7.

Train K. E., Davis, W. B., & Levine, M. D. (1995). Favoring Feebates. *ITS Review, 18*(4), 2–3, 8.

Train, K. E., Davis, W. B., & Levine, M. D. (1997). Fees and Rebates on New Vehicles: Impacts on Fuel Efficiency, Carbon Dioxide Emissions, and Consumer Surplus. *Transportation Research E, 33*(1), 1–13.

Transport Canada. (2003). *Straight Ahead: A Vision for Transportation in Canada.* Ottawa, ON: Transport Canada.

TRB (Transportation Research Board). (1993). *Primer on Intelligent Vehicle Highway Systems, Transportation Research Circular 412.* Washington, DC: National Research Council, Transportation Research Board.

TRB (Transportation Research Board). (1994a). *Curbing Gridlock: Peak Period Fees to Relieve Traffic Congestion.* Special Report 242, 2(Vols. 1 and 2). Washington, DC: National Research Council, Transportation Research Board.

TRB (Transportation Research Board). (1994b). *Road Pricing for Congestion Management: A Surevy of International Practice, NCHRP Synthesis 210.* Washington, DC: National Research Council, Transportation Research Board.

TRB (Transportation Research Board). (1995). *Expanding Metropolitan Highways: Implications for Air Quality and Energy Use.* Special Report 245. Washington, DC: National Research Council, Transportation Research Board.

TRB (Transportation Research Board). (1996). *Paying Our Way: Estimating Marginal Social*

Costs of Freight Transportation. Special Report 246. Washington, DC: National Research Council, Transportation Research Board.

TRB (Transportation Research Board). (1997). *Toward a Sustainable Future*. Special Report 251. Washington, DC: National Research Council, Transportation Research Board.

TRB (Transportation Research Board). (2002a). *The Congestion Mitigation and Air Quality Improvement Program: Assessing 10 Years of Experience*. Special Report 264, Washington, DC: National Research Council, Transportation Research Board.

TRB (Transportation Research Board). (2008). *Potential Impacts of Climate Change on U.S. Transportation*. Special Report 290. Washington, DC: National Research Council, Transportation Research Board.

Tromp, T. K., Shia, R.-L., Allen, M., Eller, J. M., & Young, Y. L. (2003). Potential Environmental Impact of a Hydrogen Economy on the Stratosphere. *Science, 300*, 1740–1742.

United Nations Conference on Trade and Development. (2003). *E-Commerce and Development Report 2003*. New York: United Nations.

United Nations Framework Convention on Climate Change. (1999). *Kyoto Protocol*. Retrieved from: .

United Nations World Commission on Environment and Development. (1987). *Our Common Future*. Oxford, UK: Oxford University Press.

Upham, P., Maughan, J., Raper, D., & Thomas, C. (Eds.). (2003). *Towards Sustainable Aviation*. London: Earthscan.

U.S. Bureau of Transport Statistics. (2009). *National Transportation Statistics 2009*. Washington, DC: U.S. Department of Transportation.

U.S. Department of Energy. (2006). *Hydrogen Cost Competitive on a Cents per Mile Basis—2006*. DOE Hydrogen Program Record. Record # 5038, May.

U.S. Department of Energy. (2007). DOE Selects Six Cellulosic Ethanol Plants for Up to $385 Million in Federal Funding. Retrieved from: .

U.S. Department of Energy. (2008a). Gas Guzzler Tax. Retrieved from: .

U.S. Department of Energy. (2008b). *2005 Hydrogen Cost from Water Electrolysis*. DOE Hydrogen Program Record. Record # 5040.

U.S. Department of Energy. (2009). Clean Cities Alternative Fuel Price Report. *Clean Cities*, April.

U.S. Department of Energy and Environmental Protection Agency. (1993). *Gas Mileage Guide*. Washington, DC: U.S. Government Printing Office.

U.S. Department of Labor. (2009). Quick Stats on Women Workers, 2008. Retrieved from:

USDOT (U.S. Department of Transportation). (1993). *Transportation Implications of Telecommuting*. Washington, DC: Author.

USDOT (U.S. Department of Transportation). (1994). *1990 NPTS Urban Travel Patterns— National Personal Transportation Survey*. Washington, DC: Author.

USDOT (U.S. Department of Transportation). (2002). *The Potential Impacts of Climate Change on Transportation*. Washington, DC: Center for Climate Change and Environmental Forecasting.

U.S. Government (2001). Control of Emissions of Hazardous Air Pollutants from Mobile Sources: Final Rule. In *Federal Register, 40 CFR Parts 80 and 86*. Washington, DC: U.S. Government Printing Office.

Van de Coevering, P., & Schwanen, T. (2006). Reevaluating the Impact of Urban Form on Travel Patterns in Europe and North America. *Transport Policy, 13*, 229–239.

Van Seters, D., & Levelton, P. (1993). *The Costs of Transporting People in the British Columbia Lower Mainland*. Vancouver, BC: KPMG Peat Marwick Stevenson & Kellogg.

Van Wee, B., Moll, H. C., & Dirks, J. (2000). Environmental Impact of Scrapping Old Cars. *Transportation Research D, 5*, 137–143.

Vernon, D. D., Cook, L. J., Petersen, K. J., & Dean, J. M. (2004). Effect of Repeal of the National Maximum Speed Limit Law on Occurrence of Crashes, Injury Crashes, and Fatal Crashes on Utah Highways. *Accident Analysis and Prevention, 36*, 223–229.

Vickrey, W. S. (1969). Congestion Theory and Transport Investment. *American Economic Review, 59*, 251–261.

Victoria Transport Policy Institute. (2009). *Online TDM Encyclopedia*. Available at *www.vtpi. org/tdm/*.

von Weizsacker, E., Lovins, A. B., & Lovins, L. H. (1998). *Factor Four: Doubling Wealth, Halving Resource Use*. London: Earthscan.

Wachs, M. (1994). Will Congestion Pricing Ever Be Adopted? *Access, 4*, 15–19.

Wachs, M. (2004). What are the challenges to creating sustainable transportation? In *TRB, Integrating Sustainability into the Transportation Planning Process*. Conference Proceedings 37. Washington, DC: Transportation Research Board, pp. 44–52.

Wald, M. L. (1998, February 6). Cleaner Cars, No Magic Required. *New York Times*, Automotive Section, F1.

Waller, P. (2001). Speed Limits: How Should They Be Determined? Address before the Sydney Chapter of the Australian College of Road Safety, September 6.

Webber, M. M. (2006). Sustainable Transport. *Berkeley Planning Journal, 19*, 183–184.

Webster, P. J., Holland, G. J., Curry, J. A., & Chang, H. R. (2005). Changes in Tropical Cyclone Number, Duration, and Intensity in a Warming Environment, *Science, 309*(5742), 1844–1846.

Wegener, M. (1995). Accessibility and Development Impacts. In D. Banister (Ed.), *Transport and Urban Development* (pp. 157–161). London and New York: Spon.

Weiner, E. (1992). *Urban Transportation Planning in the United States*. Technology Sharing Program, U.S. Department of Transportation, DOT-T-93-02.

Wellington, A. M. (1888). *The Economic Theory of Railway Location*. New York: Wiley.

Wheeler, J. O. (1967). The Transportation Model and Changing Home-Work Location. *The Professional Geographer, 19*, 144–148.

Whitelegg, J. (1993). *Transport for a Sustainable Future: The Case for Europe*. London and New York: Belhaven Press.

WHO (World Health Organization). (2001). *A 5-Year WHO Strategy for Road Traffic Injury Prevention*. Unpublished document WHO/NMH/VIP/01.03, available from Department of Injuries and Violence Prevention. Geneva: Author.

Wohl, M., & Martin, B. V. (1967). *Traffic System Analysis for Engineers and Planners*. New York: McGraw-Hill.

Wright, J. P. (1979). *On a Clear Day You Can See General Motors*. New York: Avon.

Yvkoff, L. (2009). California to get 46 retail hydrogen stations by 2014. The Car Tech blog. Retrieved from: .

Zobel, R. (1999). In NHTSA *Proceedings of the 16th International Technical Conference on the Enhanced Safety of Vehicles* (p. 729). Washington, DC: U.S. Department of Transportation.

Index

Page numbers followed by *f* or *t* indicate figures or tables.

About the Author

William R. Black, PhD, is Professor Emeritus in the Department of Geography at Indiana University in Bloomington. He has written numerous articles in the general area of sustainable transportation and planning. Several articles have focused on those factors that make current transport systems nonsustainable, while others have looked at the related problems of the impact of global warming on transportation infrastructure, social barriers to sustainable transport, full costing of transportation, and the development of indicators of sustainable transport and mobility. Dr. Black was North American chairman of the National Science Foundation (NSF) and the European Science Foundation Conference on Social Change and Sustainable Transport held at the University of California at Berkeley in 1999 and, along with Peter Nijkamp, edited a volume of papers from that conference titled *Social Change and Sustainable Transport*, published in 2002. He served as coordinator of STAR, an NSF-funded thematic network on sustainable transport analysis and research, and as North American coordinator of STELLA, a thematic network on transatlantic sustainable transport research funded by the European Commission and the NSF. He has served on numerous Transportation Research Board (TRB) and National Research Council panels and committees and is currently a member of the International Activities Committee and the Social and Economic Factors of Transportation Committee, which he formerly chaired. He has also been a member of the TRB Committee on Transportation and Sustainability since its creation. In 2007, Dr. Black was recognized for his contributions to sustainable transportation by the Chinese Institute for Transportation.